To Marge —
I hope you enjoy
following the 90th P.V.
through camp, march,
and battle.
Best Wishes
Jno Nurkin

Mullica Hill 1998

"This War is an Awful Thing..."

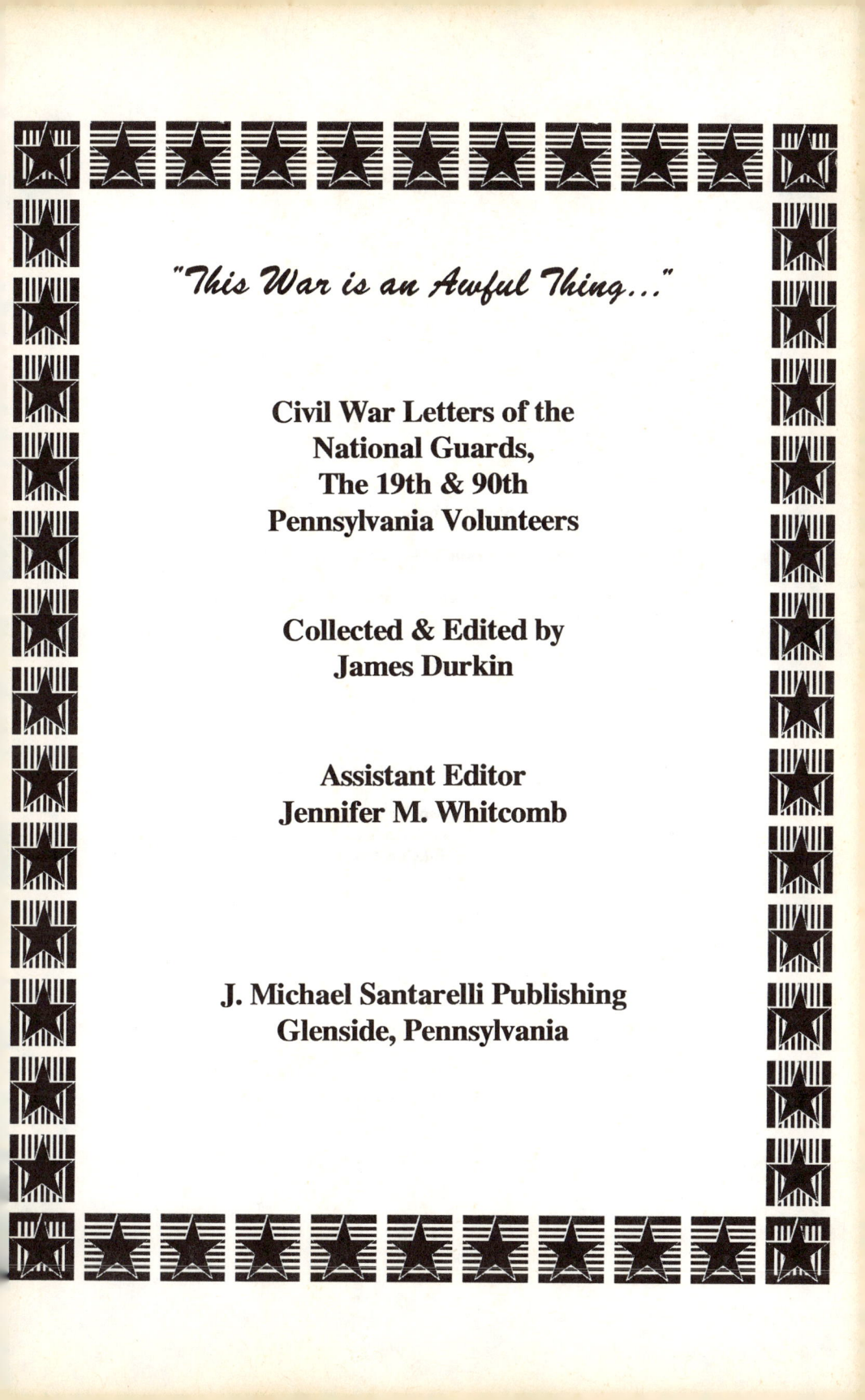

Civil War Letters of the National Guards, The 19th & 90th Pennsylvania Volunteers

Collected & Edited by
James Durkin

Assistant Editor
Jennifer M. Whitcomb

J. Michael Santarelli Publishing
Glenside, Pennsylvania

International Standard Book Number IS-0-9631314-1-9

@James Durkin, 1994, All Rights Reserved.

Permission to reproduce in any form must be secured from the author and the publisher.

First Edition

Please direct all correspondence and orders to:

J. Michael Santarelli Publishing
226 Paxson Ave.
Glenside, PA 19038

Acknowledgments

This book is a result of research I began in 1991 on the 90th Pennsylvania Volunteers. It was my intention, both then and now, to write a complete history of the regiment. That project continues. However, as I gathered these letters, I hoped that I should not be the only one to read them. When others found them interesting, my decision was reinforced. I am very grateful to Michael Santarelli for having enough faith in the material to assume the risks of publication.

When the civil war began in 1861, the National Guards Regiment of Philadelphia was among the best known Militia units in the United States. The Guards became the 19th Pennsylvania Volunteers in the 90 day service and the 90th Pennsylvania Volunteers in the three years service. In the more than 125 years since, almost nothing has been written about the National Guards. Most of the regimental records have been lost.

My hunt for the 90th P.V. has been most successful in two places, The State Archives of Pennsylvania and the National Archives. I am grateful to the staff of the State Archives of Pennsylvania for their assistance in locating and duplicating the records of the 90th P.V.. I am also deeply grateful to the staff of the National Archives, especially to Mr. Mike Music, Mr. Mike Maiers, and Mr. William Linn. I also thank the entire staff of the Central Research Room of the National Archives for their courtesy, especially Archives Technician, Sharon McCoy-Holley who was always pleasant, helpful, and efficient. I also appreciate the help of Mr. Todd Butler of the Civilian Records Branch. He was a great help in obtaining and wading through the pension files of the 90th P.V.

I must also thank the staff of the United States Army Military History Institute, especially the Photograph Branch for their assistance.

I owe a debt of gratitude to a number of Philadelphia institutions for their assistance in tracking down the boys in the 90th P.V. The staff of the M.O.L.L.U.S Library and Museum on Pine Street in Philadelphia has been a constant source of information and assistance in the completion of this project. The same is true of the staff of the G.A.R. Museum on Griscom Street, especially Mr. Bud Atkinson and all of the reenactors of the 28th P.V..

I need to especially thank Civil War Times Illustrated Magazine for allowing me to reproduce here the letter of Sergeant Frank Jennings to his brother and sister, located in the Civil War Times Illustrated Collection of the United States Army Military History Institute, Carlisle, PA.

I also owe special **thanks to** the following descendants of soldiers in the 90th P.V.:

> Mr. William H. Gallop **for allowing** me to obtain photographs from his copy **of the** Survivors Association booklet published at the **dedication** of the regiment's Gettysburg monuments in 1888.

> Mr. Alan Duke for providing me **with the** photograph of Lieutenant Charles Wilson Duke **and the Poem** written by Private William Fayette, "Fredericksburg".

> Mr. Keith Thomas for the poem "Antietam" **by** Sergeant John Candelet

I am also in the debt of Mr. Scott Hahn for providing a copy of the photograph of Captain Anthony Morin and for his permission to use the photograph.

I wish to thank Mrs. Mary Cullen for suggestions and criticism which contributed to the development of this project. I also am grateful to Chief Inspector Edward Rauch, Retired, Philadelphia Police Department, for his assistance in some of the research, and suggestions and encouragement in the development of the manuscript. I would be remiss if I failed to Thank Mr. and Mrs. Walter Tellegen for their financial encouragement of the research related to the 90th P.V.. I owe special thanks to Jennifer Whitcomb for her assistance to the editing process. Her contribution was huge and her work excellent. I am deeply in her debt.

Last, but certainly not least, I am forever in the debt of Ms. Marie Lally. I am constantly amazed by her unsolicited generosity. Ms. Lally gave me access to her home in Delaware during my research at the National Archives. Her kindness saved me hundreds of hours of research time, thousands of miles in travel, and, certainly, thousands of dollars in hotel bills. I don't know how I will ever repay this debt, but I will never stop trying.

                                          James Durkin
                                        Philadelphia, Pennsylvania
                                        January, 1994

A Few Editing Notes

Since the letters printed in this volume are historical source material, I have attempted to change them as little as possible in the editing process. For this reason errors in grammar, capitalization, and spelling have been left largely uncorrected. I have edited only when it was necessary to make the letter more understandable to the reader. For this reason, the vast majority of changes are made in the punctuation of the letters. Most of the Civil War soldiers were very inept at the use of this particular skill. In some cases, the letters as written were impossible to understand clearly without significant revisions of the punctuation. In these cases, changes have been made. I have chosen not to correct the punctuation of the opening and closing salutations of the letters, simply because, the majority of the men used no punctuation at all when opening and closing their letters. Since the correct punctuation was the exception and not the rule, I have chosen not to change these sections, and to let the reader experience them as written.

Contents

Prologue

1. Fredericksburg by Private William Fayette, 1.

2. The National Guards, 3.

3. 1861, 17.

4. 1862, 27.

5. 1863, 101.

6. 1864, 146.

7. 1865, 194.

8. The Watson Case, 196.

9. To My Brother & Sister, 220

10. The Fate of Charles Ricketts, 232.

11. Recovering The Body of the "Perfect Soldier", 240.

12. Letters to the National Tribune, 243.

13. The Slowest Mail of All, 256.

14. Antietam by Sergeant John Candelet, 269.

15. Sources, 270.

16. Notes, 273.

17. Index, 274

Photographs & Illustrations

The Baltimore Riot, 7
General Nathaniel Banks, 11, Library of Congress
Colonel Peter Lyle, 11, Survivors Association, 90th P.V.
Negro Slave with Cotton Sack, 35
Chaplain Horatio Howell, 52, Survivors Association, 90th P.V.
Howell Memorial, 52, Survivors Association, 90th P.V.
Dedication of Howell Memorial, 52, Survivors Association, 90th P.V.
Captain Anthony Morin, 72, Courtesy of Scott Hahn
National Guard's Armory, 76,
Newspaper Delivery in Camp, 79
Lieutenant Charles Wilson Duke, 95, Courtesy of Alan Duke
Major Alfred Sellers, 98, USAMHI
Dedication of the Tree Monument, 100, Survivors Association, 90th P.V.
Recruiting Poster, 90th P.V., 118, Courtesy of Alan Duke
Sketch of Soldier, 118, National Archives, Joseph Temple
Major A. J. Sellers wearing Cngressional Medal of Honor, 123, USAMHI
Execution of a Deserter, 135,
Andersonville Stockade, 176
Building Fortifications on the Weldon Railroad, 180,
Lieutenant Hillary Beyer, 213, USAMHI
Soldier with Rifle and Spade, 226, Library of Congress
General Phillip Kearney, 242
Soldiers in Libby Prison, 267

For Jack who died a warrior

&

For Debby who touched my heart.

Prologue

In 1861, almost an entire generation of American young men marched off to war. They went voluntarily. There was no draft until two years later. Most of them believed it would be a short war with no more than one battle. They expected a quick dash to glory. What they got was a long march through hell. The letters which follow have been unread for at least one hundred years. They tell the story of what the young men of one regiment saw, and felt, and did in the Civil War, the greatest American tragedy. This war was one in which men who were born to be brothers, spent four years trying to kill each other in every conceivable way, and, for the most part, succeeded nicely in their attempts.

For most of these young men the war was the defining event of their lives. Those who survived it were still thinking, and talking, and writing about it forty years later. Those who did not survive left only their letters to speak for them. Some are simple and straightforward. Others possess an eloquence which seems to have been abundant among the soldiers of this particular war. Together they are the largest source of eyewitness testimony about the activities of the 90th P.V. which has been assembled since the war ended.

"This War is an Awful Thing..."

Civil War Letters of the National Guards,

The 19th & 90th Pennsylvania Volunteers

Battle of Fredericksburg
A poem
By
William Fayette
Drummer, Co.C, 90th Regiment
Pennsylvania Volunteers

As a Tribute in Memory of
Captain Charles W. Duke

The First Officer Killed in the Engagement And who so valiantly gave his life in saving that of another in the first hour of that memorable battle on December 13th, 1862

'Twas on the 13th of December,
    Silently we lay,
But too well can we remember
    All the scenes that day;
Cannons roaring, shells were ploughing,
    O'er our dauntless line;
Many a spirit then was sorrowing
    From its humble shrine.

Chorous

Rest warrior though thy slumbers,
    Ne'er shall waken here,
There are true friends without number,
    Holding thy memory dear.

Hastening from a couch of sickness,
    Girding on his sword,
Showing all who looked for weakness,
    That he was no coward.
Heeding not the bullet's whistle
    Sounding his death knell;
Till at last a rebel missle
    Struck! and poor "Duke" fell.

    Chorous

There poor "Sweigert" wounded lying
    With his latest breath,
Cried "Oh God"! brave boys I'm dying,
    'Tis a glorious death."
Hotly fought our little band,
    Fierce the contest raged,
Oh May God pity the land
    Where Civil war is waged.

    Chorous

With our war cry: "For the Union:
    Death unto its foe."
Still we fought the rebel minions,
    'Till many a one laid low;
We retreated to the river,
    Silently we crossed--
Then we knew we were defeated,
    Fredericksburg was lost.

    Chorous.

The National Guards

The most important election in the history of the United States of America took place in November of 1860: Abraham Lincoln was elected as the 16th President. His election divided the nation. One month later, South Carolina passed an Ordinance of Secession, declaring that it was no longer a part of the Federal Union. Within 3 weeks the other six states of the deep south seceded from the Union. For the next few months these states—South Carolina, North Carolina, Georgia, Florida, Mississippi, Alabama, and Louisiana—would seize property belonging to the United States, unopposed by the lame duck Buchanan Administration. The seceded states occupied post offices, customs houses, arsenals, and forts. The Federal government took no action to stop them. As a result, the new administration took office facing a crisis.

After Lincoln's inauguration on March 4, 1861, things began to speed toward an inevitable clash between the opposing sections. On April 12, 1861 the rebel guns in Charleston harbor opened fire and the guns of Fort Sumter responded. The North and the South were at war. Two days later on April 14, 1861, President Lincoln issued a call for 75,000 Volunteers to serve 90 days to assist in putting down the rebellion. As a direct result of these events, several million young American men would spend most of the next four years fighting and killing each other. One such group of men was the 19th Pennsylvania Volunteers, known as the National Guards. They volunteered in Philadelphia on April 16th and were accepted by the Government on April 27, 1861. In several weeks, they received arms and equipment and began moving south.

This Pennsylvania State Militia organization, which eventually became the 19th and later, the 90th Pennsylvania Volunteer Infantry Regiment had been in continuous existence as a military unit since December 11, 1840. On October 3rd of that year a number of persons in Spring Garden, a suburb of Philadelphia, met to organize a company of militia infantry. In December the company was organized with the title of National Guards. This is believed to be the first use of the title now common to the organized militia of the United States. The Guards were attached to the 1st Regiment, 1st Brigade, 1st division of Militia. The National Guards took part in their first street parade, celebrating Washington's birthday on February 22, 1841. During that year the National Guards participated in ten parades with a turnout of about 50 armed men in each parade. The company attended the inauguration parade of President William Henry Harrison; one month later it took part in the President's funeral parade as well. In 1844 the Guards were on duty in

Philadelphia during riots which broke out in May and again in July, as a result of conflicts between the members of the Native American Party and Irish Catholic immigrants. Before the militia suppressed the violence, members of both groups were murdered in the streets and a number of Catholic churches burned to the ground.

In 1846 Peter Lyle became Captain of the company, He would remain the commander of the unit for the next thirty years. Under Captain Lyle, the company became famous as a crack militia unit. Lyle offered the Guards for service in the Mexican War, but the offer was not accepted as the quota for troops was filled. Between 1840 and 1860 the company took part in numerous dinners, field days, parades and reviews. Occasionally they invited other units as guests to parade with them. Among these organizations were the Ancient and Honorable Artillery Company of Boston, the 7th New York Regiment, and the Richmond Blues. Throughout the 1850's the company grew in popularity and recruits filled the ranks. With the units rapid growth, a decision was made to break with the 1st Regiment and form the 2nd Regiment of Militia. On December 11, 1860, the Guards paraded as an eight company infantry regiment. It was their twentieth anniversary as an organization. Peter Lyle was elected as

Colonel of the new 2nd regiment.

Shortly after the organization was formed as a regiment, expectations of war began to increase as the Southern states seceded from the union. Recruited up to ten full companies, the 19th Pennsylvania Volunteers, with Colonel Lyle in command, formed in Franklin Square in the evening of May 14, 1861. Several thousand people assembled to wish the troops well as they marched off to war. When the command, "Forward!" was given, the crowd roared. As the soldiers stepped off, the crowd surrounded them and marched beside them to the railroad station at Broad and Prime Streets (now Washington Avenue), cheering every step of the way. The regiment boarded the train and rode as far as Perryville. There, the troops transferred to a steamer for the trip to Locust Point in Baltimore.

When the National Guards arrived in Baltimore on May 18, 1861, they entered a divided and bloodied city. Maryland was a divided state. This was reflected in Baltimore, where Union and Confederate sentiments were mixed to an explosive degree. There was a great deal of resentment over the movement of Federal troops through the State. Southern sympathizers were outraged that these troops, moving across Maryland, would be used to intimidate their southern brethren. These feelings had exploded on April 19, 1861, when the 6th Massachusetts

The Baltimore Riot, the 6th Massachusett's Infantry is attacked by a mob of Southern sympathizers on April 19, 1861. Both soldiers and civilians were killed and wounded.

Regiment moved through Baltimore. Because there was no direct rail connection to Washington from the North, it was necessary to move cars through the city by teams of horses for a significant distance. On that day, while the Massachusetts troops, were making this connection, they were attacked by a mob of Southern sympathizers. At first they were stoned and cursed. However, the situation quickly deteriorated, and shots were fired by both sides resulting in both soldiers and civilians being killed and wounded.

After the Baltimore riot, Washington was in danger of being isolated from the Northern states. The governor of

Maryland, the mayor of Baltimore, The Baltimore chief of police, and many citizens believed that the railroad bridges connecting the Northern states to Maryland should be burned. This suggestion was made allegedly to prevent further violence, however, many of those recommending such a course did have Confederate sympathies. General Winfield Scott, commanding the Federal armies, believed that if the capital lost the railroad connections with the north for more than ten days; it would fall into southern hands. It was clear that the railroad connections through Baltimore had to be maintained. The department commanders, initially, General Cadwalader and later, General Banks, and General Dix used Federal troops to prevent southern sympathizers from interfering with the war effort. The 19th P.V. served in this capacity in Baltimore. The National Guards camped near Fort McHenry with two other Philadelphia regiments, still expecting to move south. On May 21st Private Oakley accidentally shot himself in the regiment's camp. The soldier's pocket pistol discharged striking him in the chest. Private Oakley turned out to be the only man in the regiment wounded in the 3 months service.

 The Nineteenth P.V. performed its duties in Baltimore without serious incident. The men were mainly detailed to search for caches of weapons, purchased by the City

8

Government for defense by the City Council after the April 19th riot, and hidden throughout the city.

In early June, the soldiers learned of the death of one of their own. James Hamilton, of Company C, had come down with smallpox and was sent to a Baltimore hospital. Left unattended for a short time, he disappeared. On June 5, a body was found floating in the Patapsco River, and identified as Private Hamilton by his Lieutenant. An investigation into his death did not indicate any foul play. However, his death saddened the regiment.

Also in June, General Cadwalader was transferred from command of the Department of Annapolis, at Baltimore, to command of a division of troops in General Patterson's army. General Banks succeeded him in command of the department. The new commander soon discovered that there were in Baltimore, groups of men who had intentions of defeating the Government's attempts to subdue the rebellion. He also learned:

"...that Marshall Kane, chief of police, was not only aware of their existence, but in contravention of his duty, and in violation of law, was both witness and protector to the transactions and parties engaged therein."

There were rumors that hostile organizations were about to seize the Customs House, the Post Office and other key points.

On June 24, General Banks received orders authorizing him to take action to deal with secessionist sympathizers. General Winfield Scott wrote the General:

"Mr. Snether of Baltimore, a gentleman of standing, will deliver to you this communication. He has just given to the secretary of war and myself many important facts touching the subject of the Union in that city. It is confirmed by him that, among the citizens, the secessionists, if not the most numerous, are by far the more active and effective than the supporters of the Federal Government. It is the opinion of the secretary of war, and I need not add, my own, that you should take measures quietly to seize at once and securely hold the four members of the Baltimore Police Board, Charles Howard, William H Gatchell, J. W. Davis and C. D. Hinks esquires, together with the chief of police, G. P. Kane. It is further suggested that you appoint a provost Marshall to superintend and cause to be executed the police law provided by the legislature of Maryland for Baltimore. Your discretion and firmness are equally relied upon for the due execution of the foregoing views."

Baltimore Chief of Police, George Kane, had well known secessionist sympathies. In a telegram sent after the riot of April 19th, Marshal Kane made his feelings clear. This telegram sent to a Frederick Militia Company read:

"Thank you for your offer. Bring your men by the first train and we will arrange with the railroad afterwards. Streets red with Maryland blood; send expresses over the mountains of Maryland and Virginia for the rifleman to come without delay. Fresh hordes will be down on us tomorrow. We will fight them and whip them or die."

When this was added to reports, that Kane had openly refused to provide any police protection for Abraham Lincoln, when he was scheduled to pass through the city on his way to his inauguration; it was clear the Federal Government had reason to be concerned, that George Kane

On the night of June 27, 1861, General Nathaniel Banks, Commanding the Department of Annapolis, ordered Colonel Lyle to take his regiment into the City of Baltimore to arrest Chief of Police George P. Kane.

General Nathaniel Banks, Commander, Department of Annapolis

Shortly after midnight, Colonel Peter Lyle led the 90th P.V. from Fort McHenry into Baltimore. The regiment marched quietly to George Kane's residence. The police chief was taken into custody between 4:00 and 5:00 A.M. without incident.

Colonel Peter Lyle, 90th Pennsylvania Volunteers.

11

commanded the Police Force of Baltimore.

When General Banks made his move to take the Police Board and Police Chief into custody, he decided to deal with George Kane first. On June 27, 1861, Federal troops were sent into Baltimore to arrest Marshal Kane. Late in the evening of June 26th, Colonel Lyle formed up the 19th P.V. near Fort McHenry, and selected six companies to take part in Kane's arrest. The Colonel arranged his force to deal with any contingency. He chose from each company five of the most dependable men and skilled riflemen, and ordered them to march on the sidewalks on both sides of the regiment. Lyle ordered these soldiers to keep abreast of their companies, which marched in platoons of ten in the street.

A little after midnight, accompanied by some Maryland troops, the National Guards moved quietly into the city. In order to prevent any alarm from being given, Colonel Lyle ordered his troops to seize all persons found on the line of march. The soldiers seized both civilians and police, placed them in the center of the column, and forced them to march quietly along.

The odd procession arrived at the residence of Marshal Kane on Saint Paul Street between Monument and Madison streets, at 3:00 A.M., and immediately placed guards in the streets nearby for several squares. An officer knocked on the door of the Marshal's residence, George Kane appeared, and was taken into custody. He was quickly placed in a waiting carriage, surrounded by a heavy guard, and taken to Fort McHenry. The column returned to the fort, taking the same precautions used on the march to Kane's residence. All civilians and police officers encountered were brought along until the Marshal was safely in custody at the fort. Once the police chief arrived safely at Fort McHenry, all those detained were released. The soldiers made the arrest so quietly that few people knew of their presence.

The next morning there was a great deal of excitement when Kane's arrest became known. A large number of people flocked to the newspaper offices, to try to separate rumor from fact. As the crowds gathered, and formed into groups of Northern and Southern sympathizers, they exchanged heated words; but no disturbances occurred, except for a few cheers for Jeff Davis. Ironically, it was a soldier from the National Guards who came closest to inciting violence on June 27th. On the corner of South and Baltimore streets, Private James Manley of Company H, of the regiment approached the crowd:

"...and made a remark relative to Marshal Kane, being down at the fort, and that he would be hung. Someone in the crowd retorted that they would hang Manly, on which he

13

threatened violence. A large crowd quickly gathered around Manly, and threatened to do him harm, when Captain Bowens with a posse of police, interposed and took Manly away thus restoring quietness."

The 19th P.V.'s duties in Baltimore, after the arrest of George Kane, consisted mainly of guarding the Customs House and the Post Office. General Banks had decided not to seize any particular buildings. He choose to have his troops guard these places from the streets, maintaining a visible Federal presence at all times. In a report to his superiors, the General informed them, that the reaction to the arrest was calm. The initial step taken had been successful. The potential threat posed by Marshall Kane had been neutralized. The Baltimore Police Department would never be used to aid or encourage any secessionist actions. Several days later, the police board of commissioners was taken into custody, once again, without incident. The 19th P.V., however, played no part in these arrests.

Later, there were protests to the congress in Washington. Congress would request the president to provide information as a result of the arrests and complaints stemming from them. Abraham Lincoln refused to comply, stating on July 27, 1861:

"In answer to the resolution of the House of Representatives of the 24th instant, asking the grounds, reason, and evidence upon which the police commissioners of Baltimore were arrested and are now detained as prisoners at Fort McHenry, I have to state that it is

14

judged to be incompatible with the public interest at this time to furnish the information called for by the resolution."

In short, it was contrary to National Security.

Once the City of Baltimore came under firm Federal control, the Nineteenth's duty in that city was uneventful. General Dix succeeded General Banks as commander. Shortly thereafter, the terms of service of the three months regiments expired. General Dix addressed the troops of his command and requested them to remain with him until he could obtain replacements. When he addressed the Guards, the decision was unanimous. They would stay, until relieved; however, they were only held four days beyond their term of service.

The regiment returned to Philadelphia shortly afterwards, and officially mustered out of the service on August 27, 1861. They had not fought in any battle and, except for Private Oakley, they had no one killed or wounded. However, their successful, non violent arrest of Marshal George Kane on June 27th, helped defuse a potentially explosive situation in Baltimore. Control of the Baltimore Police was placed firmly in the hands of loyal men, and the State of Maryland was, now, more securely within the Federal Union.

Once the National Guards returned to Philadelphia, they provided an even greater service to their country than their

15

service in Baltimore. After the Confederate victory at Bull Run on July 21, 1861, President Lincoln called for 400,000 volunteers to serve three years or the war. The State of Pennsylvania would provide over 200 regiments of troops to the government. There would be a great demand for experienced officers to lead these units. The National Guards provided more than 450 members of the original regiment to serve as officers and non-commissioned officers in these other Pennsylvania regiments. In the long term, this was their greatest contribution to the war effort.

1861

Official Records, Series 1, Volume II, page 622.

Headquarters
2nd Regiment Infantry, 1st Brig., 1st Div.
Philadelphia, May 4, 1861

General George Cadwalader

   An examination of the muskets furnished to my command by gunsmiths and machinists has demonstrated that a great proportion of them are defective and wholly unfit for use. In tapping the nipples in they have not been inserted straight, and the iron forced around them split. They will not bear a pressure of air, which escapes around the nipple. Numbers of the locks are insecurely fastened, and many of the barrels have flaws and holes in them 1/16 of an inch deep. They are also filled around the nipple with some soft metal. The number thus defective and useless are two hundred and forty-six. The balance are reported to be only in tolerable condition, and if taken apart and critically examined, would no doubt be unsafe and useless.

Peter Lyle Colonel

George Cadwalader Collection, Historical Society of PA

Headquarters
2nd Regiment, 1st Brig., 1st Div.
Philadelphia, May 4, 1861

General,

   Enclosed you will find the resignations of Lieutenant Colonel George Megee, Major D.W.C. Baxter-Captain J.W. Fritz of Company A-and 1st Lieutenant Christian Bird of Company H of my command-Your acceptance of them will greatly oblige.

Yours Truly

P. Lyle Colonel

George Cadwalader Collection, Historical Society of PA

Headquarters
Department Pennsylvania
Philadelphia, May 9, 1861

Special Order #34

I. The arms in possession of Colonel Lyle's regiment will at once be packed up and returned to the Commanding officer of Frankford Arsenal who will furnish good muskets of the same caliber. The Colonel of the regiment will equip his regiment without delay.

By order of

Major General Patterson

Fitz John Porter A.A.G.

Brevet Major General Geo. Cadwalader 1st Div., Pa. Vol.

Colonel Lyle furnished with a copy from this office.

George Cadwalader Collection, Historical Society of PA

Camp Pennsylvania
Headquarters 19th Regiment P.V.
Baltimore, May 23, 1861

General

  I deem it my duty to communicate to you, that, information has been lodged with a Private of Company H of my command, by a citizen of Baltimore, that a large quantity of Powder, has been concealed in the vaults in Green Mount Cemetery, York Road and is now there.

Very Respectfully Your Obt. Servt.

P. Lyle Colonel

P.S.   When information of this kind is given at the
       Encampment, would it not be proper to detain
       the informant and report forthwith to you?

P.L.

George Cadwalader Collection, Historical Society of PA

Headquarters
Dept. of Annapolis
Baltimore, Md. June 7, 1861

Special Order#19

   Colonel Peter Lyle of the 19th Regiment Pa Vols. will detail one company from his Regiment to proceed with a large gun from Baltimore Md. to Fort Monroe, Va., guarding it against injury. The company detailed will take with them four days rations and forty rounds of ammunition, and will be ready to take the steamer at Locust Point at half past three o'clock this afternoon. Upon the completion of this duty the company detailed will rejoin the regiment to which it belongs.

By order of Brvt. Major General Cadwalader

Thomas H. Neill Capt. 5th Infty. A.A.A.G.

Library of Congress, Nathaniel Banks Papers

United Sates Military Telegraph

Winfield Scott Received June 27, 1861

From Baltimore

   The Chief of Police, George P. Kane was arrested this

morning at five, 5 o'clock upon my order by Colonel Lyle nineteenth, 19 Regt. Pennsylvania Volunteers. Colonel Kenly first, 1 Maryland Volunteers appointed Provost Marshall to execute the Police Law. All is quiet. Further instructions will be duly executed

N. P. Banks Nathaniel Prentiss Banks

Pennsylvania State Archives, Regimental Records, 90th P.V.

Headquarters, 19th Regt. P.V.
National Guards Philadelphia,
September 12, 1861

His Excellency A. G. Curtin

    Governor of Pennsylvania

        Governor

   Upon the recommendation of Major General McClellan my regiment was accepted upon the 3rd Inst. by the Secretary of War for 3 years or the war; would you please give me permission as the companies are organized to encamp them near Philadelphia for the purpose of instructing the recruits; so that they may be efficient when we receive marching orders? Also inform me whether I shall retain the original number, 19th Regt. In a few days I will forward you a roll of the Officers for your approval. An answer at your earliest convenience, will greatly oblige.

Yours truly

Peter Lyle

Colonel

   The response to this letter by Governor Curtin resulted in the National Guards entering the three years service with a new designation, The 90th Pennsylvania Volunteers. Despite losing so many experienced men to other regiments, the 90th P.V. soon recruited enough new men to fill the ranks. After spending the winter in Philadelphia, the regiment left for the front on April 1, 1862. The 90th would perform valiantly throughout its three year term of service. From the Battle of Cedar Mountain, which was their baptism of fire, to the siege of Petersburg, the regiment fought with distinction. The battles stitched onto the regimental flag read:

Cedar Mountain	Chancellorsville	Cold Harbor
Rappahannock Station	Gettysburg	White Oak Swamp
Sulphur Springs	Mine Run	Petersburg
Thoroughfare Gap	Wilderness	Jerusalem Plank Rd.
Bull Run	Todd's Tavern	Weldon Railroad
Chantilly	Spotsylvania	Poplar Springs
South Mountain	Laurel Hill	Ream's Station
Antietam	Guinea Station	Hatcher's Run
Fredericksburg	North & South Anna	
Fitzhugh House	Bethesda Church	

Of course, the regiment did not fight in all these engagements without suffering heavy losses. The casualty lists revealed the following:

Killed in Action	108
Died Disease or Accident	157
Wounded Not Fatal	426
Captured	329
Discharged Medical Disability	226
TOTAL	1,238

This total of 1,238 men killed, wounded, captured, and disabled by their service in the regiment amounted to 66% of all of those who fought in the 90th P.V. This was due to the fact that the regiment was involved in some of the hottest fighting which took place throughout the war.

In the second battle in which they fought, The 2nd Battle of Bull Run, the ninetieth fought for only one hour on Chinn Ridge and suffered about 200 casualties as a result. A few weeks later, while fighting beside the famous cornfield at Antietam, the regiment was engaged for about 20 minutes. In that 20 minutes, 36% of those engaged were killed or wounded. At Fredericksburg in December 1862, the 90th P.V. attacked Stonewall Jackson's lines and suffered an additional 80 casualties, most of them in killed and wounded.

The 90th was in luck when Joe Hooker led the Army of the Potomac down to Chancellorsville in April of 1863. In spite of having to do a great deal of hard marching, the regiment had the good luck of being engaged in no actual fighting. All of their 9 casualties resulted from one well placed rebel shell which exploded among the men on April 30, 1863 near Fredericksburg.

Three months later at Gettysburg, the 90th, once again, found itself in the midst of the hottest fighting. On July 1st along Oak Ridge, the 90th was engaged with the rest of the I Corps in holding off a large part of Lee's army until the rest of the Army of the Potomac could reach the field.

In four hours of fighting, 48% of the men in the regiment were killed, wounded, or captured; as the I Corps was driven back through the town of Gettysburg to Cemetery Ridge. After Gettysburg, the Army of the Potomac was only engaged sporadically until the spring of 1864. When the I Corps was disbanded, the 90th, with the rest of the Corps was merged into the V Corps. In May, the men of the 90th fought throughout the "Forty days" and sufffered through two truly disastrous days. Late on May 5th in the Wilderness fighting, the 90th was ordered to make a charge by General Griffin and lost 124 men in an attack which was made and repulsed in only five minutes. Two days later, the regiment was sent forward in another charge at Laurel Hill, near Spotsylvania; and suffered 40% casualties in that fight. As the Army of the Potomac ground its way down to Petersburg, the 90th P.V. continued to see hard fighting. However, losses were lighter in the trench warfare which developed there. The regiment would, however, suffer one more terrible day. In the fight for the Weldon Railroad on August 18th and 19th, on the afternoon of August 19th, General Mahone's Division trurned the Union flank and swept down the lines in the rear of Crawford's Division. Almost two entire brigades were captured by the rebels that day including more than 120 officers and men from the 90th Pennsylvania. After this incident, there were only about 50 enlisted men and half a dozen officers still in line to answer the call to arms.

In April 1862, almost 1,100 officers and men were in the ranks when the National Guards left Philadelphia to serve three years. On November 26, 1864, when the regiment was mustered out in front of Petersburg, only 22 of the original privates remained in the ranks and were mustered out of the service.

Pennsylvania State Archives, Regimental Records

Skippensville December 28, 1861

To His Excellency the Governor of Pa.

    About six weeks since, I received a letter from Colonel P. Lyle requesting me to come to the City. I complied with his request and met him in the Armory(National Guards). He said he had been informed that I intended raising a company of Infantry. I replied that I had written to his Excellency some time prior but did not receive any answer. He said I should join his Regiment, which should be one of the best that has left the State. He said he would give me a position as Captain, of Company D, John Magee being the Captain of the company at the time, but he should be promoted to Major. As soon as I returned to my home, I relinquished my practice and commenced recruiting. I had my men mustered into Company D, and now I find that Captain Magee is doing all against me he can. The Regiment cannot be filled out by the 16th of January, and I suppose he does not wish to have a Republican take charge of the Company. I have spent upwards of $200.00 for the sake of filling out my company, and now after spending all that money and six weeks of incessant labor, I am to be wheeled out of my position. The fact is simply this, the Field Officers and nearly all the line officers are Democrats, and I being a Republican, they wish to dispose of me the best way they can. I am a poor man and have gone to a great deal of trouble and expense in recruiting, it would, thereupon, be hard if I should not receive a commission. I hope his Excellency will remember me once it is within his power to give me a position in the 90th Regiment. I should be very much obliged to his Excellency. I have done a great deal for the party and have never received any compensation, nor have I asked any prior to this...There is too much of the New Republican in me to remain at home when my country is in danger. If the Regiments are consolidated, the officers cannot all remain, and I know there will be more or less dissatisfaction among the officers of the 90th, and I still think I can get charge of Company D. If his Excellency wishes any references, I can give any amount. I will give a few if they are now required. I can give them

        from Norristown   Daniel Snyder Esq.
                                            Joseph Allebach
                                           H. W. Bonsall
                                           D. H. Mulvaney
                                           J. M. Moore

        Reading, Berks Co.   Dr. Suthen
                                           Dr. C. Hoffman
                                           Dr. J. Spotz
                                           J. S. Richards Esq.

I am very truly your obed. Servant

T. N. E. Shoemaker M.D.

This letter from Dr. Shoemaker was the first indication that politics might play a part in the formation, and day to day operations of the newly organized regiment. While it is true that most of the officers in the regiment were Democrats, this situation appears to have been a simple case of a promised appointment which never developed. Captain Magee did leave the regiment, but he was replaced from within by Captain John Gorgas. This was not the last claim that politics played a part in the operation of the regiment and the assignment and promotion of officers.

1862

Pension File, Matthew Mason, National Arhives, RG#15

Baltimore, April 2, 1862

Dear Father

   I have taking the opportunity of writing, a few lines to you to let you no how I am and ware. I am very well at presant and hope that you are well, and awll the rest are the same way. Give mi lofe to mother and to awll the rest of the family. We live very nice. We got a dining room and bed room. Give mi love to all mi invoiring (inquiring) friends.

                      Pattison park Baltimore

                      Captain Rouh Co. H, [Rush]

                      Your affectinit son Matthew Mason

   The above letter and the three that follow it are part of a number of letters written by Private Matthew Mason. These are divided into two groups. I believe that the first letter was most likely written by Private Mason. I suspect that the letter dated April 11th was most likely written for Mason by another more literate member of his company. The differences in grammar, capitalization, and spelling are just too drastic for them to have all been written by the same person. A possible suspect as Private Mason's ghostwriter is Private William Lelar who was a member of Company H, Mason's

Company. I believe that he wrote the majority of Private Mason's letters home.

Pension File, Matthew Mason

April 6, 1862 Baltimore

Dear Father and Mother

   I take the opertoneity of writing a few lines to you to let you no how I am. I am very well at presant. I was very glad to heare from you. I wich you would send me a raser and some stamps and paper. Give my lofe to...Ant Mason, and to Mrs. Gillen, and Frank, and to all the Griffens, and Miss Duffy, and other inquiring friends. We are very comfible here. We get fat pork and beans and hardbiskets. I must close.

                              Your affectinit son
                              Matthew Mason

Pension File, Matthew Mason

Patterson Park April 11, 1862

Dear Father & Mother

   I received your letter on the 10th and I was very glad to hear from you that all are well. Mother, Sam Bartin is not in this regiment and I don't know where he is. Mother, I live right comfortable down here and we got plenty to eat and I am enjoying very good health. We received our muskets yesterday and our accoutrements. We are stationed in a very nice place. We can see four Forts from our camp. They took us to one of them last week and showed us all around. It looked right nice, mother. You wrote for me to tell some news about the war. Mother, you know more about the war than I do for we don't get any news here at all. Mother, I want to know who wastelling you that I kept correspondence with a woman and what said woman you was alluding too. I was really surprised to read it for I never done anything of the kind. I would like to know if you mean Sirrey, for it seems as if you do. I think Sirrey is a respectable girl, as I never seen her do anything out of the way. She always treated me first rate, and she done more for me when I left Philadelphia than some o f my good friends. Mother, we have a very poor arrangement here for washing. I have to get my washing done in Baltimore which I have to pay for, and we ain't payed off yet and I have not got any money. Mother I would like you to send me $2.00 in your next letter for I ain't got any money at all and I will be allright when we get paid. Mother, give my best respects to Aunt Bonn, and to you and father, and to my brothers and sisters, and to Michael Mason and family, and to Miss Griffin, Mr. and Mrs. Dougherty and the two Miss Duffys, and Mr. and Mrs. Bullin, Mr. Ryan and family, Mrs Gillan and family and all my inquiring friends. As I have no more to say I will close for the present so I bid you all goodbye for a while. Hoping that this letter may find you in as good health as I am enjoying at present is the best wishes of your

        Obedient son

        Matthew Mason

        write soon again

Pension File, Matthew Mason

Aquia Creek, Virginia April 23, 1862

Dear Mother

 I received your kind and welcome letter on the 26th, and I am very sorry to hear that father is unwell. I hope he is well again by the time I receive another letter from you, mother. We left Baltimore about 2 weeks ago, and we arrived in Washington safe. When we got there, they put us in an old depot first up, a little place called the Soldier's rest; and we got our meals right off at a place called the Soldier's retreat, such as it was. They gave you the samething at every meal. Well, the next day we got orders to march into Virginia and we all got ready and we was ready to move in 15 minutes and we marched up along the Capitol to Pennsylvania Avenue and then turned in some street. The rain made the roads very muddy. In some places it was nearly up to our knees. We marched as far as the Long Bridge when the orders was countermanded, and we all had to turn back again. About 2 days later we got orders to march again, to go to Aquia Creek. We all got ready and marched to the boat, and it rained hard that day. The Captain of the boat said that he could not start until the next morning for the rain made the Potomac very rough. Well, we started the next morning up the Potomac and we had to go 55 miles up. It was a pretty sight. We passed fort Washington, Alexandria, and Mount Vernon, and some other places. When we got to the place, they did not land us for some time, for the rebels had burnt the dock and the railroad depot. They broke the telegraph and tore the railroad up for 2 or 3 miles. We are right busy fixing it. We have to work on Sunday. It is this railroad goes strait to Richmond. I have not seen any rebels yet. The rebels were strongly fortified here. They had 4 batteries and rifle pits dug for 1/4 of a mile long but they took all the guns with them. Our regiment camp is right on the banks of the Potomac, and we got plenty of fish to eat. There is 3,000 men here and we expect 7,000 more soon. General McDowell is here very often. Mother, we are about 40 miles from Yorktown. We go further south in a few days. Our regiment will get paid off in a few days but I will not get any, for we have to be in the service 4 months before we get our first pay. Write an answer as soon as you get this letter, mother. Give my love to father, and brothers, and my sisters. Tell them that I am right well. Also, to Aunt Mason and family...

Matthew Mason

When the 90th P.V. arrived at Aquia Creek in late April, it was assigned to General Irvin McDowell's Corps. The men of the regiment expected to move quickly to the peninsula to join in General McClellan's campaign against Richmond. While they waited, the men of the 90th kept busy making repairs to wharves, bridges, and railroad lines destroyed by the retreating rebels. On April 30th the soldiers of the 90th, who had been members of the old National Guards Regiment were taken out for target pracice. Evidently, the newer soldiers were judged not to be ready for this exercise at this point in their training. Each day brought more and more contraband slaves into the Federal camps. When one of these women had a baby after arriving in camp, the boys of the 90th designated the new arrival Peter Lyle. Even though the regiment was kept busy chopping wood and unloading railroad iron from barges, a few of the officers managed to slip away and do some fishing without being discovered.

   On May 3rd the camp was visited by some high ranking dignitaries. General McDowell brought with him to camp Secretary of War, Stanton and Secretary of the Treasury, Chase. That evening, the regimental camp was visited by dignitaries of a different sort. A slave couple came into camp leading their fifteen children and a single yoke of oxen. The work of repairing the facilities surrounding Aquia Creek continued through mid May. It was interrupted on May 11th by some skirmishing south of Fredericksburg. The 90th had the opportunity to watch the Signal Corps communicating with rockets. Later in the week, a balloon train arrived at Aquia Creek, and a guard of ten men was detailed from the regiment to escort the train to Falmouth. There was another break in the camp routine when President Lincoln and Secretary of War, Stanton came down to review General McDowell's Corps on May 23rd. Two days later on May 25th, the Federal soldiers would march away from Aquia Creek. Their destination would not be the peninsula and General McClellan's Army. They would, instead, march hard for the Shenandoah Valley where Stonewall Jackson was giving the Federal commanders lessons in quick movements and slashing attacks.

On May 25, the 90th left its camp near Fredericksburg. The 90th and the remainder of General Ricketts' Brigade, accompanied by General Hartsuff's Brigade, began their move toward the valley. On this march, the 90th P.V. had its first soldier wounded by gunfire. In a ridiculous incident, Private Samuel Anderson, of Company D, became lost in the woods while on the march, and while dragging his musket through the bushes, the weapon discharged and shot off one of the Private's fingers. As a result, Private Anderson never made it into combat. He was discharged on a certificate of disability in July, 1862 before the regiment saw its first real action at the Battle of Cedar Mountain.

Pension File, Frank Wise

On the banks of the Rappahannock
Opposite Fredericksburg
May 10, 1862

Dear Mother,

    We were yesterday paid off. I send you $22.00. I am very well. We had a long march of 15 miles the day before yesterday. Don't expect we will stay here very long. Write and direct to

Frank Wise
Company H,
National Guards
90th Regiment P.V.
Washington D.C.

                          Love to all Your son

                          Frank

    Corporal Frank Wise volunteered on November 4, 1861 and was assigned to Company H. He survived all the hard marching and fighting of the fall campaign of 1862. His luck held out from the regiment's first fight at Cedar Mountain all the way through the Battle of Chancellorsville. It ran out on Oak Ridge outside the small town of Gettysburg.

Corporal Wise was killed in action July 1, 1863 in the first days fighting there. When Frank Wise's mother applied for a pension, she used the letters her son had sent to her to prove that they were not estranged, and that her son had contributed to her support. In the pension application, Mrs. Wise revealed that her son was unable to read or write and all of the letters he had written home, were written by an unknown member of his company.

Pension File, Edward Cole

Falmouth May the 10th, 1862

Dear father and mother and sister

    I take my pen in hand to let you know that I am well at presant and I hope that you are all the same. I received your letter and the $1.00 that you sent to me. I had been paid off about too hours before I received your letter. You wanted me to let you know whether the farmers farmed anything or not. I will tell you the truth: thare is farm after farm and no one to run them, for wat people is left, they say that all the men that was able had to go in the army. If they did not go, they would come at nite and make them go, and if they don't go they will take them out of the house and home. That is wat they say, that is left behind. There is the oald men and weamen a lementing for there family, and the darkeys ar in as much trouble as the wite. There masters and all left them and joined the army. They are in a hell of a muss for they don't now ware to go to get any thing to eat. Thare is some of them a going to Washington and some of them ar a going with the...and everywhere they can go. If you ask them anything they will say, "Me don't no sir." If you ask them how old they are, they will say they dond no. If you ask one of them when thare birth day is, they don't no. If you ask them how far it is to any place, they will say, "yes it is a pirty smart

As early as 1862, the war was devastating the Virginia countryside. Those who lived where the armies traveled and fought, found their lives changed dramatically for the worse. Even the slaves who remained, suffered with their owners. Private Edward Cole described their condition in one of his letters home.

distance", and that is all they no. They say that they hante got any birth day nor they dond now a thing, but if you ask them if thare master ever whips them, they will say that master has flog them so hard as to fetch blood. Here I send $20.00 to you. I don't mention any one in particular, for I send it to who eaver wants it. I don't care who gets it, in particular, so that u get it at home. Whe ar agoing on fother in a weak or so and whe do intend to halve a fite about 12 miles below Fredericksburg, for there is about 50,000 of the army and we halve got about 100,000 of a standen army here. I send this $1.00 note home to you, and I am a thousand times oblige to who sent it to me, for that $1.00 note that I got at Baltimore. It did not do me any good, for no one won't change a $1.00 note down there. I want you to send me some post stamps for thare is none to get down thare. I borrow all that I had, and they don't want to part with them. Send a piece of paper if you can. Send it by male. I want you to send me the postage stamps in the next letter. No more at present but I still remain your effectionate son soldier. The money is sent to no one in particular; there is twenty and one that you sent me.

Edward Cole

Direct the letter the same way, by the way of Washington for the 90th regiment for the National Guards, Colonel Peater Lile to Washington and forworded.

Private Edward Cole enlisted in Company E September 24, 1861. He spent the winter of 1861-1862 with the regiment training in Philadelphia and moved South in the ranks of the regiment. Although his command of grammar and spelling left a lot to be desired, his description of the people and the places he observed is quite vivid.

Pension File, William Phillips

May 13, 1862

Fredericksburg

Dear Mother & Father,

We left Belle Plain on the morning of the 9th instant about 12 o'clock noon without knapsacks on our backs. After marching four miles in the hot sun, and dust all over our shoe tops we halted. We waited for our wagon train to come up. Then, our Lieutenant Colonel ordered us to unsling knapsacks; and put them in the wagons. Then, we took up our line of march. We kept on until we arrived at this place, where we met the balance of the regiment. That night we laid down without tents and the next day we commenced and made shelters out of our India rubbers. That is all the tents we will have this summer.
    Yesterday the paymaster made his appearance in camp very suddenly. Then there was rejoicing among the boys you may

bet, especially among the married ones. I sent $20.00 home by the chaplain, and he will advertise it in the paper and then you can go and get it, but whether you go or not, he will deliver it to you. We are in General Ricketts' Brigade and yesterday we had a general inspection and now we have a rough time of it. It is nothing but dull from morning to night.

Glorious news just came into camp of the sinking of the Merrimac and the occupation of Portsmouth & Norfolk by our troops, and then there was nine hearty cheers given and the band struck up the Star Spangled Banner. It is roasting here but thank haven we have a little shade to get into. Colonel McLean's Regiment is in our brigade and a hard looking set they are. We expect to move away from here everyday for the city. I hope you have got well, also Caroline. I have been sick with the diarrhea for the last two weeks, but now I have got over it. I wish you would send me some postage stamps as they are not to be had here as they are very scarce. You would laugh to see Billy—he has got his head shaved just for devilment. He sends his best regards to all hands and also, Lieutenant Morin.

I am going to send home $30.00 every pay day. I was very glad to hear from Sam and john and that they have taken a prize. Let me know whenever you hear from Charles. Remember me to all inquiring friends, and tell John to write. Don't forget to send out some postage stamps.

From your son,
Sgt. William Phillips

Sergeant William Phillips was mustered into the regiment on September 17, 1861. He had been a Private in company K in the 19th P.V. Sergeant Phillips came from a large family. He was one of nine children. Of the nine, three had volunteered for service in the army. In the regiment's first fight at Cedar Mountain, Sergeant Phillips disappeared, and he was listed as missing in action for the remainder of the war.

Personal Papers, 90th P.V., National Archives, RG#94
William Drinhouse

Philadelphia, May 18, 1862

Dear Son

    I am very sorry to inform you, that your beloved Brother Edward has been sent home to us in a dying condition, having been mortally wounded in a battle of New Berne, North Carolina. Indeed, it was rather sudden as we knew nothing about it until last Friday. I wrote to you about it last week, Saturday, but have not received any answer. Your mother is lying very low. From the effects, the Doctor says, of the sudden news. Her recovery being very doubtful. We would like to have you, if possible, to arrange matters for your little brothers and sisters. I would be under a great obligation to your Colonel if he could spare you for a few days. Things are in a hopeless condition here. No one but myself to take care of anything. Your brothers and sisters send their love to you, also, your mother; and wishes you to take care of yourself and be a good boy when she is gone.

                                        I remain your
                                        affectionate father

                                        A. Drinkhouse

                                        Goodbye William

    Corporal William Drinkhouse volunteered in Philadelphia on January 29, 1862 and was assigned to Company G. This letter from his father concerning the death of his brother, Edward, was one of hundreds of thousands which were sent and received by soldiers and their families during this terrible war. Once William Drinkhouse found himself at home, among his grieving family, he could not bear to tear himself away. The grief of his family proved more than he could deal with. When his furlough expired, Drinkhouse did not return to the regiment. On June 4, 1862, he was listed in the company and regimental records as a deserter. Eventually William Drinkhouse did return to the army. He joined the 4th Delaware Volunteers and later served in the 105th Company, 2nd Battalion of the Veteran Reserve Corps. His service in these organizations proved honorable. When William Drinkhouse applied for an invalid pension in June 1865, despite his desertion from the 90th P.V., his pension was granted.

Pension File, Frank Wise

>Banks of the Rappahannock
>Opposite Fredericksburg
>May 20, 1862

My Dear Mother,

    Having a few hours to myself this morning, I thought I could not employ my time better than to write a few lines to you. Hoping when they reach you, they will find you and all the family enjoying the best of health, as I am at present. Thanks to God for all his kindness. Dear mother, we got paid off on the 10th of this month and I sent you $22.00 by our chaplain. I have not received any answer yet whether you received it or not. If you did not receive it, send word right away so I know what to do. I wrote a letter to my sister Hannah, on the 12th and received no answer. Send me word if she received it or not. Dear mother, I am still cooking and getting along very well with the boys. I am fat and as hearty as ever, nothing to trouble me. I take the world easy, and intend to do the same until I return home. We intend to make a move this week or next. I think we will march on Richmond. I have nothing more to say at present, only to send my love to father, and sisters, and brothers, and my sister's family, and in particular to Sally. Syl Byrne sent some money home. Find out if they received it and send him word when you write to me. He sends his love to you and all the family and to Hannah and Sam and inquiring friends.

Give my best respects and Syl's best respects to Pat Kelly and all his family and to Mr. and Mrs. Sipe.

No more at present
From your affectionate son

Frank

Private Frank Wise, like many soldiers in the 90th P.V., sent money home to his family as often as possible. There were several different ways available to the soldiers in the regiment to get money back home. Of the different methods available, each possessed different levels of risk. Some men sent money directly to their families inside their letters through the mail. This was the riskiest method, because, there were frequent thefts of money sent by mail. Others in the ranks sent money through Adams Express, one of the largest express companies in the country. There was some risk in this method also. Although safer than the mail, thefts sometimes occurred, and packages were sometimes lost before delivery.

The safest way for soldiers in the 90th to get money home was to send it to Philadelphia in the care of some trustworthy person. For some of the men, this meant sending it with an officer of their company when they returned to the city. Many men chose this method, and it was usually reliable.

However, most soldiers choose to send their money home in the safest possible way. They forwarded their hard earned pay to Philadelphia in the custody of the Chaplain, Reverend Horatio Howell. The Chaplain made numerous trips home to Philadelphia on regimental business. He frequently carried money with him for delivery to the families of the soldiers. On some occasions, Reverend Howell carried more than $10,000 in cash back to the families of the soldiers in the 90th P.V. There is no indication that the chaplain ever failed to deliver any of the funds entrusted to him.

Pottsville Miner's Journal, Lewis C. Crossland

May 21, 1862

I write to inform you of the movements being made by the rebels. They are gathering in great numbers on the other side of the Rappahannock River and are constantly shooting down our pickets, whenever opportunity offers. It is impossible for any of the troops of this division to get across the river until the bridges are rebuilt. The railroads and bridges have been destroyed all along this line but have been repaired only by the members of this regiment. It is composed of a great many men from Pottsville and vicinity which is one reason why I write. Old Schuylkill County has men everywhere, ready to face the enemy. This regiment is in General McDowell's Division, and in fine condition. The bridge that was commenced over the Rappahannock was completed yesterday, and an engine that was used on the Reading Railroad is now running on this road from Aquia Creek. This road is a direct route to Richmond.

The troops of this division have been reviewed by General McDowell and a number of other officers of the division. He spoke a few words to them. He said, "We will make a move in a few days, and I hope you will all do your duty." The men replied that they would. They then cheered him, and he rode quickly off. The health of this regiment is good, and the weather is pleasant for the troops. It is a melancholy sight to see the deserted farms and houses. There was recently a rebel Major blindfolded brought into General McDowell's headquarters, with a flag of truce. He was afterwards escorted back until he reached the rebel lines. What the flag of truce was for I cannot say. Deserters are coming continuously up to our pickets, and delivering themselves up and laying down their arms. They say that the rebels are gathering in large numbers, but that a great many of them were deserting. They say they hardly got anything to eat, and are badly in want of clothing, etc.
I remain your obedient servant.

L.C.C.

On May 21, 1862, the first of a series of long detailed letters was printed in the Pottsville Miner's Journal, a Pottsville Weekly newspaper, written by a soldier in the 90th P.V. who signed them only L. C. C. The writer of these letters was Lewis C. Crosland, who joined the regiment in January 1862. He proved to be both a good reporter and a good soldier.

Pension File, Frank Wise

Banks of the Rappahannock
Opposite Fredericksburg
May 23, 1862

My Dear Mother,
    I received your kind and most welcome letter this morning which gave me much pleasure. I hope that you and all the family are well. I was very glad to hear that you received the money I sent to you; I was very worried about it until I received your letter.
    Dear Mother, do not share any of the money I sent to you. I sent it to you thinking you might want it. I am glad to hear that George and pop is working. I would like to have a plate of pop's ice cream just now, for it is awful hot down here. I am glad to hear that my sister, Hannah, received my letter. Tell her to write to me soon and let me know how Sam and all the family are, and Sally and all the girls are.
    Dear Mother, when you answer this letter send me word whether Mrs. Byrne received Syl's money or not, for he is very uneasy about it. He has not received a letter for over two weeks. We are still expecting to move every moment. I am well and hearty and I am still cooking. I have nothing more to say just now, only to send my love to you and pop, and George and son, and John. Give my love to Hannah, and Sam, and all her family. Give my love to Sally and all inquiring friends.
    Sylvester Byrne sends his love to you and all the family. Remember him to Hannah, Sam, and Sally, and all friends. Remember both of us to Mr. and Mrs. Sipe and to Mr. and Mrs Kelly. Give our best wishes to Ned Kleper and all the boys around the corner. Tell Syl Byrne's folks that he sends his love to all of them <u>and wonders why</u> they don't write to him.

                  No more from your affectionate son

                            Frank

    In this letter you will find $25.00. When I receive word that you received it, perhaps, I will have some more to send. I will send a small bundle to the hall; you can go down there and get it. It will be there some day next week for sure.

Send me word about the money right off.

Do not go to the hall after my bundle. Go to 201 Vine Street to Captain Rush's house. Tell them that you want the bundle marked Frank Wise and you will get it.

This letter from Frank Wise illustrates the extent to which the Union soldier was concerned with getting money safely home. After their concerns about getting killed or wounded, and worrying about where their next meal would be coming from, the Federals appeared to worry most about supporting their families back home. In this letter from Fredericksburg, Frank Wise inquires whether his money arrived safely, and also whether or not money sent by Sylvester Byrne had been received by Byrne's family. Sylvester Byrne was a friend of Corporal Wise and a member of Company H. Byrne would be captured just two months later at the 2nd Battle of Bull Run, when Longstreet's attack shattered Tower's Brigade and drove it from Chinn Ridge late in the afternoon of August 30, 1862. Byrne was later exchanged and served with the 90th P.V. until the regiment was mustered out. By that time, Sylvester Byrne had attained the rank of Sergeant. He finished out his term of service with the 11th P.V.

Pension File, Matthew Mason

May 24, 1862

My Dear Mother

           I received your kind and welcomb letter, I am most happy to find you ware in the injoyment of good health. I am glad to here that father is better, dare mother. It is the first time that I heard of any of houre men being over powerd. I got a long first rate and I am well at present and hope to find you and all the rest of the family. We are in the same place but we espect to move soon on to Richmond. We are in General McDowell's Division and General Ricketts' begade. Dear Mother, you wanted me to let you know that man was drowned; he wase caring railrode iron off the boat.

   Dear Mother, I dow not espet any thing from you. Keef is well and stood the marching first rate. I have seen George Barton and Tom Warde. They are both in Bellmans regiment. They are very near and are both well. Dear Mother, I had to throw away all of my under clothing and borrow some money to bye some clothing and a pair of boots. I want you to send any clothing and tell Aunt mason that I will write to her as soon as I get cance. We are very busy, dear Mother. Do not worry about me, I get anof to eate. We have to carry houre tents on houre backs.

   Give my kind love to father. Also, my brothers and sisters. Giv my love to Mr. and Mrs. Dougherty. Also, Miss Griffen, and Miss Duffy, Monty Blumm, Aunt Mason, Mrs. Gillen, Mrs. Ryan, Mick Mason and family, Mr. and Mrs. Collem, Mr. and Mrs. Bowler, also grandmother.

                                  Your affectinet son

                                    Matthew Mason

In the letter dated May 24 and the undated one which follows, Matthew Mason writes about John Rose of Company K, who met an untimely death at Aquia Creek. Private Rose had joined the regiment in February 1862. He was the second man in the 90th to die, preceded only by Private Joseph Jones of Company E. Jones had died of disease in camp on April 28, 1862. Private Rose was killed accidentally on May 11, 1862. The boys of the 90th were unloading railroad iron from a barge at night, at the landing near Aquia Creek. Rose was loaded down with iron and missed his footing on the gangplank. He drowned quickly before any help could reach him. His body was recovered several days later.

Pension File, Matthew Mason

         In Camp Opposite Fredericksburg
         Undated

Dear Mother

   I received your welcome letter yesterday and I am sorry to hear that father is no better. Well, we got the railroad finished at last, and we got orders to leave for Fredericksburg. We got on the cars and our regiment was the first Union troops ever passed over this railroad. We are encamped on the banks of the Rappahannock River and Fredericksburg is on the other side. We expect to march into Fredericksburg soon. There is 40,000 rebels across the river. We can see them.
 It is very hot down here now and cold at night. We had to march miles before we got here, mother. Mr. Harington is sick in the hospital at Washington and I do not know what is the matter with him. I seen Billy O'Keefe. He is right well and sends his respects to you all. When we got here it was very dark and we had to sleep without tents. We were paid off yesterday but I did not get any money. I will not get it until next pay day. There is about 50,000 men laying about here. It is a pretty sight to see all them tents.
 Mr. Morrison died suddenly of the heart disease, so one of his friends told me. Give my best respects to Mr. and

Mrs. Dougherty and family...I will have to close now as the mail starts in a few minutes. I hope that this letter finds you all in good health, as I am enjoying at present, is the best wishes of your son.

                                        Matthew Mason

Pennsylvania State Archives, Regimental Records

                                        General Hospital
                                        Judiciary Square
                                        Washington D.C.
                                        May 28, 1862

Sir:

    Private G. B. Kellar, 90th Pa. Vols., a cook in this hospital, deserted from here on the 26th inst. Today a letter from him to one of the house surgeons, states that he received a "telegram from Gov. A.G. Curtin of Pennsylvania authorizing me to bring a company from my district as soon as possible to Harrisburg and thence to Washington D.C."
    This man is a deserter from this hospital, and I will arrest him as such when he appears here. He left his post of duty in the kitchen, without any complaint or warning.

                                        Very respectfully
                                        Your obd. servant

                                        Edward P. Vallium

                                        Asst surgeon in
                                        Charge

To Governor A. G. Curtin
Harrisburg
        Penn.

    George B. Keller enlisted in the 90th P.V. on March 22,

1862 and was assigned to Company A. In May, Private Keller became ill and was sent to the Judiciary Square Hospital. He deserted, and despite the claims made in his letter, there is no evidence that he ever recruited any other soldiers. He also never returned to the army, and was carried on the rolls as a deserter.

Pension File, Matthew Mason

Manassas Junction
May 28th, 1862

Dear Father

    We arrived here at 4:00 o'clock yesterday morning in good health and spirits expecting to meet the enemy. We were disappointed, but I understand they are not far off. We struck tents near Fredericksburg Sunday afternoon and marched to Aquia Creek, 18 miles. We rested for the night being pretty tired. On Monday morning the Brigade started on schooners in tow of steamboats, for Alexandria where we took the cars for this place. I saw George Barton and Tom Ward at Fredericksburg. They were in good health. We are in a nice place here but we expect to hear the long roll every hour to march towards the enemy. We marched in quick time from Fredericksburg to Aquia Creek. Many of the men were obliged to drop out of the ranks, as it was a very warm day. John Rose was drowned while unloading a canal boat of railroad iron. While on the gangplank he missed his foothold and fell overboard. It being a dark night, nobody could see to help him. Billy O'Keefe stood the marching first rate.
    I shall conclude as the mail is near ready to start. With my love to you, mother, and sisters, and brothers, and all enquiring friends.

Your Affectionate Son
Matthew Mason

Pension File, Edward Cole

June the 4th, 1862

Dear Father

I will let u now that I am well and I hope that this letter will find you all as it has left me. Whe are not at Fredericksburg now. Whe left Fredericksburg on Sunday May the 25th and whe went to Elexandria, and from there to Manases Junction, and from there to Manases gap, all over the Blew ridge mountains. We went on threw the Manases gap railroad on to Falmouth station. There they give us 3 days rations and they tok our nap sacks from us. We thout that whe would have a fite in a couple of day or so, for they giv us 50 rounds of amunition, then, whe went after Jackson to reinforce Banks ware he was drove back threw the mountains. He was reinforced with three brigaids and General Shields division of about 16,000 men. All together thare was 40,000 men, but Shields men got thare the day before whe got to Front Royal. He had a skirmish, and he took 150 prisoners, and he got 9 men killed. They was shot in the brest on Sunday.

We ware drawn up in line of battle on the Shenandoah River. Thare was the greatest cannonading that ever was heard at Bull Run. It was Banks and Jackson. They drove him back in the mountains and captured near all his baggage wagons and some 400 prisoners. It was the greatest site ever I seen, to see batrys and artilary a flying all along the road from Front Royal to Strausburg. The distance is 12 miles. The road was black and as thick as hops with cavalry, artilery, and infantry. Jackson flew to the mountains and thare was not much fite...A great deal of our boys is not as brisk as they was, for they had to march about a hundred miles...The chaplen is a taken this money for me; send the letters to him, and he will bring it to me. Send it to the armery, or to the Captain, and he will giv it to him for I don't now wat his name is. Give respects to everyone; no more at present but still remember yours truly.

Edward Cole

Private Cole again provides a vivid description of some

of the scenes which the men in the 90th were exposed to in their travels. The regiment did some hard marching from Fredericksburg to the Shenandoah Valley to reinforce the troops opposing Stonewall Jackson, as he wreaked havoc up and down the valley. Fortunately for the 90th P.V., Jackson had retreated prior to their arrival and they were merely observers in this campaign, suffering no battle casualties.

Unfortunately, for Private Cole, his health began to deteriorate. He did not survive the strenuous marches the regiment made in this campaign. He died on July 7, 1862. His service record listed the cause of his death as "exhaustion".

Pension File, Frank Wise

Camp near Brooks Station, Virginia

June 4, 1862

Dear Mother,

    We got paid off today and we were all very glad when we seen the paymaster coming. We all commenced cheering him. The Chaplain of our regiment is going to take our money home and he is going to advertise it in the paper. So you take a good look out for him when he comes. That will be tomorrow. I am sending $40.00. I must come to a close. My best to all the family. I am well and getting fat.
    My best respects to Hannah, and Sam, and Sally, and all inquiring friends.
Write and let me know when you receive the money.

                         From your affectionate son

Frank Wise

Frank Wise has the distinction of being one of just a few men of the 90th to make the claim that camp life was making them fat. Once again Private Wise sent money back to his family with Chaplain Howell. On May 24th the chaplain had safely carried more than $10,000 back to the soldier's families in Philadelphia. Now, he was making another trip. The chaplain was a regimental jack of all trades. In addition to taking money safely back home, the Reverend also brought packages for the soldiers up to the front. On at least one occasion, he did some recruiting and brought the new men up to the regimental camp. Of course, all this was in addition to his usual duty of tending to the spiritual needs of the men.

Chaplain Howell continued to serve the regiment in many ways until his tragic death at Gettysburg, on July 1, 1863, on the steps of Christ Lutheran Church on Chambersburg St. An unknown Confederate cavalryman shot Howell to death, as the Reverend tried to explain that he was a non-combatant and that his sword was ceremonial. In the heat of battle,

Chaplain Horatio Howell of the 90th P.V. was killed on July 1, 1863 in the streets of Gettysburg.

The Howell Monument, Christ Lutheran Church, Chambersburg st., Gettysburg.

Dedication of the Howell Monument at Gettysburg by the Survivor's Association of the 90th P.V., September 1888.

the explanation proved unacceptable. The rebel fired, and Howell fell dead on the steps of the church. He was one of only three Union chaplains killed in action during the war.

Pension File, Frank Hollis

Virginia, June 5, 1862

Dear Father,

    I received your letter last night, which gave me very much pleasure, for it has been so long since I got one from you. You said that you had not got a letter from me for a long time. Why, I wrote to you two weeks ago and have been waiting for an answer ever since. We left Fredericksbrg on the 25th of May and marched 30 miles to Aquia Creek, and took the boat for Alexandria, and then took the cars for Manassas Junction. We stayed there one night, and marched 25 miles and stopped for the night. In the morning, about 5:00 A.M, we were on the march again for about 30 miles, and so on for eight days. I have been in better health since I been away. In regard to my money, I will send it home as soon as I get it. All that I have eaten since we have been marching was nothing but raw bacon, and coffee, and crackers. I like the bacon better raw than I do cooked.
    We were only one mile from the Battle of Strausberg, and we have been following Jackson up, but we are at a stand now. The rivers here flow so fast that three bridges have been carried away in less than 24 hours. As I have no more to say, I will close. As I am doing so, I will send my love to you and all the family.

From your son

Frank Hollis

P.S

    If you would call at the N. G. Hall, I think that you would find my overcoat as all of them were sent there about three weeks ago. If you do let me know in the next letter.

Pension File, Lewis Wollenweber

								Front Royal
								June 5, 1862

Dear Father,

   I received your letter of the 21st of May, and it has given me great pleasure to hear from you. We Was paid off yesterday and I will send you $10.00. As soon as you receive it, let me know by return mail.
   We have now but very little time to write, as we was on the march since last Sunday, the 25th of May. Since then we have come from Fredericksburg in eastern Virginia to Alexandria by railroad to Manassas Junction, and from there we marched to Front Royal through the Blue Mountains, and will perhaps soon march again. I have endured a great deal of hardship since we left Fredericksburg. It has been raining for five successive days and we was without any shelter at all. We had left our tents and knapsacks at Piedmont Station so that we could march faster. The only thing I had to eat was a piece of raw bacon and hard crackers.
   As the mail will soon close I must bring my letter to a close. As soon as you hear that our chaplain has arrived, take the order which I send you enclosed, go to the armory of the National Guards and show it to him. He will pay you $10.00. I have received the post stamps, and you would oblige me, if you would send me a few more. As soon as we get time, I will send you a description of our march in pursuit of General Jackson and its adventures. I am as well as can be expected after the fatigue of a long march. You must excuse me for writing so poor a letter, but it is as good as can be expected under the circumstances, when you have to sit under a board for a shelter and a piece of a board for a desk. Give my best regards to all and write as soon as you can. Direct your letters to Washington and from there they will be sent on to the regiment.

						I remain your affectionate son

						Lewis Wollenweber

Private Lewis Wollenweber volunteered in Philadelphia on October 28, 1861. He was assigned to Company K and campaigned with the regiment through some of the hardest fighting of the war. Private Wollenweber passed safely through Cedar Mountain, Rappahannock Station, 2nd Bull Run, Chantilly, and Antietam. Finally, fate caught up to him. He was killed in action when the regiment charged Stonewall Jackson's line along the railroad outside of Fredericksburg on December 13, 1862.

Pension File, Henry Snyder

                                    Camp near Front Royal
                                    June 12, 1862

I am quite well and so is the rest of the boys.

Dear Parents,

    I take the pleasure of writing a few lines to you to inform you that I am well, and hope that these few lines find you all the same. Dear parents, how are you getting along?...The creek must have been purty high. We was on an island when it rained so. The whole brigade was encamped, and it was raining as hard as it could rain and we got orders to march. We got wet through and through. We just got out when the bridge went down. It rained for three or four nights and we had no tents. We had to stand out in the rain and take it all of those three nights. We were on a forced march. We marched 26 miles that day. It was on Sunday when we got in Front Royal--Sunday morning--and then we was within 20 minutes march to catch Jackson. He was seen about 20 minutes before we got there.
    Dear parents, have you got the $20.00 yet that I sent

you? I am very anxious to hear whether you got it or not. Minister Howell took it to Philadelphia and from there he would express it. Write to me when you get it and let me know. We expect to leave here and go to Richmond. Our company goes out on picket duty tonight. We was encamped on the other side of Front Royal. All at once we heard cannons commence to roar, and in about half an hour we got orders to march to Shields, and Banks, and Fremont; but Fremont was fighting him. We went out on double quick. You ought to seen the people come to the doors to see the troops rushing through and howling as hard as they could. It was fun to see them, but we did not go far, for Fremont soon made him run... As we was goin through the city was, we had our guns right shoulder shift arms. I was just pitchin the gun down to a shoulder arms when the sargeants gun struck a tree and hit him in the mouth and as it happened, it struck my gun and did not hit me. If it had, it would have knocked me down. Much love from your son.

Henry C. Snyder

Henry Snyder was one of the few non-Philadelphians in the regiment. He came from the small town of Delaware Water Gap in Monroe County, Pennsylvania. He and several others from that town had joined the regiment early in 1862. Henry Snyder proved to be an excellent soldier, working his way through the ranks to the position of Sergeant.

Pension File, Matthew Mason

Ricketts Brigade
Near Front Royal
June 12, 1862

Dear Mother

I received your welcome letter of the third this morning. I was glad to hear that you all are well. I am very well, and have been so ever since I left home, and I think I can stand it as well as anyone. I do not want any clothes at present, but you can send me a ounce hat(light color). You had better send it by mail; wrap it up very small. It will take about three stamps, but you can find out at the post office how many it will take. I think this is the best way to send it, as some of the boys have had boxes sent to them by express and they have been over a month coming, and some have never been received at all.
   You must not believe what you see in the papers about our regiment, as they often receive false reports. We have had a hard time the last three weeks. We left Fredericksburg Sunday, May 25th about 4:30 o'clock P.M., marched till 2:00 that night when we found we was at Aquia Creek. It is about 15 miles by railroad, but the way we came, about 18 miles. We left Aquia Creek, and the next day(26th) about 10:00 o'clock A.M., embarked on board boats for Alexandria, Virginia. We arrived there about 6:00 P.M. and staid there till 10:00 P.M., when we was packed on freight cars for Manassas Junction. We arrived there early the next morning, encamped, and just as we got fixed, orders came to march. After marching about two miles we again encamped in the center of a large clover field, and sure enough, the next day all the bridges was carried away. As soon as we got on the other side of the river about 10 of us left the company and put up in an old house. We killed a small heifer and we had plenty of fresh beef for two days, when we was ordered back to camp, our knapsacks having arrived.
   Since then, nothing of interest has transpired except General Banks arrived on the other side of the river yesterday. On the 10th, our company was out on picket; nothing happened. We are under marching orders. Some say we are going to Richmond via Fredericksburg, but we do not know when or where we are going...
   Somewhere the rest of our regiment was encamped wet to the skin. The next morning (31st), we marched about four miles. When we arrived at a town named Piedport, we left our knapsacks there and was told we would we would have to make Front Royal that night. We drew three days rations... We halted about two miles from Front Royal after a forced march of at least 20 miles over a very bad road, dark and raining all the time. The next morning(1st) we encamped on the other side of the town. In a few hours we received orders to cross the river and we encamped about 1/2 a mile

on the other side of the Shenandoah River, raining all the time, and we was without blankets, tents, or knapsacks. 1st, 2nd, 3rd, 4th it rained all the time. On the 4th a bridge over the north branch of the river was carried away and we was ordered on the other side of the river for fear the main bridge would be swept away.

Matthew Mason

The above letter signed by Matthew Mason is one of the group of letters which, I believe, was written for him by another soldier. The grammar, spelling and punctuation is far superior to the letters which Mason had sent home from Baltimore, when the regiment first left Philadelphia. The letters clearly could not have been written by the same person.

Pension File, Henry Snyder

Camp near Front Royal
June 14, 1862

Dear Sister

    I got a letter from home yesterday and was very glad to hear from them. She said that they got a letter from you and that you did not get a letter from me in a good while. I ain't had much time to write, for we are marching all the time till a week back. I just come off picket duty this morning, so I thought I would write a few lines to you, being that I have the time. Dear sister, you must not think hard of me for not writing to you, for I have not got time, for we have been on a forced march and we left our knapsacks behind. Writing paper was very scarce and we just got our knapsacks. Dear sister, send me a dollars worth of post stamps for they are very scarce. I don't want them all, but I'll sell some of them for I can't send you less than a dollar. Send them to me as soon as you can, for I can't write any letters home.

Dear sister, how is little Mary getting along? I would like to see her and the dear little baby, also.

Dear sister, there was 400 wounded men came in yesterday into Front Royal. They were coming in all day. They do not know where to put them all. They are cut all to pieces by shells. It is horrible to see them. It is a sad looking sight. There was one that had a ball hit him in the throat and it just missed his wind pipe. He was laughing about it, and he said, "a miss was as good as a mile."

If you can't get me a dollars worth, send me just a few—even if it is just two or three. I will send you the money as soon as I get them. What is Abe doing now? Do you do anything in your store? It must be very dull(business) now. I guess we will have to go to Richmond; I suppose in about a week. That is the place where the fighting is going to be. The rebel, Jackson, was here Sunday before last, where we are now, with 30,000 men. Here was where Shields drove him away and took two or three hundred prisoners. Jackson was seen 20 minutes before we got here and when he seen us coming, he left(General McDowell's Corps). They are giving him rats. They are after him as hard as they can go.

Once in a while he gets a couple thousand of our men, then about 20,000 of rebels, then he fights. That is the way he done with Shields. The other day he attacked two thousand of his rear guards and cut them all to pieces.
As soon as Shields got there with his full force, then he retreated. He may take all of his force, which I suppose is 40,000 men, and we take 15,000, but he wont stand that many. He is a coward. He keeps retreating and making guerrilla bands out of his men. When we get after him, he scatters them all over. Our men is capturing them all over. He is purty near played out anyway. He won't stand it much longer the way they chase him. I would like to get a chance at him. I would like him to be tied to a tree, then, I would like to charge bayonets on him. I don't think I would leave much of him till I got done. The more I hear, the madder I get at him, the dirty rebel.

I wrote a letter home a couple of days ago. I sent $20.00 home by express. Now, I intend to send twenty home every two months. There is two months pay coming to me yet. So, maybe I can send next month twenty more...

Henry Snyder

In the above letter, Henry Snyder unknowingly pays tribute to the very man he claims to hate so much. He credits Stonewall with having a force of 40,000 men with him in the Shenandoah valley. Unfortunately for the Union cause, just about everyone on the Federal side believed the same thing. Jackson and his force of about 17,000 men gave the impression of much larger numbers because they marched hard and fast and they struck hard. It was easy for the harried Union troops in the valley to believe that Stonewall had a large force.

Life In Southern Prisons, Charles Smedley

Front Royal June 18, 1862

Dear Parents

After traveling through the different parts of the country, and witnessing the state of things caused by this rebellion, I, by degrees, made up my mind that the larger the force we could put in the field, the sooner would this rebellion be crushed; and it was the duty of every person who could, to volunteer. Having no business to require my attention, that I liked, and believing that if ever I lent my aid in suppressing this rebellion, now was the time.

If I were at home, perhaps I would find more pleasure; but to take everything into consideration, it is every man's duty to try and put down this rebellion. I did not expect to like a soldiers life when I left home, but can honestly say that I like it better than I expected to.

Charles Smedley

Charles Smedley was a unique soldier. He was a Quaker from Lancaster, Pennsylvania. He decided to join the 90th P.V. in May 1862 because he opposed slavery and the men who had rebelled to maintain it. He risked rejection by his family and his religion in taking this action. Private Smedley was taken prisoner at the 2nd battle of Bull Run. He was paroled and went home on furlough until he was exchanged. He returned to the regiment in time to fight at Gettysburg, where he was hit slightly in the neck and hip. While Charles was off defending Pennsylvania from invasion, tragedy struck the family farm. Shortly after the battle, Private Smedley received the news that his mother and brother had both died of fever. Despite this terrible news, Charles continued to do his duty, and was promoted to Corporal shortly after Gettysburg.

Pension File, Henry Snyder

                                      Camp opposite Front Royal
                                      Undated

Dear Parents

    I received your letter yesterday and was very glad to hear from you dear parents. I got that dollar that you sent me. I am very much obliged to you for sending it. Dear parents, we got paid off last night. I got $25.10. I did not quite get two months pay, all except three days. I did not get that half months pay, for I did not get paid in our company. Next payday I will get paid in our own company. So the Captain said that he would see that I get it. The three days and the half months pay will make 17 days, and next time I will get paid in our company. I will get it and send you $20.00. That is all I can send you this time for I paid a dollar towards the sword, and half a dollar to the cook and band, and the sutler three dollars for things I had to have when we would march. I would generally get something to eat. Dear parents, that $20.00 I sent you, if you want to use it you can. Dear mother, who is going to help you wash or ain't you going to wash? Dear father, you want to know whether my boots was purty near worn out. I wore them purty near out, then I sold them. I got a good pair of shoes. I could have had two pair but they would be too heavy to carry. Write to me and let me know when you get the money, for I am very anxious. I am quite well and hope these few lines may find you all the same. No more at present from your son.

Henry Snyder

Pottsville Miner's Journal, Lewis C. Crosland

Front Royal
June 16, 1862

I write again to let you know what has been going on with us since I wrote you last. After writing you my letter of the 21st, we were called on to march. Our regiment left Fredericksburg on the 25th day of May, and met with a great many ups and downs during the march, both day and night. The weather was very bad and the roads in a bad condition for marching, still the men went over the ground as fast as could be expected. Our regiment, along with a number of other Pennsylvania regiments, moved on toward this valley in a hurry. We passed through Manassas and a number of other small towns. We are now encamped on a hill about a mile from Front Royal, which commands a good view of the town. Where we are at present encamped is the place where the late battle was fought. We have been here some time. Our march

to this place was forced, I can assure you, as the rebels had not left long before we arrived. Jackson's forces were in the Valley not far from where our regiment halted. The men had hardly rested themselves before the roll was beat to fall in. There was heavy cannonading not far off. The men were ready in a short time for battle in case Jackson on his retreat should come this way. But he made his way to the mountains on another road. Our men then retired to camp. The health of the regiment is good; the men are in a fine condition, and no doubt, will make their mark should the opportunity offer. The bridges that crossed the Shenandoah River are all destroyed by the late combat, and have not been repaired yet. Colonel Ashby's death has been confirmed by men that were in the late battle. The wounded are being brought into Front Royal from the fight at Port Republic. They have been sent to Washington.
I remain yours truly.

L. C. C.

Pension File, Frank Hollis

Manassas Junction
June 26, 1862

Dear Father,

    I thought that I would write to see what is the reason why you have not written to me. I have not got but one letter from you in six weeks. I have written to you every week. There must be something wrong, because I have written to others, and get answers in return. My health is better now than ever it was. When I left Philadelphia I only weighed 110 lbs. and now I weigh 132and 1/2. What do you think of that? We have a good many sick just now, but I happen to be one of the lucky ones. As I do not know what else to say I will come to a close. In doing so I will send my love to all of the family.

From your son
Frank Hollis

Philadelphia Evening Bulletin, J. T. H.

Camp near Manassas Junction
June 29, 1862

The quiet of our present camp life is extremely monotonous. Now and then I ramble over the old camping grounds where the rebels held their sway--but aside from this, there is nothing to change the usual current of our tropical life. We have fitted up to the grounds adjoining our tent, and while "at home" we have the comfort of a fair shade from a row of transplanted trees, and in full view of the immense plain that spreads itself for miles around us, resembling somewhat the prairies of the west. Contrary to expectation, we have remained a fixture at this point, and there are no signs of removal. The vast changes consequent upon the acquisition of new commanders in our division, have caused considerable commotion among the various departments. The promotions among the most prominent positions runs thus: Major General over the division recently commanded by General Ord has been conferred upon our late Brigadier General Ricketts. Lieutenant Tower of the "Topographical Engineer Corps" (in service during the Mexican campaign) has been placed as our brigadier general, and other minor changes have taken place; not important to mention.

In my visit to Bull Run battleground, I was surprised to find it a most magnificent spot for contending armies to meet upon. It is nearly a year since the painful history attached to this spot was inaugurated--and still the desolation occasioned by the conflict of the 21st July, 1861 has not been removed. Prior to that date, agricultural pursuits had made it a perfect garden scene, the land being of excellent quality and under good cultivation. Now it is a barren plain--fenceless and overgrown with grass. On all sides it is skirted with a dense wood, the northwestern portion of which seems to have been visited by the sternest strife. Near this wood is where Sherman's battery (Union) was taken, the horses which had assisted in dragging the battery over the plain, driving the enemy before it, had reached the wood just in time to receive the charge of the Black Horse Cavalry, and a pile of their bones, now lying where they fell, is a monument to the memory of the occasion. But the horrors of the results of the fray are exhibited by the bones of our brave soldiers strewn around the field! Here, a trench, wherein our troops were thrown and meagrely covered, stretches over the ground they had endeavored to wrench from their foe. Individual graves are numerous everywhere. Clothing, such as coats and pants of blue used by our troops, is scattered over the surface of the earth--in some instances, the bones of the owner still within its folds--and the trunk of a soldier I gazed upon, that had been recently torn from its grave by some ruthless hand, possessed me with horrible reflections; and turning from the melancholy scene, I retraced my steps to camp, pondering upon the utter want of humanity among our barbarous foe, and the want of appreciation of a brave soldier after "shuffling off this mortal coil." Pieces of cartridge boxes, bayonet belting, and other small utensils of an equipped soldier, lay about promiscuously. The trophy hunters had been over the spot in large numbers, and everything that could be used as a memento had been secured.

From the battle-field following Bull Run, still remains the long rifle pit, over two miles in length, through which I strolled on my return. With General Pope at our head, we will no doubt be heard from occasionally--quite refreshing, for it will let the mass know that there is a corps d'armie in Virginia worthy of note. Tomorrow will be brigade inspection; the entire division turning out in their best style. I must now go to work and "brighten up."

J. T. H.

The above letter sent to the Philadelphia Evening Bulletin and published in that paper, was signed only with the initials J. T. H. Unfortunately, when checking the complete list of soldiers serving in the regiment, there are so many men with those initials in the 90th, it was impossible to identify the writer any further.

Pension File, Frank Hollis

Manassas, June 30, 1862

Dear Mother,

I have just got the letter that father sent to me and it gave me much pleasure, for I have not got one for three weeks. Where is it that father says he is going to that he will not be able to write to me for some time. I could not make it out. We are still in the same place, but we expect to go to Richmond very soon. I expect to be paid after 3 or 4 days, and I will send it home as soon as I get it.

There are a great many sick in our regiment, most of which is got the typhoid fever. We also have several at Alexandria and Washington, but my health is excellent. As I have no more to write just now, as the mail is going out now, I will come to a close. In doing so, I send my love to you and all the family.

From your son

Frank Hollis

From the beginning of the war to the end, disease was epidemic in the camps of every army. The medical science of that time was simply unable to deal effectively with the most serious contagious diseases. More men on both sides died of disease than were killed in battle.

Life In Southern Prisons, Charles Smedley

July 4, 1862

Dear Parents

I am sorry to hear that you cannot help being uneasy

about me. This regiment as yet has not been in any dangerous positions, and may not during the war. As far as myself is concerned, I have no fears and feel it is my duty to go wherever the regiment is ordered. The question often comes into my mind, "Have I done right?" To this my conscience answers that I have and must continue to do my duty. The longer I remain, the more firmly I am impressed that I am doing nothing but my simple duty and all will come out right in the end. And being thus impressed, I move along with a light heart and nothing to fear. To be frank, I put my faith in the Almighty ruler above, and believe whatever my fate shall be, in accordance with his will. I know that my course is inconsistent with our discipline, but I believe that at present I owe a higher duty to my country...If it is my fortune to get back safely home, I can congratulate myself on having done my duty.

Charles Smedley

Charles Smedley was a soldier who always did his duty. When he recovered from his Gettysburg wounds, he returned to the regiment and served as Corporal of Company G. At the battle of the Wilderness, near the end of the first day of fighting, General Griffin ordered the regiment to cross an open field to attack and recover a battery of captured Union artillery. Colonel Lyle ordered the men forward and the 90th charged across the open ground toward the guns. There was a short burst of hand to hand fighting, and the regiment was driven back with heavy losses. The charge took only five minutes. Of the 250 men who charged across that field, 124 did not return. Half the regiment was killed, wounded, or captured as a result of that hopeless attack.

One of the prisoners taken by the rebels was Charles Smedley. He spent the next six months in rebel prison camps. He survived four months in the camp at Andersonville. When Federal troops threatened that place, Smedley and most of the camp population were transferred to another camp in Florence, South Carolina. The corporal died in the Florence camp on November 11, 1864. He had kept a diary during his imprisonment, which was later returned to his father by another prisoner. In 1867, Joel Smedley, Charles father, published his sons diary to publicize the suffering undergone by the soldiers held in Confederate prison camps. When the 90th P.V. was mustered out of the service on November 26, 1864, the fate of Charles Smedley was still unknown to the regiment. On the final muster roll for Company G, beside the name of Corporal Charles Smedley, three words were written, "an examplary soldier."

Pension File, Henry Snyder

        Seven miles the other side of
        Warrenton
        July 4, 1862

Dear Parents

 I received a letter from you dated the 20th and, was very glad to hear from you. Dear parents, it has been a good while since I wrote to you. It never gives me more pleasure in my life, than to get a letter from you, dear parents. We got paid off at Warrenton, and I will send my money home as soon as I can, for I don't want to send it home in a letter for fear I will lose it. So, I think Mr. Howell will soon go to Philadelphia, then I will send it home, dear parents. I am only going to send home $15.00 dollars, for I want the rest. I asked Mr. Howell about it, and he said I better send only $15.00, for I will want money worse than anything else. You must not think that I spent it for nothing, for I buy things to eat. John is going to send $10.00 home. Always you wrote that if I wanted money I should let you know. That is something I won't do, to send home for money. Since I have been in the army, I have wanted money many a time but never sent for it.

Dear parents, how I would like to see the baby. It has got a very nice name. I was so glad to hear that you named it Tilly. I suppose that you named it after Tilly Evans. Dear parents, how does the boys get along with the boats? What is Sam Williams doing? Has he got his boats at the gap this summer? I was going to have my likeness taken, then we left Warrenton. I was going to have it taken and send it home. If I ever get a chance, I will have it taken yet. It is not so about Lewis being put in the guard house for getting drunk. I will have to bring my letter to a close. No more at present from your son.

H.C. Snyder

Pension File, Matthew Mason

Warrenton 7 July 1862

Dear Mother

I received your kind and welcome letter and wase happy to here that you are all well. I am very well at presant and injoying myself. We had a very long march: 15 miles in 5 hours in the scorching hot son to Warrenton. It was very hard on the men. We was the advance regiment, and our company was the advance company. I was the advance guard. We got into town before the rest of the regiment and the people in the town was said...and thought that we wold kill the women and children but sone found that we behafed well. They were sirprised and wase glad to see us look so well.

I was citing down in the shade and a gentleman and a lady

come along and the lady torned round and said, "ware are you going tomorrow?" I told her that we were going to stay here. She said you better go on, we don't want you here. This is the hottest place for cessinest that we hav been in yet. We haft to be very carful how we go a round. It is a very nice place. I have no idea of getting home. The way things look down here at present we can't get any ferlow for anything wat ever.

I wood like you to send on that hat. I want it very bad. I want a light one; light if you can get it for me. I haft to come to a close. Give my love to father, and brothers and sisters...

Your affectinit sone

Matthew Mason

Pension File, William Phillips

July 7, 1862
Warrenton, Va.

Dear Mother & Father,

   I wrote a letter to you from Manassas saying we were going to celebrate the 4th. We had no chance to do it after all. On the 3rd we went to work and each company made 2 arches in front of their street and planted trees all over the camp. We had everything fixed up even to our having fireworks on the road. Reveille was beaten at daybreak and every body was gay as a lark. Just after breakfast, the Sergeant's call was beaten and the order given to pack up as soon as possible, and by 8:00 o'clock we were on the march. The way we had to celebrate the 4th was marching in a broiling sun, uphill. We reached Gainsville where we went to camp, and the next morning at 6:00 o'clock we took up the line of march and marched until we reached this place, which is the prettiest town we have been in yet. The distance we marched in two days was twenty three miles. This is the hottest part of the country. They say that the thermometer in the sun was 120 degrees on the second day. I keeled over from the effects of the sun. Let me know what kind of a fourth there was in Philadelphia. There was an excursion from Washington and Alexandria on the fourth to Manassas to visit the camps, and you may judge of their surprise when they found us all gone. We got news here of McClellan being in Richmond, and they say it is official. I must close for the want of something more to say. I wish you would send two large silk pocket handkerchiefs and direct them to me. Take them to the armory, and tell whoever you see there to send it on at the first opportunity, as that is the only way I can get anything. Write to me as often as you can, and send me a few postage stamps. Remember me to all inquiring brothers and sisters and friends, and Mr. & Mrs. Tufts. Was that money in time for the 4th for Ed & Caroline?

From your son
William Phillips

When Sergeant Phillips disappeared at the battle of Cedar Mountain, he was listed as captured. However, the officers and men of his company did not believe that Phillips had been taken prisoner. On the morning of the battle, Lieutenant Anthony Morin, of Company D, had ordered William Phillips to fall out beside the road. The sergeant had suffered from diarrhea for several days, but he had managed to remain in the ranks. Lieutenant Morin, seeing Phillips weakened condition, had ordered him to fall out and remain behind.

That night as the regiment moved into position to relieve General Banks troops, Pegram's battery opened fire on the moving column from a range of only 400 yards. The exploding shells, landing among the ammunition and baggage trains, created a stampede. Frightened teamsters fled the hail of

Captain Anthony Morin, after the Battle of Cedar Mountain, his request to exhume the bodies of freshly buried soldiers to identify Sergeant William Phillips was refused. Phillips was listed as "Missing In Action" for the rest of the war. He was not reclassified as "killed in Action" until 1867.

iron in confusion, down the road where Sergeant Phillips had fallen out. Several men were killed in the confusion. The runaway teams crushing soldiers under the wheels of the heavy wagons. The dead men were buried where they fell beside the road.

Lieutenant Anthony Morin believed that Sergeant William Phillips was buried with the men killed in the stampede. He requested to exhume the bodies of those men in order to identify Phillips. Higher authority denied the request, and the sergeant was simply carried as missing in action. His family never heard from him again after Cedar Mountain.

When William Phillips' father applied for a survivors pension in 1867, it was approved with payment dating back to August 9, 1862. Lieutenant Anthony Morin made a statement to the government saying he had no doubt William Phillips had been killed that day as, "He was unable to desert."

Pottsville Miner's Journal, Lewis C. Crosland

Warrenton, Virginia
July 17, 1862

Since I wrote you last we have advanced to this place, where we will remain encamped until further orders. Since my last letter from Front Royal, we were marched back to Manassas, where I had an opportunity of seeing the Bull Run Battlefield. The bodies of human beings are still to be seen scattered on the field. We were there until the Fourth of July. Our men made great preparations to celebrate the day of independence, but when that glorious day appeared, we were ordered to march. The men were sorry to leave their camp that day, but as it had to be done, there was no help for it. About 11 o'clock A. M. the regiment moved off under a broiling sun. We arrived at Gainesville at sun set on the same day, where we halted for the night. Next morning the men were ordered to march. After marching under the heat of the sun all day until 6 o'clock, we came to Warrenton. After passing through the village some distance, the men were halted for the night, where we are now encamped awaiting further orders. The men enjoy themselves eating fresh cherries. The views here are splendid, but the weather is hot. Still, the men stand it well. There is no news of importance with us. I hope we will soon have something besides marching to do. I think now that General Pope has command of this army, he will move the men quicker than McDowell and do more fighting. The men are all willing to make themselves useful should they have the chance. The health of our regiment is good, and the men are in the best of spirits, hoping this rebellion will soon close that we may give England a chance as soon as possible, as our flag shall not be insulted with impunity by any nation. I remain yours truly.

L. C. C.

The 90th P.V. was now part of the newly formed Army of Virginia, under the command of Major General John Pope. Pope had been brought East due to the administration's concern and dissatisfaction with the performance of George McClellan. Unhappily for the men who served under his command in Virginia, General Pope would find himself overmatched by the Confederate Generals he would face in the East. First Jackson, then Lee, confused and defeated Pope and his Army of Virginia.

Pension File, Frank Hollis

Warrenton, July 20, 1862

Dear Mother,

I take the pleasure of sending you $15.00. I would of sent $20.00, but I lost $5.00 and kept $6.00 for myself. I hope you will not think it hard in me not sending more, but next pay day I intend to send $20.00. Please write and tell me if you got it, so I will not be worried about it. I will send it by the Chaplain. I think that he Will come at the hall in Race Street. As I have no more to say, I will close. In doing so, I will send my love to you.

Your Son
Frank Hollis

Once again, Private Hollis sent money back to his family with Chaplain Howell. The destination of the money was the National Guards Hall, located on Race St. below 6th St. The hall was one of the best known buildings in the city. In 1856, the National Guards, then a State Militia Company lost most of their uniforms and equipment to a fire in a rented building. Shortly afterwards, the men of the company decided to build an armory of their own. Despite the enormous cost, $110,000, the National Guards raised the needed funds. The construction of the armory began on September 17, 1856 and the dedication took place on November 16, 1857. Once the building was constructed, the

The National Guards Armory was located on 6th St. below Race St. in Philadelphia. It was constructed in 1856-1857 at a cost of $110,000. There was a great deal of traffic between this building and the regiment in equipment, packages, and letters sent to and from the front.

Guards continued to grow in popularity until they became a four company battalion in 1858 and an eight company regiment in December 1860. Throughout the war the hall was a two way conduit for mail, packages, and equipment from the front to the city and back again.

Pottsville Miner's Journal, Lewis C. Crosland

Warrenton.
July 22, 1862

    We have not received orders, yet, to advance since we came to this place, but our camp has been moved about a mile from where it was at, it being an unhealthy camping ground. The weather is very warm here, but that will not last long as the fall months are near at hand. The health of the men will then improve fast and the troops can move further south. There has been a highly important movement made lately. That is the advance to Gordonsville, Virginia--it is a great blow to the rebels. It is the junction of the Orange and Alexandria and Virginia Central railroads. Three fourths of the troops, munitions, and supplies of all descriptions for the rebel army, at Richmond, passed through Gordonsville by rail. It has now been stopped since General Pope has got command of this army. He had issued orders that suit the men exactly. They like the way he speaks about all things. The rebels will soon be cleared from their positions when his army advances. They have been for some time at Culpeper Court House, but have now left. They intended to fortify the place and make a stand there. The secesh of Warrenton thought we would have a battle before getting by it, but the troops went by safe enough, but had they met the enemy there they would have routed them quickly. The place is now occupied by General Hatch, a portion of Pope's army. I cannot give you any more news of importance. Our regiment is in good health and fine spirits. The weather has now changed. It is raining.
I remain yours most truly.

L. C. C.

The next two letters, from Matthew Mason and William Lelar, illustrate just how deadly a place the army camps of this war could be. Private Matthew Mason had been sharing a tent with and taking care of a sick soldier. When the second letter by Lelar was written, one week after the first, it informed Mason's parents of their son illness but attempted to console them by stating that he was not seriously ill. Unfortunately for Matthew Mason, William Lelar was mistaken. Private Matthew Mason had contracted Typhoid Fever. He died in camp on August 4, 1862.

Pension File, Matthew Mason

Waterloo July 25, 1862

Dear Mother

    I received your welcome letter and was very sorry to hear that you and father was in bad health but I hope that you will soon get well. I am very well at presant. I am still in the same tent with the same young men. One of them was very sick and I was very busy attending to him that I could not rite sooner, but he has got well. I was very sorry to here that my friends are getting wouned. I am at a place called Waterloo aboote 7 miles from Warenton. We are incamped in the woods. We half to go aboote a haff a mile for water. I was on picket the other day. We had a very good time of it. We ron short of rashings, so we had to kill some pigs for to get something to ete. We can't get anything aboote this place for love nore money. George Worthing is well. I want you to tell Jesse Griffen that I wil rite as soon as I get a cannch. We are moving aboote so from one place to another, that I can't get a cannch to do anything. We get the papers here every day. I want you to send that

It was not uncommon for papers such as the Philadelphia Inquirer to be delivered in the camp of the Army of the Potomac.

hat as soon as you can. I am in nedde of it very badely, for the son is vary hot down here. I will send my likeness as sone as I can get it tacking. Give my love to father, and brothers, and sisters...I have to come to a close.

                                              your Deare Sone

                                              Matthew Mason

Pension File, Matthew Mason

                                      Camp of the 90th P.V.
                                      Near Waterloo, Virginia

                                      August 2, 1862

Mr. James Mason, Esq.

Dear Sir

      Your Son(Mat) requested me to write you a few lines, as he did not feel well enough to write himself. Mat has not been well for 10 days past, but it is nothing serious, and if he should get any worse, I will let you know right away.
  Mat is a good soldier and has never given out on the march yet, and I can assure you that is what a good many are not able to say. We left Warrenton about the 21st of July and as this place is only 6 miles from W—, we arrived here the same day. We do not like this camp as well as our old one; we are not near enough to a town to buy what we want. We are near Waterloo, but you cannot call it a town or even a village. July the 21st, the regiment was on dress parade and the official order on the death of President Van Buren was read to us. At dawn, 13 guns was fired, and during the day at intervals of 30 minutes. The order also says that the officers are to wear crepe on the left arm and on their swords. The colors of the regiment are to be put in mourning for 6 months. Yesterday, General Pope reviewed our brigade and I believe he is to review the brigades that are here. I believe I have told you all the news about our camp, but, I do not think, as well as Mat would. I will now close so as to be in time for the mail.

                      I remain
                            yours truly

                      Wm. D. Lelar
                      Co. H, 90th Regt. P.V.

Pension File, Henry Letherbury

                                  September 4, 1862

My Beloved Mother,
  I just received your loving letter and how glad was I to receive it, it being the first that we were allowed to receive or send since the 9th of August. Since then, Dear Mother, we have had a very hard time of it. We have been fighting and marching night and day. We have not rested more than one day at a place since the fight on the Rappahannock River. Some days without a mouthful to eat but what green

fruit and corn we could pick up on the road. Our feet are all sore and swelled, some poor fellows without a shoe to their foot(although mine is pretty good). With the long marches and hardships, I have been afflicted with piles very bad, so much so I can hardly get along. Sometimes I would be compelled to drop out of the ranks and not get up with the regiment until the next day.

  My dear mother, thank almighty God that I am still alive and unhurt after the terrible battle of Bull Run on Saturday. Our brigade was on the extreme left, just where the rebels tried to break us, which they succeeded in doing by outnumbering us 3 to 1 on that flank. Our brigade was terribly cut up. My company lost 2 killed, 7 wounded, and several taken prisoner. Mother, I thought about you and your prayers in my behalf all the time. I was almost certain God would answer; it was that that cheered me up and gave me confidence. Now, dear mother, still continue to pray for me. Do not get so low spirited, for you will surely lose your mind, and myself a kind and loving mother. Do cheer up, and live for my sake. That you can pray to God for my safe deliverance from this terrible war.

  My Beloved Mother(I say again for I cannot repeat it too often), since the late, terrible battle our brigade has been reported unfit for duty on account of the hardships we have undergone lately. We are now in camp(since yesterday) to recruit our health and get new muskets and clothing. Everything will be new again: uniform, underclothes, shoes, stockings and in fact everything that we have lost. We left our knapsacks on the field of battle with everything we own in them, and were compelled to leave them there in the hands of the rebels, escaping with what we have on our backs.

  How I would like to have some of the good things you tell me you make. We have had nothing but hard crackers and coffee, and once in a while fresh beef. Yesterday, was the first time in three weeks that we had bacon or pork but now in camp we will have everything the same as ever. Our rations will be made regular now that our supply wagons are with us. I forgot to tell you that our General, Z. B. Tower, was very badly wounded.

  Give my love to Pop, Aunt Liddy, Mrs. Clayton and family and all the rest of the family, and inquiring friends. My undivided love to you and a thousand kisses my dear mother, and may God bless you and strengthen you in these trying times. How I would like to be with you once more. Good bye, and may God bless you.

                                      Your affectionate son
                                      Henry Letherbury

                              Company E, 90th P.V.
                              Colonel Lyle
                              Washington D.C. or elsewhere

N.B.
   The post stamps will come in first rate as this is the
last one and I have no money to get more, for what little I
had I spent to get enough to eat by buying hoecakes at 25
cents a piece--about as big as a dinner plate and worth
about 10 cents.

Henry Leatherbury wrote only this one letter home to his family. Whether his concern for his mother's health overwhelmed him, or the bloody Antietam fighting shattered his nerve, is not known. What is known is that Private Leatherbury deserted from the regiment on October 7, 1862. He was never apprehended.

Philadelphia Inquirer, Writer unknown

                                        Early September 1862

   The writer had just arrived in Alexandria with a heavy
mail from the regiment, that being the first mail sent by
the guards for 15 days. The Guards had not heard from
Philadelphia for about that length of time.
   For five days and nights the Guards had been under fire
of the rebel batteries, night and day. In the fight of
Thursday, at Thoroughfare Gap, the Guards kept the rebel
General Longstreet at bay for twelve hours, though they were
only required to perform that desperate service for four
hours. In the fighting of Sunday at Bull Run, the Guards
took part. The fighting was terrible and there was much
confusion when the writer left the scene. Captain P. H.
Jacobus of Company F, who had been sick, took his place in

line and was shot in the leg during the battle. He was carried to a temporary hospital on the field, and it is not known whether the Captain's life was saved or not. 1st Lieutenant Raymond of Company F was badly wounded and left on the field. Sergeant Harry Sellers of Company B was shot and killed while cheering on the men. Sergeant Iseachar Baker of Company F was killed. Some twenty-five or thirty of the regiment were wounded, but the writer was too hurried to be able to think of their names. He says: "We all think the war is about to close. The old Bull Run battle-ground will finish it." In a postscript the writer states that he has not changed his clothes for eighteen days, nor slept in a tent for that period of time.

Writer Unknown

Pottsville Miner's Journal, Lewis C. Crosland

September 8, 1862

In the battle of Bull Run on Saturday, our regiment suffered very heavily, standing their ground like regulars, and at the same time giving the rebels a ring of their metal, which the enemy did not fancy. In the engagement, General Tower was wounded while leading his gallant men on to victory. He was taken from the field, handing over his command to Colonel Lyle. Lieutenant Colonel Leech taking over command of the 90th. The loss of the brigade was heavy, including officers. None of our regimental staff was hurt. It is impossible for me to give the names of the killed and wounded of our regiment. The list will be made up soon. There are a great many of our men missing, yet some are returning every day. All is quiet about Bull Run and Centreville at present. The rebels are hovering towards Maryland, and it may be that they have crossed the river and gone into the state. Jackson has the main body with him, and from some rebel prisoners with whom I had a conversation, I learned that Jackson had said he would soon be in Pennsylvania. It may be that he will try to do some damage if possible, but the men are not going to be silent while he is making his appearance here. He will meet with a warm reception should he attempt to carry out his plan. They are now in large force at Poolsville. Our army is after them, and it is reported that they have had a fight in that direction. General McDowell is relieved from his corps. His command has been given to General Burnside. Since writing the above, I have received a full account of the killed, wounded, and missing numbering in all about 250 men. There is no use my giving the list of names as they are undoubtedly in print now. There are some from Schuylkill County in the list. Those that are mentioned are nearly all from Philadelphia. It has been another good trial by the regiment, it being the second time they were engaged. The officers of the regiment are well satisfied that they can depend on their men doing their duty. The 90th regiment is said by General Ricketts to be the best regiment for drill and military duty in his division. Our regiment, among other noble regiments of Pennsylvania are now in pursuit of Jackson and his band of traitors. Should he make his way into Pennsylvania, let it be the duty of everyone, young and old, to take hold of the musket and be ready for the coming foe. It is now time this war was closed, and it is the only way, as I have said several times, to crush this rebellion at once. If there are any secesh sympathizers at home, send them away to their friends who are now trying to ruin the country. Give no traitors quarter, but send them adrift and let them seek their rebel friends. I know some who are in favor of the rebels. They should have some of our Schuykill County men, who have been in many battles since this war has commenced, at home. They would show them how to use traitors that are at home enjoying themselves, while many a volunteer is falling each day. I have seen many a hard rub since I have been in the service, and I am willing to take what comes. I have raised the stars and stripes, and I will spend my last days defending them. I have the spirit of the Union soldier. That is the first thing that is needed in a war of the kind that is now before us.

Yours Respectfully

L. C. C.

This was Lewis C. Crosland's last letter home from the 90th P.V. The description of the Bull Run fighting had to be provided to the soldier by his friends in the regiment. Private Lewis Crosland was lying wounded in a Washington

Hospital when he wrote this last letter to the Pottsville newspaper. He had been struck down at the Battle of Cedar Mountain. As the 90th P.V. moved into position to relieve the battered troops of General Banks on August 9, 1862, Tower's Brigade came under artillery fire from Pegram's battery. A shell exploded close to the regiment, and Private Crosland was wounded in the left knee. The concussion of shell knocked him unconscious. Lewis suffered a severe knee injury. The shell had broken his left knee and severed several ligaments. Private Crosland was discharged from the regiment on a surgeon's certificate of disability on October 3, 1862.

Despite suffering a severe knee injury, Crosland's service to his country was not over yet. He served in the 27th Pa. Militia Infantry(One of the 90 day units recruited when Lee invaded Pennsylvania), and again in Company I, 7th Pa. Cavalry.

Both of the two letters which follow were written for the soldier by staff members of the General hospital at Alexandria. This soldier, William Crale, joined the 90th on January 13, 1862 and was assigned to Company I. He contracted Typhoid fever, which was still present in the ranks of the regiment, several months after the epidemic began. Private Crale, however, was one of the fortunate few. He recovered from the disease, and eventually, returned to the ranks.

Pension File, William Crale

>General Hospital
>Alexandria
>Undated

Mrs. Crale

  Your son William Crale requested me to write to you. Your son is varey sick with the typhoid fever. But there is hope of him yet. We do all we can for him. He is varey sick. His fever is not yet broken up. I havn't time to write nothin else.
>from hospital clerk
>James Zilsay

Pension File, William Crale

>Alexandria, October 6, 1862
>Monday Morning

Dear Madam

  Your son received your letter on Thursday of last week and is sorry that you have been unwell, but hopes you will soon recover from the neuralgia. It pleases him to learn that his sister, Mary, is getting better.
 The box you speak of forwarding on the 2nd of this month has not yet arrived. There is almost always an unavoidable delay of several days, when the boxes are sent by express in these times, and so that we could hardly expect it so soon.
 William, I found in the hall this morning looking out on

the river from the back window. He is much better(though his ear runs a little) and he hopes that he will be ale to get downstairs this week.
He is anxious to see his brother in law and trusts he will visit him soon after his arrival in Washington. He sends much love to you, his Father, and all inqiring friends, and hopes you will write soon.

Yours most truly

A. M. Mervin

Pennsylvania State Archives, Regimental Records, 90th P.V.

Philadelphia October 11, 1862

Honorable Andrew Curtin

    Dear Sir

As a citizen of Pennsylvania I desire to enter you, my complaint of the ill treatment to which a number of the invalid soldiers of said state are subjected to in the Grovenor House Hospital at Alexandria, Virginia. The facts of which I complain are contained in the following "extract" taken from a letter written me by a relative (Theodore Robinson, 90th Regt. P.V., Co.E) and I unhesitantly vouch for the correctness of every word therein contained.

"Those who are **Patients** in this **Hospital** are **treated** more **like dogs** than men. Several days ago a young man was **ordered** upon **guard duty** at the **gate** leading to this building **he had been severely shot** through the **shoulder** recently, and from **weakness** was **unable to stand** for **any length** of **time**. During the time the young man was **on guard**, the **Surgeon saw him sitting** for the **purpose** of **resting**, **whereupon he was immediately arrested**, **confined** and **fed upon bread** and **water for some time**. **So it is with most of us** we are **not allowed to lie down** for rest with **our clothing on**, nor approach the fence surrounding the building. We have no kind of seats provided us and must use our cots for that purpose. One thinks himself favored if he is allowed an absence of two hours. There is a **camp hospital** outside of **the house** containing **32 patients**, and for **ten days** the **surgeon has not examined their wounds** nor **even inquired** as to **their**

condition. The convalescent soldiers are compelled to assume entire control of these poor fellows so that their condition is most miserable. In a word, such brutal treatment as we receive is discouraging to all patriotic men."
    The writer off the foregoing "extract"(Mr. Robinson) we commend as being a reputable, extremely sober, industrious, and truthful man who, although beyond the age proscribed by law for a soldier, yet patriotically enlisted in the cause of the Union, supposing that he would receive at least human treatment, were he so unfortunate as to have his health impaired by exposure or be wounded in battle. Permit me to assure you that had I known of any other method by which the evil complained of could be remedied, I should not have troubled you with the subject. Sincerely trusting that in view of the above facts you will endeavor to afford the desired relief by having Mr. Robinson removed to a hospital within your own jurisdiction.

                                    I remain respectfully
                                                   yours

                                    John E. Baum
                                    No. 235 So. 12 St.

    I should have before stated that Theodore Robinson has been suffering for five months with a severe attack of inflammatory rheumatism.

                                    J. B.

John Baum was related to Private Theodore Robinson of Company E, 90th P.V. In his letter to the governor, Mr. Baum complained that Robinson's medical care consisted of confinement, brutality, and bread and water. Private Robinson had joined the regiment on February 1, 1862 in Philadelphia. He lied about his age when he enlisted. This soldier claimed he was 43 years old when, in fact, he was 52 years of age. Sometime in May, the strenuous life of a soldier began to take its toll. Robinson was sent to the hospital for treatment of Inflammatory Rheumatism.

It is possible that Private Robinson's hospital stay was as unpleasant as Mr. Baum described. However, it is more likely that Robinson disliked army life, realized he was too old to be a soldier, and wanted to get out of the service. Another possibility is that the soldier just wanted to get placed in a hospital back in Philadelphia. A great many soldiers tried to get transfers out of Washington hospitals and into hospitals in their home states. Once a soldier was safely in a hospital in his own state, it was often impossible for the U. S. army to ever get him back again. There was politics involved in the appointments of doctors to positions in these hospitals in states like Pennsylvania. Sometimes an injured soldier, once he became comfortable in a hospital at home, could by the use of political favors, insure that he never returned to active duty. They sat safely at home, collecting a soldiers pay, while their companions fought and died at the front. This is not necessarily what took place in this case, but it did occur. Private Robinson's problem was solved quickly, however, when he was discharged on a surgeon's certificate of disability on November 5, 1862.

The three following letters were written by Private William Crale as he recovered from his bout of Typhoid fever. He was one of those lucky enough to recover completely enough to return to the ranks. Private Crale rejoined the regiment in time to fight at Gettysburg in July, 1863. He was taken prisoner along with about 40 others in the regiment, when the 90th retreated from Seminary Ridge through the town of Gettysburg, late in the afternoon of July 1, 1863.

Pension File, William Crale

> General Hospital,
> October 19, 1862

My Dear Mother,

    I received your kind letter yesterday and was very sorry to learn that you had a bad cold. Dear mother, my shirt and cap suited me first rate and so did the rest of the things, all but that twenty five cent note you sent me. I was out in the market yesterday and bought a few apples and gave the man three cent pieces. I haven't seen anything of William yet. I asked the doctor about a furlough and he said he didn't think there was any hope of getting one...
    Give my love to father, Mary and all inquiring friends.

> Your affectionate son
> William Crale

Pension File, William Crale,

General Hospital
November 2, 1862

Dear Mother,

    I received your kind letter dated the 28th but I am sorry to hear that father has a bad cold, but I hope he will soon get better. I am pretty well myself, all but the my legs. If I walk too much they pain me when I go to bed and the doctor says that I will be so fat that I can't get in a barn door.
    Dear Mother, you need not worry yourself about me not having warm drawers, for I expect to get paid next week. If they ain't warm enough, I will buy drawers. You need not trouble yourself about my descriptive list for I can draw my money without it for we was mustered in. Tell that brother Willie says...tell the Breyer girls that I send my best respects to them, and when they write to Charley, tell him to keep up good courage and I will try to be with him soon.
    Give my love to Mary Anna and all inquiring friends.

                                Your son
                                William Crale

Pension File, William Crale

General Hospital
Alexandria,
November 13, 1862

Dear Mother,

    I now take the present opportunity to write to you to let you know that I am going to leave the hospital today by order of the doctor, but I don't know where abouts.
    Dear mother, you need not worry about me for I am all right. When you write to William do tell him that I am well at present.
    Give my love to Father, Mary Anna and all inquiring friends.

                            Your affectionate son,

William Crale.

Private Frank Hollis wrote the following letter not knowing it would be his last. He would not need the items he requested from his parents. A stray bullet found him. On December 13, 1862, as the 90th P.V. charged into Stonewall Jackson's lines outside of Fredericksburg, Frank Hollis was killed in action.

Pension File, Frank Hollis

> Warrenton,
> November 15, 1862

Dear Father,

    I have just received your letter, which gave me much pleasure. I have not got my overcoat yet but I would like to have it for it is very cold down here without it. We have left Maryland and are at Warrenton, Virginia. Mind, and send me some cigars and a pair of gloves for I miss mine very much. Send my overcoat as soon as possible. Direct as following:

> F. H. Hollis
> Company I, 90th Regt. P.V.
> Ricketts' Division
> Warrenton, Virginia.

    I have no more to say at present, so I will close by sending my love to you and mother, and all of the rest.

> from your son
> Frank Hollis.

Pension File, William Crale

>Convalescent Camp,
>Alexandria, Virginia
>December 2, 1862

Dear Mother,

   I now take the opportunity of writing to you to let you know that I have arrived at camp and have remained here until the present time, which is about three weeks. They sent me from the hospital without an overcoat or blanket and one pair of drawers. I have caught a bad cold and my legs are worse than they were before I came out of the hospital. This camp is situated about a mile from Alexandria and I was down to the hospital yesterday. I saw Doctor Belinger and he said that I didn't gain much. I have got clothing now and you need not worry about me getting along after this. I sent for my descriptive list before I left the hospital. If I had it now I could get a discharge. They are discharging very fast. If you should answer this letter, direct it so it will follow if I should happen to go to the regiment. There are a great many of our boys here; Corporal Shay and MacIlwain. The reason I didn't write before was because I hadn't a sheet of paper, or envelope, or stamps.
   Give my love to Mary, Father, Anna, and all inquiring friends.

>Your affectionate son,
>William Crale.

   The two soldiers mentioned by William Crale in the preceding letter, Corporal Shay and Private McIlwain, both suffered from serious medical problems. Private McIlwain of Company I, had contracted tuberculosis and would be discharged on a surgeon's certificate in January of 1863. Corporal Shay had been captured at 2nd Bull Run, and was now recovering from the effects of his captivity. Shay's good health never completely returned. He also obtained a surgeon's certificate of disability; and was discharged in February 1864 due to heart disease.

Private Crale recovered from Typhoid Fever and was exchanged from captivity after Gettysburg. He remained with the regiment, and suffered from sunstroke on July 30, 1864, while working on the construction of Fort Warren in front of Petersburg. Once again, he recovered and survived the war, living until 1907.

Pension File, Henry Snyder

December 3, 1862
Camp near Aquia Creek

Dear Parents,

    I sit down to inform you that I got a letter from you tonight, so I thought I would answer it right away for we are going to move tomorrow morning towards Fredericksburg. We are going to White Plain and there we are going to cross the Potomac. Then, I suppose we will attack Fredericksburg.
    I sent you twenty dollars this morning. I kept twelve dollars. I owed five dollars to the sutler. I am well and hope these few lines may find you all the same. Mag DePuy will have to come down a notch lower, poor miserable wretch as she is. I would like to see her go to the poor house. Our 1st Lieutenant Duke joined us tonight. He just came from Philadelphia. We have got plenty of clothes also of grub pleasant to eat. I just got two shirts; also two pairs of drawers. You must not send me my things till I send for them. If I live I will be home this winter on a furlough. We will go into winter quarters soon. I got one of those papers. I have not got that dollar that you sent me. I

Lieutenant Charles Wilson Duke, the first officer in the 90th P.V. to be killed in battle. He was at home sick in Philadelphia, but returned to the regiment when he learned of the impending Battle of Fredericksburg. He was survived by a wife and four children.

suppose I will get it some time this week. No more at present from your son.

> Henry C. Snyder
>
> Delaware Water Gap
> Smithfield Township
> Monroe County, PA.

If the privates in Burnside's army could figure out that their commander was going to attack Fredericksburg ten days before the attack was made. It is no surprise that General Lee's army was so well entrenched when the attack was finally made.

Lieutenant Duke, when he returned to the regiment on December 3rd, had only ten days to live. He had been home sick in Philadelphia but returned to the regiment when he learned of the impending battle. He was killed in action while leading his men. Lieutenant Duke was survived in Philadelphia by his wife and four young children.

Pension File, William Wright

Pollocks Hospital
Near Fredericksburg, Virginia
December 14, 1862

Mr. James Wright,

Sir, I write these brief lines at the request of your

son. In the terrible battle of yesterday, your son fell while nobly doing his duty. He is not considered to be in danger, so do not be alarmed. The ball passed through the left breast lodging near the surface of his back. It has since been cut out. He rests quite comfortably, and will, in a few days, be sent to some hospital in or near Washington, where every attention will be paid him.

Yours etc.
A. J. Sellers, Major
90th Regiment P.V.

The above letter written by Major Alfred Sellers to the father of Private William Wright describes William being wounded at the Battle of Fredericksburg. Private Wright enlisted in the regiment on December 16, 1862 in Company G. He survived the chest wound at Fredericksburg and eventually returned to the ranks. Wright fought in the Wilderness campaign and all through the summer in front of Petersburg. The rebels captured Private Wright on the second day of fighting at the Weldon railroad. He was sent to the Confederate prisoner of war camp at Salisbury, North Carolina. On December 30, 1864, William Wright died of chronic diarrhea in the Salisbury camp. His three year term of service had expired exactly two weeks before his death.

Pension File, Lewis Wollenweber

Major Alfred Sellers was an outstanding combat soldier. He earned two Brevet promotions at the Battle of Antietam. Later, for his outstanding leadership on July 1, 1863 at Gettysburg, he would be awarded the Congressional Medal of Honor.

```
                                        Pollocks Hospital
                                        December 14, 1862
```

Mr. S. A. Wollenweber

     Sir, at the request of your son, I transmit these few lines to you. He is safe and out of all danger. In the terrible engagement of yesterday, he fell while nobly fighting for his country's honor and maintenance. He was wounded in the knee, a mere flesh wound. In a few days, he will be removed to one of the hospitals in Washington. He is well cared for now.

        Yours with respect

         A.J. Sellers, Major

         90th P.V.

 Majors Sellers was an outstanding combat soldier. However, his skills as a diagnostician were very limited. Unfortunately for Lewis Wollenweber, the mere flesh wound which Major Sellers described, proved to be fatal. On January 7, 1863, Lewis Wolenweber died of his wounds

---

Major Alfred Sellers was a man who was in his element on a battlefield. After the Battle of Gettysburg, Major Sellers commanded the regiment for a time. Twenty five years later he would lead the regiment once again, on the battlefield at Gettysburg. In 1888, the 90th returned to that field to dedicate their regimental monuments.

1863

Library of Congress, Nathaniel Banks Papers, Peter Lyle

>Headquarters 2nd Brigade
>2nd Div., I Army Corps
>March 9, 1863

Lieutenant D.P. Haviland
Adjt. 12th Regt. Mass Vols.
      Adjutant

      Having learned with great regret that in consequence of ill health brought on by exposure in the service, and while in confinement as a prisoner of war at Richmond, Va. You have resigned your commission as 1st Lieutenant and Adjt. of 12th Mass. Vols. I deem it but just that I should bear testimony to your gallantry in action and good conduct and efficiency as an officer, and I know that when you are again restored to health, you will rejoin the service which at any time can ill afford the loss of an officer of your ability. Trusting that you may return with rank and a command that your past services so justly entitle you to.
      With my best wishes for your health, I am

>P. Lyle C.O. 90th P.V.

>Commanding Brigade

Pension File, Thomas Benner

>Camp Pratt's Point, Virginia
>Thursday Evening, March 19, 1863

My Dear Parents

      I wrote to you just after the Battle of Fredericksburg and I answered your letter respecting my being killed, and still I have received no answer from you. It may be on account of my coldness in writing to you but, you must excuse the manner in which I have wrote. You must not complain. I would not have written to you in such a manner but George sent a letter to me at Washington about three years ago, which I have since never forgotten, nor I never will, if I should live to be a hundred years old. It was written by your consent and by your dictation, so you must know that he was the one that has tried to widen the break between us, for which I am very sorry.

Dear Father, I wish you would let me know how you found out that I was a Sergeant and that I was reported killed in the <u>Fredericksburg Slaughter Pen</u>. I wrote to you from the Battlefield, and I have never received but one letter from you, Dear Father. I suppose you must feel proud of me; at least I feel proud of myself, having raised from 5th Corporal to 2nd Sergeant. It may be that I will be a Lieutenant before this unnatural war is over. It is said that self praise is half scandal but this much I can say: that no one ever entered the ranks with a more full determination to redeem himself or die, than I did. If I was in any other regiment than this, I would have been a lieutenant before this time. The regiment is an old organization and none are promoted but those who belonged to it before the war commenced. So if you would like to see me in a higher position than I am now, you have it in your power to have me promoted. I am sure you are acquainted with the Governor of Maryland, A.W. Bradford. A line from him to Colonel Lyle, stating that he would like to See me promoted, would do business for me. Such influence as that or any one high in military power would.

Dear Father, I was in Baltimore on the 8th of February and again on the night of the 17th. I went to see Tim Echols and heard that he was buried that day, so I went on to Washington to join the regiment. I expect to be again in Baltimore on or about the 10th of May, when I will see you. Hoping to see you and hear from you soon, I remain your

                                         outcast Son
                                         Thomas S. Benner alias
                                         Thomas S. Gibney

Give my love to mother and direct Thomas S. Benner
                                         Co. A, 90th Regt. P.V.
                                         Washington, D.C.

Thomas Benner enlisted in Company A of the 90th P.V. on

November 25, 1861 using the alias of Thomas Gibney. He attained the rank of sergeant and served with the regiment throughout the war. Thomas Benner had originally lived in Baltimore, but had a falling out with his family sometime in 1857. Shortly afterward, he left Baltimore and went to Washington to look for work. Unable to find work in Washington, Thomas left there in 1858 and traveled to Philadelphia, where he found employment and settled down.

Pension File, Alexander Waters

> Camp Lower Belle Plain,
> Virginia
> March 19, 1863

Mrs. Anna Waters

    Madam:

      I received a letter from you in regard to Alexander Waters, a member of my company who was killed at the Battle of Antietam, September 17, 1862; but not being aware that he was a married man, I was surprised in getting a letter from you claiming to be his wife. As I know he never sent pay to anyone, and as I have had much difficulty with people saying that they are the wives of men killed in action, I have to be very particular about what I do.
  But, if you can prove to me in any way that Alexander Waters is your lawful husband, I shall be pleased to do all that I can for you.
  I shall be in Philadelphia, if the army does not move by the 27th or 28th of March, and if you arrive at Philadelphia and call at 1031 Frankford Road, I will do all that lays in my power for you; or, if you do not get to Philadelphia, let me know and direct your letter to Captain Jacob M. Davis, Company B, 90th Regiment, P.V., Colonel P. Lyle, Robinson's Division, Washington D.C.

Jacob M. Davis, Captain
Co. B, 90th regt. P.V.

Mrs. Anna Waters had written to Captain Jacob M. Davis when she learned of her husband's death at Antietam. Alexander Waters had enlisted on December 10, 1861 in Philadelphia and assigned to Company B. He was with the regiment from that day until the morning of September 17, 1862. He went into action with the regiment near the famous cornfield at Antietam. On that September morning the 90th moved through the East Woods in the direction of the cornfield. While still under cover of the woods, Colonel Peter Lyle saw Colonel Richard Coulter approaching him. Coulter had taken charge of Hartsuff's Brigade, when Hartsuff went down wounded. The brigade was fighting on the left of the cornfield and under heavy pressure from attacking Confederate troops. When Coulter rode up to Colonel Lyle, he shouted, "For God's sake come and help us out!" Colonel Christian, Lyle's brigade commander, had just fled the battlefield in terror[he would be forced to resign two days later]. Without orders, Colonel Lyle led the 90th P.V. forward to Coulter's assistance. Hartsuff's brigade was immediately withdrawn, and the 90th replaced it in line of battle. The regiment stood firm under a brutal fire from the 4th Alabama and the 5th Texas. For about twenty minutes, the soldiers of the 90th held off the attackers, exchanging heavy volleys, and taking and inflicting heavy casualties. Finally the weight of the rebel attack became too much and slowly the regiment was forced backward, exchanging fire as they retreated. The 90th withdrew fighting into the East Woods and beyond. Their twenty minute fight near the cornfield cost them a total of 95 men killed or wounded. In that twenty minutes, 36% of the 90th P.V. was left killed or wounded on the Antietam Battlefield. Private Alexander Waters was one of those casualties.

Pension File, John Stutzman

April 10, 1863   Camp near Belle Plain, VA

Dear Sister

   I take the opportunity to let you know that I received your most welcome letter. I was very glad to hear from you once more, and you write a pretty good letter and a big one. Thems the right kind of letters to send down here in this part of the country, and furthermore I like such a letter to read. We left old landing one day last week. I can't tell you what day it was but anyhow we left there to join the brigade again. Now we have picket duty to do and have a company drill at nine o'clock, then roll call at twelve o'clock. Then, another drill at two o'clock and a dress parade at sundown, tattoo at 9:00 P.M., and taps at quarter past nine. Then, we go to warm feather beds so good we can't sleep in it. Further, I let you know that we had a general muster today for pay. We had to have knapsacks on our backs, and haversacks, and canteens and go out.

President Lincoln was down here yesterday and he reviewed the four Army Corps, him and his wife and son. Well, the First was to get breakfast in the morning at five o'clock, and then clean our brass and muskets and have our shoes blackened and go out. We had to walk about four miles to go where it was. The review was to be at six o'clock in the morning, but it didn't come off until the afternoon. We was the first brigade on the ground and we had to wait till they all was there. They fired a dozen cannons when he appeared on the field. After he was there it did not last long, for he was to ride in front of the rest of them, and after we passed in review, march by companies front. After we got past him we was done and we came home and had our dinner. After we was in camp that day, we had to come out on dress parade. After that was over, we was done for.

Today, we turn over and we have that muster; (and) we had a review last week, just our division and General Hooker... I have wrote so much. I have started to write as big a letter but I am getting tired to write so much, and I'll make it a short letter. I can write a big letter if I set my mind to it. You must excuse me for not writing a big letter. I'll write you a big letter one of these days.

We had a good bit of marching these last few days, and so I get tired of writing, but I'll give you a pretty good letter. After all I must write a letter to Joseph McCarty for he wants me to write to him. I'll tell you what you can do—you can tell William Robins that me and a companion of mine is going to write to him. He wasn't discharged from the service. He is a deserter. He deserted, when we went into the Bull Run fight, and we hain't seen him since. If he ain't careful he will be caught for the government is going to conscript up in Pennsylvania, and he will get caught.

I always like to get an answer when I write to a person. Now, I must tell you that we made out right. Our new camp, when we came here, it was nothing but big trees and brush. It took us two days to clear it up and get it fixed up. We live here but know we have a log camp to live in, an live high. We get our potatoes and molasses and soft bread, and fresh beef once in five days.

There is no talk of moving yet, for I don't think the army will move before these conscripts come down. We are going to be filled up with conscripted men, then we will have a full regiment again. We heard today that the I Corps is going to stay around Aquia Creek, and if we stay here this summer, we wont have any fighting unless the rebs come over the river to attack us. Then, we would have some fighting to do, but I guess there is no danger of them crossing the river.

    I seen in the paper the other day that our fellows drove them out of Tennessee again, and the women and children is leaving Charleston, expecting a fight down there. Our skirmishers are between our pickets and their pickets, and so they expect an attack on them. I really think the war will soon be over, then, we can come home and rest awhile. After a rest, I'll go to boating again, my old job. If I am at home I'll take good care, and stay home for awhile, and have some fun there. I haven't seen any fun since I left home...but if I knowed then what I know now...

John Stutzman

    John Stutzman was another of the non-Philadelphians in the regiment. He joined the 90th P.V. in December of 1861 and became a member of Company B. Before his term of service ended he was promoted to the rank of Corporal. He received a gunshot wound in the charge, which the 90th made, on the first day of fighting in the Wilderness. However, he recovered from this wound and later returned to the ranks.

Pension File, Henry C. Snyder

April 17, 1863
Camp near Belle Plain,
Virginia

Dear Parents,

    I received your letter dated the twelfth and was very glad to hear from you. I am well and hope these few lines will find you all the same. We expect to get paid off now in a couple of days, but I won't have over twenty six dollars to send home. I am very sorry. They are going to take our clothing bite off. I have had about sixty four or five dollars worth, and they only allow us $42.00 a year. So, it will take about half our pay to settle up. That is the way the government does. I did want to send home $40.00, but I can't now, the way things is going. But I am satisfied to settle up every year, so, when we get discharged they can't take it out of our bounty.

They are going to break the regiment up and make them in three companies, and muster the officers and non-commissioned officers out. They will keep the oldest corporals and sergeants. So, I think I will stand a good chance of getting out, but we will get drafted right off; they don't know that I am underage. I won't tell them till I get out. When I enlisted I was put down as 18 years, so I will stand a good chance of getting out of the service.

So, they have got Dan Snyder in Fort Delaware. You say he was caught as a spy. If they can prove he is a spy, which they can, if they found any papers on him which concerned the government. They will hang him, that is a sure thing, but I would hate to see it done. It is his own fault. He had ought to know better to have government papers about him. Tell uncle Will or some of them, they had better go down if they want to see him before he dies, for they will hang him sure. Maybe they can get him clear by being his relatives. I did write to Lil Staples a purpose to tell Evert to leave, for they are bound to fetch him back, and Hooker will shoot him, being it is the second time he has deserted. There is no danger of them ever finding it out, so don't you worry yourself about it. Tell John that I got his letter, and answered it right away. I wrote a letter to Charley, and told him that I sent him a photograph, but forgot to put it in, so I will send it in this letter and you give it to him. So, no more at present from your son.

Henry C. Snyder

The soldier referred to in Henry Snyder's letter as Evert, was most likely John W. Staples a former member of Company K. Private Staples had enlisted in the regiment on December 3, 1861. However, Staples did not find the service to his liking. He deserted from the regiment on May 27,1862. There is no record indicating he was ever apprehended or that he ever returned to the army. Perhaps, Henry Snyder's warning motivated Staples to put himself out of the Government's reach.

Pennsylvania State Archives, Regimental Records

                                Philadelphia, April 25, 1863

To His Excellency

    Andrew G. Curtin

        Governor of Pennsylvania

Respected Sir

    I have asked my friend Colonel Chorman to call upon you in relations to my step-son Lieutenant John A. Griffin, who is, as you will see by his letter to us, at present sick at the Hospital at Georgetown, Virginia.
    A perusal of his letter will at once enable you to see the importance of his obtaining his Commission as Second Lieutenant. He has hardly as yet recovered from a wound he received at Fredericksburg, and now suffering from Typhoid fever. You may well imagine our anxiety when we hear that he is even without means. When I add to this that he has a wife in this city who has been sick since his absence, and who has now become insane, you will have some idea of our position, and of his desire to remit us as soon as possible for advances we have been obliged to make him.
    I would ask of you, therefore, under the circumstances to hand Colonel Chorman his Commission and confer a great favor upon us.

                    Very Respectfully

                    Samuel Lehr
                    1419 Spruce St.

Samuel Lehr wrote to Governor Curtin to ask for relief for his stepson John Griffin. Griffin had been a member of the National Guards in the militia and in the 19th P.V. He was mustered into the 90th P.V. on September 17, 1861. Colonel Lyle recommended John Griffin for promotion to 2nd Lieutenant on January 9, 1863. Lieutenant Griffin's promotion became caught up in the controversy ignited by Governor Curtin issuing a Captain's Commission for Lieutenant George Watson. Colonel Lyle's objections to Watson's promotion delayed official recognition of all regimental advancement until late in 1864.

Pension File, Henry Snyder

                                      April 26, 1863
                                      Camp near Belle Plain, Virginia

Dear Parents,

     I received your letter dated the twenty first and was sorry to hear that you were not all well. I am well and hope these few lines may find you all the same. I hope that Joe, and Father, and Sister is better. We expect to move tomorrow morning towards Falmouth. We are going to join another brigade, for ours is going to be broken up. I would like to have sent home more money, but I only got $34.70 out of two months pay.
     I have been on picket duty for three days and just came in. It rained for two days while I was out We were the outside pickets. We could see the rebels from where we was

on picket.

Dear father, there is men getting commissions. Can't you get me one? Charles Brodhead is in the State Senate, is he not? You and him is good friends. Can't you write a letter to him and ask him if he would not get me one? Him and Governor Curtin is good friends. If anybody could get me one, he could. You write to him and ask him. Tell him that I have been in every one of the battles that the regiment has been in; that is eight. I have always done my duty. Write to him and see what he would say. Tell him what regiment I belong to. I can give him good recommendations by the officers in the regiment. Don't tell anybody that I wrote to you about this...

The rebels said the other day that they got a new general, General Starvation. There was two hundred and fifty came into our lines while we was on picket. They said they did not get much to eat and they were starving. No more at present.

Henry C. Snyder

This letter from Henry Snyder is one of just a few found in which a soldier in the 90th asks a relative to intercede with state politicians for assistance in getting promoted. However, there were quite likely dozens of other such letters which did not become part of any official record. There are dozens of letters in the regimental records in which politicians request promotions for men in the regiment. However, it does not appear that Henry Snyder's father honored his request. There is no record of any politician recommending Sergeant Snyder for a commission.

The two long letters which follow were written by John Stutzman just after the Battle of Chancellorsville. Each went to one of Stutzman's two sisters, and describes in great detail the action of the regiment in the campaign around Chancellorsville. All of the regiment's casualties, one man killed and eight others wounded, occurred on April 30, 1863 when the I Corps was demonstrating in front of Fredericksburg. From this, it might appear that the 90th played no other part in this campaign. It is clear from these two letters that the regiment, indeed, the entire I Army Corps played a large part in everything but the actual fighting.

The only man in the 90th P.V. who was killed in this fight was Samuel R. Miller who had enlisted in Company K on November 26, 1861. Private Samuel Jackaway of Company K, who was wounded by the same shell, remembered the death of Miller saying:

"Samuel Miller was killed at Fitzhugh House opposite Fredericksburg...We were in line of battle at the time but our guns were stacked and we were lying down. The rebels got a line on us and commenced throwing shells at us from the opposite side of the river. One of the shells exploded in our ranks and killed Corporal Samuel Miller and wounded 7 or 8 men. I was slightly wounded in the right forearm. William Lodge had a leg amputated as a result of a wound.
   I remember that a large piece of shell struck Samuel Miller in the left side of his face and cut out the left eye and the whole side of his face. When I went to the hospital to get my wound dressed, I saw Miller lying on a stretcher outside of the hospital tent with blood gushing out of his

wound. He died on the stretcher where I last saw him.
   Sergeant Kitts of our company, who was a personal friend of Millers, got permission to bring his body to Philadelphia and the body was buried in Philadelphia..."

Pension File, John Stutzman,

May 8, 1863   Camp in the woods near the Rappahannock

Dear Sister,

   I take the opportunity to let you know that I received your welcome letter this morning and I was very glad to hear from you. I let you know that we got marching orders on he 30th of April and we marched that day near the river and then we dug in. Got orders to pack up our knapsacks to march again. Well, we did so and marched down to the river and we halted there till they had the pontoon bridges across the river. One of our brigades went over the river...we didn't get across the river, still, and we stayed there along that river. The next day about five o'clock the rebels commenced shelling our division and one came over in our regiment and burst in our company F and killed one and wounded seven besides in one company.
   We had to get out of that, and move back further in a ditch, and laid there that night. Orders came in that night to be ready the next morning to move at daylight, and so we did, and I commenced to answer mother's letter and we had to go before I had it finished. Well, we got up and marched that day, all day, until we got above Falmouth, about ten miles. We crossed the river that evening, and then we halted, and just was a going to put up our tents and the orders came in again to pack up. We formed a line of battle there, and kept there awhile. I couldn't make out what it's for, and directly we hear that there has been a fight between 5 and 6 o'clock. The IX corps broke and ran, and the rebels drove our men, and that's the reason we had to march that night. Well, we laid there about twenty minutes and the words was "Forward, march" and we marched out to where the battle was fought, and just as we got out there, we turned to the right.
   You never seen the like before, running in all directions, getting in ditches in every direction, and so we went back in the rear where they couldn't hurt us that

night. We was the last regiment off that field.   All the rest of the regiments all run away from us, and we come off the field by a flank and got in a ditch.   We were safe for that night. I received a letter from home that night. We got in the ditch, and the order came that night to march at daylight in the morning.   I sat down and commenced to write a letter but I couldn't finish it...We marched that morning, and I thought that we would only go only 2 or 3 miles, but they took us 27 miles that day.   We had our heavy knapsacks to carry,   and it was   awful warm that day, but we had to stick it out. We crossed the river that evening about six miles above Banks Ford. Just as we got across the river, we put up our tents to have a good nights rest, but as luck happens we had to be drawn up in line of battle, for there was a general engagement that evening and reports came in from the front that General Reynolds should get his corps in line, and not leave a man go through our lines. So we stayed there about a half an hour, and we started to march again, and marched purty near all night. We got there at last, and just as we got to the road where the fighting was that evening, the XI Corps opened a fight just as we got there. I thought we would get in it that night, but we didn't get in it. I wasn't a bit sorry that we didn't get in it.

  We went about half a mile on the right of the battle and we stopped there.   General Robinson told us to throw up breastworks, it would help us a good bit, and we went to work, and worked all night. In the morning I thought sure we would get in it, and at daylight they commenced firing and fought about four hours, but we didn't get in that. Just ought to hear the firing and roaring with cannons and muskets. I thought the whole world was coming to an end.

  When the fight was over some of our fellows went where the battle was fought, and allowed that a body could see half a dozen men piled up on top of each other. A body couldn't walk for dead men. That wasn't only our men, it was the most of the rebels. Them that got out safe, they told us that the rebels lost two to our one. So you may think it was a hard battle...

  On Monday the officers came around and told us that there was going to be a fight, and we should keep our guns capped. That was about five o'clock in the evening. A brigade of the 1st division came up the road and went in front of us for fear old Johnny Reb would come. General Baxter came along the line and told us that the Bucktails was out in front of us, and that we shouldn't fire on our own men. That was our own general of our brigade, and he allowed that if the rebels would come, that we would have two hours of daylight we could give them enough of fighting until dark...

That was on Monday evening and we stayed there till Thursday night about nine o'clock. We got orders to pack up and we did so. It was raining awful hard but we had to go, and then we was drawed up in line and we stood there three hours. Orders came to make ourselves as comfortable as we could, and we put our tents up again and stayed there about three hours longer. Then we all thought we would have to cover the retreat. I thought surely that our whole division would be in Richmond insides of ten hours, but we didn't have no trouble at all. It was daylight before we got to the river and in the morning the old bull dogs began to growl again. I thought then that we would catch it when the rebels commence to fire on the pickets.

We had eight days rations in our knapsacks and we was to drive the rebels into Richmond, but we couldn't go that far with our eight days rations. I began to think that them eight days rations would carry us to Richmond, but as prisoners. So, we was glad to get out of that again. Since we recrossed the river, the rebels holler over to our pickets,"How do you like Hooker?"

We marched back to Falmouth that day and stayed there all night, and no wood there, and it was raining purty near freezing that night for the want of fire, but we had no wood. The next morning we packed up again and was to go over to our old encampment, but we didn't go there. We marched awhile and turned toward the river again. You ought to see the boys all cry, "Hooker is going across the Rappahannock, We'll have some more slaughter", but we got camped about a mile from the river. We are here yet. We have been in the woods and had a beautiful camp, and the doctors allowed that it wasn't healthy in the woods, so we had to move outside where there is no shade.

I let you know that we had the 136th P.V. went home on Wednesday morning, and we had a big time of it. They got a band of music and escorted them down to Falmouth. Before they left the brigade, they came in front of our Colonel and gave him three cheers for Colonel Lyle and, three cheers for the 90th P.V. We had a merry time of it, but they were merrier that I was...

Now we are in camp again and intend anyhow to have the rebs come and try us. We have tried them often enough. I don't think we will go across the river in a hurry again... We was very lucky this time. We wasn't engaged at all. We didn't get no ticket for the ball this time.

This thing of going into a fight is pretty nasty. Some poor fellows never see their homes. The rebels lost about ten thousand, but we lost a good many. Well, I must close now...

Your brother,
John Stutzman

Pension File, John Stutzman

May 21, 1863   Camp near Falmouth, Virginia

Dear Sister,

I take the opportunity to let you know that I received your kind and most welcome letter this afternoon. I seen the mail carrier come through the camp, and I told one of our boys,"There goes Charles Simmons with the mail and just look what a big mail he has got tonight." I told the boys, "there ought to be one for me tonight." Our 1st Sergeant brought our letters to the company and called out the names. I began to think, at last, that I won't have one tonight, but it came at last, and I was very glad to hear from you once more. I knowed where it was from as quick as I had it in my hand. I wasn't sure if it was from you or from Lib, but I soon found out where it was from. The boys allowed that I had the Philadelphia Inquirer to read tonight.
Further, I let you know about this last battle we had down here. I forgot most all, anyhow, we got marching orders on Wednesday, and we marched that day inside of a half mile of the river. We halted that night and put up our tents, and slept till two o'clock in the morning. We was routed out of our tents, cook our coffee, and got our breakfasts as fast as you can, and take down them tents to march again. When daylight came, we thought we would have to go across the river in the morning. We didn't get away until two o'clock in the afternoon. While we were laying there some of the boys howled out, "There comes some rebel prisoners." I went down a few yards to the road where they was coming. I counted 80 men and 1 Lieutenant, and a Major from the 22nd North Carolina. I was talking to some of them and I asked how they got taken prisoner...They said they didn't know nothing of us crossing where they was, and so our fellows made a charge on the rifle pits and took them unexpected.
We marched down to the river that day. That was Thursday and we put up our tents and have a good night, and the next day we marched down close to the river. About 5 o'clock, the rebels commence shelling and throwed about five or six

shells and directly one come right at our regiment. Sure enough, it did come. I thought it would come right for our company. It burst in among Company K and killed one and wounded five in the same company. It wounded a sergeant in Company F and one private in C Company. The same shell killed a Lieutenant in the 136th Regiment P.V. and five men besides. It was a 20 lb. shell, and it tears things when it bursts. When it strikes, it counts one and no more. You ought to seen us get out of that.

Right along our picket lines, all at once, they commenced firing. That was the III Corps. I thought the rebels was coming right into us, but they didn't come, and the next day, I heard that General Jackson couldn't get in line at all. He was marching his men by a flank, and our men cut them to pieces. That was the rebels General Jackson, and our men cut them all up, so it went on a while. We went about a mile to the right of the pickets, and we halted there and laid there awhile. Orders came to fall in, well, we fell in and formed a line of battle there, and one of the regiments of our brigade went out as skirmishers. Well, we thought that we would get it that night. We moved in the woods, and they told us to throw up breastworks to defend ourselves from any attack. We laid there in line of battle that night, and didn't get no sleep that night.

Well, it went on till the next morning, but we didn't get into it the next morning. We didn't get into it at all, and about daylight they commence fighting on the right. That was Sunday morning. Well, it continued about four hours and I thought we would be engaged that day. We had our rifle pits to go in, and when they commenced fighting on the left of the line, we get in our pits thinking they would open down there, but they didn't.

The fight stopped and it was all quiet. That day our men cut the rebels down, and our fellows took about five hundred prisoners. They was all wounded and didn't expect to live any length at all. It was a regular slaughter pen there, and that night we throwed up breastworks, so we wouldn't get cut up so.

On Monday morning we was there, and expecting an attack every minute. The officers kept saying, "Get in your ditches men, the rebels are coming." On Monday the rebels made an... on our batteries and got repulsed every time. The way our men drove them, the skirmishers would advance on the rebels and drive them...our fellows would let them come up to the mouths of their cannons, and then our fellows would open on them. It cut them down just like grass. On Thursday, there was another engagement of the rebels, and we fought for about two hours. They didn't gain anything of it. That was

NATIONAL GUARD,

NINETIETH NINETIETH

Col. Peter Lyle's Regt.

Above, a recruiting poster for the 90th P.V. Below, a primative self portrait drawn by Private Joseph Temple. The letter, in which the sketch is drawn, is almost totally unreadable due to fading ink.

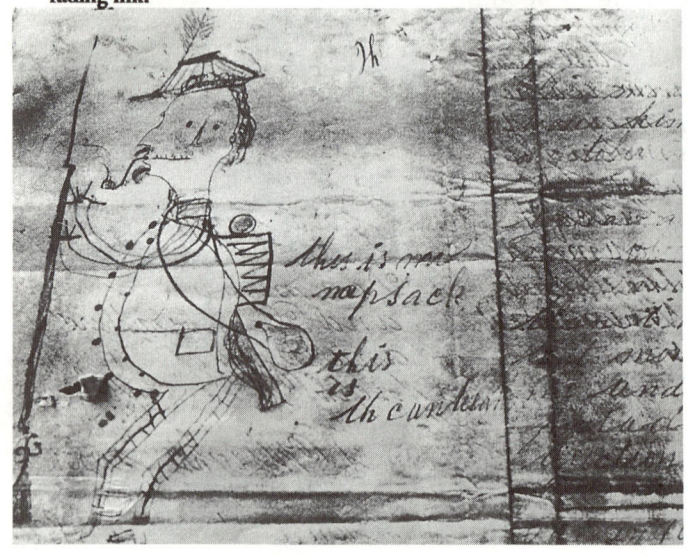

the last fight and, further I'll tell you that the VI Corps we left down to Fredericksburg. On Monday General Sedgwick's Corps made two or three charges. The third charge, they got the heights of Fredericksburg. They kept them about ten hours. The rebels come then and took them back again...

More about the 136th P.V.: Colonel Lyle said that if he gets his regiment home to Philadelphia, he could get over four hundred men out of that regiment to reenlist in our regiment. That, if he gets his regiment home. He is trying to get it there, and if we should happen to get home to get some men, I'll be at home. They say they have a notion to enlist in our regiment, but if my time was out and I was going home, I should stay at home. I wouldn't make a fool of myself twice. I should know better the next time.

We had a battalion drill this evening, and it was a good one for the first time since Nicetown. It went awkward at first but we'll soon get into it again. We have had no drilling of any account for eight months. I am afraid we will get it now while we are laying still in camp. We have splendid music down here. There is a band of music playing now. The first division is got two bands and we can hear them every evening. It sounds nice a little ways off...

John Stutzman.

The following letter, sent from Captain William P. Davis to Mrs. James Keating, is the only example of a commanding officer's letter notifying a surviving widow of the death of her husband in battle, which exists in government records. Captain Davis, himself, was wounded in the first day of fighting at Gettysburg. Lieutenant Edmund Gorgas relieved him and sent him to the rear to obtain medical treatment.

Most of the casualties suffered by the 90th P.V. occurred

on the first day. However, Private Keating of Company H was killed on the skirmish line on July 3rd. After the repulse of Picket's charge, the 90th went out on the skirmish line in front of Cemetery Ridge. At one point, the fire of the rebel sharpshooters proved so effective that the Union skirmishers were driven back to the ridge. Private Keating was killed by these sharpshooters.

Pension File, James Keating.

                         Hospital in the Field
                         Near Gettysburg, Pennsylvania
                         July 8, 1863

Mrs. James Keating

                Madam:

                    It becomes my painful duty to inform you that your husband James Keating, or James Giddons as he is known in the company, was killed during the late battle near Gettysburg while in the performance of his **duty**. The regiment was doing duty as skirmishers at the time he was shot. Being wounded myself early in the action of Wednesday, July 1st, and compelled to go to the rear, I am unable to give you any particulars of his death. But from all I can learn, his body was recovered and buried by his comrades the next day.
    While deeply sympathizing with you in your bereavement, I take this occasion to bear testimony to the good character of the deceased, he being universally beloved by his comrades and respected by his officers for his obedient and cheerful disposition under all circumstances.
    Bowing to the decrees of Providence, who giveth and taketh away, may you find consolation in the Hope that his spirit has ascended to that Happy Sphere on High and is now enjoying eternal happiness.
    As soon as my condition will permit, and the company

books can be got at, I will send you his final papers to enable you to get his affairs settled with the United States Government.

I would recommend that you place your claim in the hands of some of the different pension agents in the city for collection.

Any communications you may think fit to address me with will be attended to with promptness, and all information in my power cheerfully given.

With the greatest respect
I remain your obedient servant,
William P. Davis
Captain, Company H
90th Regiment P.V.

Pension File, William Jones

Camp Near Hagerstown, Maryland

July 17, 1863

Dear sister

    I received your letter on the 17th, and was very glad to here from you all. We left Harrisburg on the 10th and went by rail to Shippensburg. We then marched to Chambersburg. We camped there two days, and then marched to Greencastle; stopped there two days and then came here. We are now encamped in the rebel entrenchments one mile below the city. Don't know how long we will stop here. There is some talk of us doing provost duty in Hagerstown. I am siting in a woods a writing this; a stump for a writing table. No more at present, it is time for drill. I send you $10.00 in this letter. I am well and harty and wish you all the same. Give my love to Lizzie Sharp. Tell her that I would have called to see her, but we started away unexpectedly. You did not tell whether her brother was in the milichy or not. When you write again let me know. Direct your letter:

Camp near Hagerstown
44th Pa. Milichy
Captain Babe

William Jones

The above letter from William Jones was written while he served in the 44th Pa. Militia, one of the 90 day emergency militia units formed in Pennsylvania in response to General Lee's invasion. He would later serve in the 90th P.V.

The letter of Major Alfred Sellers describes the action on Oak Ridge on the first day of the battle of Gettysburg. Sellers had proven to be a good officer when under fire. At Antietam he had received two brevet promotions for his gallantry in action. The action described in this letter, waving his sword and rushing to the front of the line, earned him a Congressional medal of Honor. The position his leadership helped to establish was one from which the regiment played a major role in shattering the attacks of Iverson's and O'Neal's brigades. Later, the 90th retired to Seminary Ridge and supported Stewart's Battery B in holding off the attack of Scales Brigade. The regiment contributed to the successful Federal effort to save the I Corps Artillery, retreating only when the guns were safely withdrawn.

Brevet Colonel Alfred J. Sellers as he appeared later in life. Here, he is wearing the Congressional medal of Honor which was awarded for his gallantry in leading the regiment to the position from which it assisted in repelling the charges of two Rebel Brigades.

Letter of Major Alfred Sellers, Gettysburg National Military Park.

line of Battle, July 9, 1863

...Mostly all the time since we crossed the Potomac... used to being saturated and plodding through the mud and over the mountains. I am now in command of the 90th and have been since the 3rd of July. Colonel Lyle having been assigned to the command of the brigade commanded by General Paul who was dangerously wounded...suppose you have read of the gallant fighting of the 1st Corps, most always in the advance. The loss of brave Reynolds is much to be lamented. On the first days battle our brigade and our regiment had the first post of honor, being on the extreme right of our Corps and it was here, where we were outflanked by overwhelming numbers and in consequence of the only division of the XI Corps which was near at hand not standing their ground or even hardly exchanging a shot. It was said they afterwards on a following day redeemed themselves. We swung our right flank to the rear very near at right angles with our Brigade and fought a long while receiving the enemies fire from both fronts. Our brigade captured two rebel colors. We have only about 100 men to go in with now. About 600 in our Brigade. The I Corps is and was the smallest one in the army and fought the grand Corps of the late Jackson now commanded by Ewell who outnumbered us 4 to 1. The prisoners would not believe us when we told them that our Corps was the only one who engaged them on the 1st inst. A diary of a dead reb was found by one of our men on the 3d days fight in which he said their regiment(the 42nd Mississippi) lost 296 killed & wounded & missing. We lost near 100. Dr. Hayes of the 88th who was taken prisoner was met on the battlefield by General Ewell and staff and questioned as to what division he was attached, in answer he stated the 2nd of the I Corps, where upon Ewell allowed that it was the best fighting division of the Army of the Potomac. Upon taking up our position we were ordered to advance up a hill double quick out of the woods our right was unprotected...the right for a few moments faltered. Mustering up sufficient courage, I rushed to the front waving my sword, and it had the desired effect, our line established. We sent our compliments, Buck and Ball with a yell--the 1st Brigade relieved us, we moved to the rear and took up our line of battle in a new position supplying some

Napoleon guns which was sending grape and canister into the advancing rebs...
   The line of battle was similar to a fish hook at one time & I thought we were most surrounded. A sharp firing has been going on in our front while writing this, so make allowance for all defects for I know not what moment we will be ordered forward...

                           Major Alfred Sellers

The following letter, written by William Jones' sister Maria, was sent to Private Jones while he served with the 90 day state militia. While William Jones campaigned with the 44th Pa. Militia, the draft took place in Philadelphia. When Private Jones returned to Philadelphia, he would discover that he had been drafted into the army and assigned to the Army of the Potomac, specifically, the 90th P.V. According to regimental records, William Jones was drafted on Sept. 9, 1863. He would be wounded later in the Battle of the Wilderness in the disastrous charge the regiment was ordered to make late on the afternoon of May 5, 1864.

Pension File, William Jones

                              Philadelphia July

Dear Brother
         I hope you will forgive me for allowing so long a time to pass before answering your letter, which we were grateful to receive. I suppose you have heard of the drafting in our city. There was several Jones's in this ward

and among the rest of them William Jones, we thought perhaps it was not our William and waited for the notice. I am sorry to say we were disappointed. The unwelcome note came today for you, the other, for Richard. Write as soon as you get this, and let us know what you think of it. Is there any way you can get off? Poor Mother is nearly worried to death about it.

I saw Lizzie Sharp yesterday, she wished to be remembered to you. Her brother is in the 31st Regt. Militia under Colonel Newkurnt. His Captain's name is Horn. They have been on the march ever since they have went away and have seen some pretty hard times. Lizzie heard from Victor on Saturday. He is now a paroled prisoner at Harper's Ferry and enjoys very poor health. Mother, father, and all the rest are pretty well; they all unite in sending their love to you. Dear Brother, Mother was very glad to get the money. It came in good time, for the rent--and I have lost several days lately, work being slack. Goodbye, hoping to see you soon.

I remain yours most affectionately

Maria.

1202 Brandywine

Write as soon as you get this. The Blue Reserves came home today. When do you think of coming home?

Pension File, Daniel Kane

Rappahannock Station,
Virginia August 12, 1863

Dear Wife

Yours of the 8th is at hand and I am glad to hear that you are well, and also able to inform you that I am the same. In order to get the relief money, you will have to go to the committy of the district in which you live, and get a card. Send it to me, and I will have it fixed and sent back to you. I do not know anything else that will have to be done, in order that you can get work at the arsenal. You will have to find out, and let me know what I must do.

I did not enlist in the Corn Exchange Regiment. I went as a substitute, and am in the 90th Regt. P.V.,National Guards. You may go to Mr. McDevitt and tell him that any papers he may want me to sign in order to assist in getting the Prize Money for you, to send me and I will sign them and send them back at once.

    I enclose $10.00 to you in this. I will write to Benny's Captain, and try and find something out about him. If you should learn anything more of him in the meantime, let me know. If you can, send me your likeness and some cough medicine of some kind. I would like it very much. Ned Hunter was in this regiment before I came out, but is not now with it.

    Send me the papers once and awhile. I would like to have the Sunday Dispatch regular, direct them the same as you direct the letters. Give my love to Agnes.

Your affectionate Husband

Dan Kane

Direct George Kane
    Co. E, 90th Regt.
    Washington D.C.

Personal Papers, John S. Davis

September 10, 1863

Colonel J. H. Taylor
Chief of Staff,

    I have the honor to report that after the hour of 10:00 o'clock P.M. on the 8th inst, much disturbance was created in the several camps of this command by the sudden display of rockets and other fireworks on a hill within the limits of this camp. The affair was perfect "<u>surprise</u>" and unauthorized by me. At one time, matters assumed such a threatening appearance, that deeming it prudent, I ordered out the guard. Upon investigation it appeared that Captain John S. Davis, Company C, 90th P.V. was the cause of the disturbance. He had been by my order relieved from duty in this command and ordered to report to Major Wood at Alexandria a few days previous, for transportation to his regiment. It appears he intended to leave here the morning of the 9th isnt., went to Washington and made secret arrangements to have them fired, all apparently for self glorification and manifest insult to me as the commanding officer--without any authority whatsoever. I immediately put the said Captain Davis under close arrest and today forward to your headquarters Charges and Specifications against him with a request that you order him tried before an intelligent court in Washington. His conduct was an outrage and "good order and military discipline" demand a careful and judicious investigation of the case.

                          Samuel McKelvy
                          Lieutenant Colonel,
                          Commanding Camp Distribution

On October 26, 1863, Captain John S. Davis appeared before a Court Martial Board to answer formal charges of, "Conduct prejudicial to good order and military discipline and Conduct unbecoming an officer and a gentleman." The board quickly found Captain Davis not guilty of all charges and specifications. However, the board made these comments:

"In the case of Captain John S. Davis, 90th Pennsylvania Volunteers, it is not clear to this Department that the accused was not implicated in the discharge of the fireworks. It is certain that he purchased and distributed them, and there is some reason to believe that he was aware of the improper use to which they were applied. As he afforded the means to the guilty parties for violating the regulations, his act tended to create disorder and subvert discipline in a camp. The proceedings and findings are approved, but he is reprimanded, and is released from arrest and will return to duty.

                          E. D. Townsend
                          Assistant Adjutant General"

Personal Papers, Alfred J. Sellers

Headquarters Army of the Potomac,
Letter to Adjutant General of the Army
Washington, D.C.

September 15, 1863

Sir,

   Major Alfred Sellers of the 90th Pa. Volunteers was detailed in accordance to the order from the War Department to proceed to Philadelphia for the purpose of conveying drafted men to the regiment.
   Charges have been preferred against him for taking from this army an enlisted man without authority and under a false name.
   I respectfully request that he be relieved from the duty he is now upon, and ordered to his regiment in arrest, that he may be tried on the charges preferred against him.

                    I am Sir, Very respectfully
                    Your obedient servant,

                    George Meade
                    Major General Commanding

The charges referred to by General Meade in the above letter were brought by 1st Lieutenant Richard W. Davis. No official copy of the charges exists today. Shortly after the charges were filed, Lieutenant Davis withdrew them. It is possible that these charges were related to Major Sellers support of George Watson in his attempt to secure the Captain's position in Company H. Lieutenant Richard W. Davis was one of those whose promotion was delayed as a result of the Watson controversy. Whether this was the case or not, the charges against the major were dropped. Ironically, Major Sellers would soon face a Board of Inquiry as a result of an incident which occurred while he was in command of transporting drafted recruits to the army.

Pension File, John Gould

September 23, 1863

My Dear Mother,

        We arrived here all safe and sound on the 21st in the afternoon. I am well and I have got plenty of everything except money. I lost all my money on the boat, except about five dollars that I had in my pocketbook. The rest I had in my watch pocket, and it was all stolen away from me. There was about a couple of thousand dollars stolen on the boat from the men. I am very glad that I did not fetch it all with me, and that I took your advice and left it all with you, pretty much. Let me know whether Pop left for Chicago on Sunday last or not. I think if I had not been so wild, I would have stayed home and gone with you out west. There is one chance left for me yet. We all have to be examined again by the Brigade Doctor this afternoon, and I may get into the Invalid Corps if I don't pass before him.
  I am in the same regiment that Johnny Hughes is in, but I am in Company F and he is in Company D. We expect to move in a few days and cross the Rapidan River, and they say we will have to fight to cross it. The rebels are right on the other side in a very good position for a fight, and the boys here all think we will have to fight before we can cross.
  They treated us like dogs when we were coming here on the boat. They had us down in the hold of the vessel, and any one that attempted to come out, a loaded gun was soon pointed at his head and told to go down again. There is five substitute deserters that are going to be shot next Friday out of our division, and we are going to be drawn up in a line around them and see them shot. I want you to tell Len McDaniel to send me that receipt that he was going to send me. I want you to send me twenty dollars in a letter. Don't have it registered. I would have it sent by express, but I could not get it if it was sent that way. Give my love to

Pop & Bell and kiss all the babies for me and write soon is the request of your affectionate son.

John Gould

P.S. Direct your letter to John Gould
    Co. F, 90th P.V.
    2nd Brigade
    2nd Division
    I Army Corps

Private John Gould was drafted on September 16, 1863 in Philadelphia. One week later, John Gould traveled South to the regiment with a boatload of draftees and substitutes under the command of Major Alfred Sellers. Many of the men included in this group were tough customers. There were thieves, cutthroats, and professional bounty men among those transported. One man became so intoxicated on the trip, he had a seizure and died. Others in the group attempted to escape by jumping overboard. Major Sellers ordered one man to be shot as he tried to escape. The man was killed, and the remainder delivered without other serious incident. A Court of Inquiry tried and acquitted the major of any wrongdoing in the death of the escaping soldier. Private John Gould was assigned to Company F when the draftees arrived at the regiment.

Service Record, National Archives, RG#98, Herman Barber,

Barber, A.K.A. Edward Von Heinecke

Rapidan, September 25, 1863

Mr. Consul:

At the request of Mr. Edward William Von Heinecke I am obliged to apply for your patronage, and state the circumstances of this unhappy man.

E. W. Von Heinecke arrived as a first cabin passenger on board a steamer in July last. Immediately after his arrival he put up at Rauh's Hotel. Some days after, he went out entirely unacquainted with the language and with very little experience which a stranger in New York stands greatly in need of; he fell on the company of some young men with whom he was not acquainted. They gave him a sophoric. At his awakening, he found himself robbed of his effects, of something over $400.00, of his watch, and watch chain. He continued sick for some days by the potions administered to him. Being without money, he could not stay at Rauh's, and hoping to meet a relation of his wife, he went to Philadelphia. There, he remained at Uhlmann's Hotel about a fortnight, during which he was unable to find his friend. Mr. Uhlmann took pains to obtain work for him; but being unacquainted with the language, and unable to do hard work; he was compelled to turn soldier.

He expected his wife to come here, and requested Mr. Rauh to receive her at her arrival, and notify him immediately. He intended to apply for furlough, place her in an honest family and then return to his regiment; then, if his wife should desire, he intended to return himself, or to furnish a substitute, without any intention of deceiving the government. He was unacquainted with the laws, and believed it could be legally done, especially as some German had so taught him. He told several persons that he desired to go to New York for receiving his wife, and had by somebody asked the Lieutenant to obtain furlough for him from the Colonel, which, however, could not be obtained.

Now there was a young man whose name was Schmidt who called on him to accompany him, and told him that nothing would happen to him, if he returned. They left the regiment on the 13th of August, at 7:00 o'clock A.M., were arrested the same day in the evening, and recognized as deserters. Schmidt is also a German.

Edward Von Heinecke, when he became a soldier, had assumed the name of Herman Barber, as he was ashamed of his family.

There is abundant proof that he never intended to desert, but left only in ignorance. He was taken to the Provost Marshal, where he had an interpreter whom he could not understand but half, the same being a Frenchman and not master of the language, nor would he allow him so much time as required to make himself understood to the court. He was sentenced to be shot on the 25th of September, but by the kindness of General Robinson, it was postponed to the 2nd of October. On that day, we shall be able to obtain the witnesses.

You are entreated in the name of the Generals of the Division, and of the staff officers of Major General Newton to lay the matter before the President without delay.

Respectfully

F. Gerber

Private Herman Barber and Private William Switz deserted together sometime on August 12, 1863. The Provost Guard captured both men, in civilian clothes, the next day near Catletts' Station, Virginia. Private Switz did all the talking when the two men tried to pass the guard posts, as he spoke English and Barber did not. This turned out to be very important for Private Barber because William Switz told all the lies when the two men tried to pass the provost guards. When Barber requested and was denied a furlough, Switz had convinced him that he could desert, and nothing would happen to him as long as he returned to the army later. At his court martial, Barber made the following statement in German, and it was translated into English as follows:

"I lost $4,000 in New York when I came over and I came to Philadelphia and while I was hard up I went as a substitute. I received a letter from my wife from Germany. She has considerable money with her, and I thought they might do the same with her as they did to me, rob her, and I was trying to get to New York, and I had an idea I could buy a man in my place. I was dumb and green and did not know any better, and it was more worryment on my mind, that made me leave than anything else. I intended to come back again if I could not get another man in my place."

The court then closed for deliberation and promptly returned a verdict of Guilty of the charge of Desertion. The sentence imposed in this case was, "prisoner to be shot to death with fire of musketry." It was at this point that the letter sent by Captain Gerber brought the intervention of the German Government. The Generals of the I Corps felt that Barber had not received justice and interceded on his behalf. The result was that President Lincoln did intervene in the Barber case. Herman Barber had his sentence commuted to five years at hard labor by the President. Private Barber was transferred to Fort Jefferson in the Dry Tortugas in Florida on May 6, 1864. He did not serve the five year sentence. Herman Barber was released from confinement on July 21, 1865 as a result of a pardon from President Andrew Johnson.

Private William Switz met a much different fate. Nobody intervened in the case of William Switz. His execution was delayed only until a priest could be obtained to attend him.

134

The execution of a deserter with soldiers drawn up in formation to witness the offending soldiers death. The scene is likely very similar to the execution of Private William Switz.

On October 2, 1863 he was shot to death by a firing squad.

A soldier in the 88th P.V. described the scene:

"About 1 O'clock P.M. the bugle called to arms. We were at once under arms & in line & marched to an opening nearby. Here we found about a dozen regiments drawn up in a 3 sided square to see a deserter shot who belonged to the 90th P.V.
 I shall never forget this scene, so long as I live. We were drawn up in line patiently awaiting the arrival of the culprit. The rain had ceased falling. At length the low mournful notes of the dead march was heard & soon the cortege entered the arena. First came a file of soldiers then an ambulance with the coffin & the prisoner & the priest; then the Provost Guard-12 men to do the shooting. The whole was literally a man going to his own funeral.
 The procession moved very slowly, & it seemed a terrible thing to know a man's minutes were known by his fellow men. At last the funeral reached the grave. The deserter, who was a young sallow looking fellow of perhaps 18 or 19 years of age, descended from the ambulance. The coffin was placed near the grave. The priest prayed with him. The guard seated him on the coffin-tied his hands behind his back -bared his bosom-bandaged his eyes & left him.
 The guards stepped to the front, the officer gave the command, 'Ready, Aim' & oh it was a solemn moment. Strong &

great men who had faced death many a time without quailing or faltering, now turned away their heads & silent tears run down bronzed cheeks, for sympathy for a fellow being. 'Fire', came the next command & the body of the victim fell back on the coffin like a log, while the cloth of his clothes flew like raveling. Just then the rain came down in torrents & we were marched from the grounds."

Service Record, Herman Barber, A.K.A Edward Von Heinecke

New York, September 28, 1863

To His Excellency

        Edwin M Stanton,
            Secretary of War
                Washington, D.C.

    Sir,

        I take the liberty to enclose a letter-with English translation attached-received today from Captain Fred Gerker, 2nd Division, I Corps, Army of the Potomac. in relation to

Herman Barber, alias E.W. Von Heinecke, condemned to be shot as a deserter on the 2nd of October.

    I feel it to be my duty to bring this matter to Your Excellency's notice, that Your Excellency may determine, whether the statement of Captain Gerker deserves sufficient credit to induce Your Excellency to intercede in behalf of the unfortunate man.

    I am, Sir,

                Your Excellency's
                most obedient servant

                Adolph Gorting

                  Consul General
                  of Hanover

Service Record, Herman Barber, A.K.A. Edward Von Heinecke

> Office of Judge Advocate
> Headquarters General
> Army of the Potomac
> September 29, 1863

Major General Newton,

    Commanding I Corps

        General,

    I am directed by Major General Meade to say that after giving due weight to the affidavits which have been forwarded in the case of Private Herman Barber, alias Edward Von Heinecke, of the 90th P.V., and to the various representations made in his favor, he is constrained to adhere to his former decision in this case. The sentence having been suspended for one week, will therefore necessarily be carried into effect on the 2nd.

        I am General,

           Very respectfully

        Your most obedient servant

           E. R. Platt
           Lieutenant Colonel
           Judge Advocate

Service Record, Herman Barber, A.K.A. Edward Von Heinecke

        October 1, 1863

Mr. President

        This man Herman Barber alias Von Heinecke is to be shot tomorrow. The Judge Advocate called personally to say he thinks a respite of ten days or so is advisable, as the man appears, by ignorance of our language, to have created a false impression at the trial. There is said to be strong palliating evidence. The respite will allow it to be produced. I hope it may be granted. Of course it must be at once, if at all.

Your obedient servant

John Hay

I enclose form of dispatch to
save time.

Service Record, Herman Barber, A.K.A. Edward Von Heinecke

Office U. S. Military Telegraph,

War Department

The following telegram received at Washington, 8.50. P.M. October 1, 1863.

From Headquarters Army of the Potomac

Dated October 1, 1863.

The President,

     Telegram in relation to Barber, alias Von Heinecke, received. Prior to the receipt, he had been respited. The papers in the case directed to be forwarded for your action.

G. G. Meade

Major General

Service Record, Nathan Raymond

Philadelphia, October 20, 1863

To Brigadier General Lorenzo Thomas
Adjutant General U.S. Army

Philadelphia, October 20, 1863

To Brigadier General Lorenzo Thomas
Adjutant General U.S. Army

        General

      Please accept this my resignation of the position of captain of Company D, 90th regiment Pennsylvania Volunteers which I now hold. My reasons for offering this are as follows: I was severely wounded in the left ankle at the Battle of Bull Run, August 30, 1862. The bones of my ankle were very badly shattered from the effects of which I have never recovered. I was confined to the house for about five months.

    In April 1863, I was able to go about with the aid of a stout cane when I made application to be placed on light duty with the Provost Marshall of this city(By order of Major General Schenck then commanding this department), on the 14th day of April 1863, since which I have endeavored to do my duty as well as my wounded ankle would permit up to this date. I received an order from headquarters of this post relieving me from duty, and as I am not able to return to duty, being still lame, as a certificate from the Medical Director of this post will certify, tender you my resignation.

    I have made application for a position in the Invalid Corps with all the proper vouchers which are filed in the office of the Provost Marshall General at Washington, D.C. My accounts with the government are all straight. I never having command of the company; having been promoted from 1st Lieutenant, Company F, to Captain, Company D, since I have been absent from my regiment. By complying with the above you will greatly oblige.

                              Your Obedient Servant
                              Nathan Raymond
                              Captain, Company D.
                              135 N. Hutchinson Street
                              Philadelphia, Pa.

Due to the serious nature of his ankle wound, the United States Government accepted Captain Nathan Raymond's resignation, and he was discharged from the service on October 22, 1863 on a Surgeon's Certificate of Disability. The wound left Captain Raymond permanently disabled. He applied for, and was granted, a disability pension in 1871.

Pension File, William Jones

Bealton Station, Virginia
November 17, 1863

Dear Sister,

      I received your last letter, and was glad to hear that you are well. The day that I received your letter, I was expecting to have my first fight. My division was drawn up in line of battle, waiting for the rebs to make their appearance. Such bang, bang, booming I never heard! But instead of being the rebs, it was our own cavalry discharging their guns. So, I went back to my tent and read your letter.

  I seen Victor last Sunday a week at Brandy's Station. He was well and hearty. He sends his love to you. All them great battles that father talks, must be the goats about Fairmount battling. Tell the young ones that as soon as I get close enough to throw salt on a rabbit's tail to catch him, I will send him home for them. I got paid off yesterday. I gave the Lieutenant $30.00 to put into an officer's hands who is going home tomorrow. He will leave it with our Captain, that is, at his home. Our Captain lives on 1031 Frankford; Captain Davis. You go to him as soon as you get this letter. 1031 Frankford is somewhere in the neighborhood of Front and Oter.

  No more at present. I would have wrote sooner, but I have been waiting for my pay. Give my love to Lizzie Sharp and all my inquiring friends...Write as soon as you get this, that is, as soon as you get the money, and send me two or three post stamps. My candle is burnt out, and I must give over. Don't give my letters to nobody.

William Jones

Private John Bellas was drafted into the 90th P.V. on July 2, 1863. When he arrived at the front Bellas found himself assigned to Company B. The Private continued with the regiment through the spring campaign of 1864. He was one of the lucky 50% of the regiment who did not become a casualty in the Wilderness fighting. However, on May 8th at Laurel Hill John Bellas was decidedly unlucky. He was among the 40% of the men in the regiment who were among the casualties on that date. Two days later, on May 10, 1864, Private John Bellas died of his wounds.

Pension File, John Bellas

Virginia, November 18, 1863

Dear Mother

    I take my pen in hand to let you know that I am well, hoping that these few lines will find you the same. I received your letter and was very glad to hear that you were all well. The rebels tore up all of our railroad. Our men are fiching it all up again. I sold the watch for ten dollars because the last time we was on the march, I fell down and broke the glass, and the works is broke. We are going to cross the Rapadan some of these days. I got paid off today and I will send you 20 dollars. I would like to hear from May McClir in. When you see her, tell her what Ridgment I am in, and what Company I am in.
    We was on picket for three days and three nights. We caught three gerilers trying to steal things out of our wagons. I am with our sargeant in a tent with him and he takes good care of me. We drove the rebels to the Rapadan and captured 10,000 of men, and 20 pieces of cannon, and 10 rebelflags. We will son go into winter quarters.
    Tell the boys around Penn St. that I send my best

respects to them, and I send my best respects to all in the house.

>That all at present

>by your affectunate son

>John Bellas

Service Record, Richard W. Davis,

>November 19, 1863
>Bealton Station

Captain F. A. Chadwick
Captain, Commanding 90th Regiment P.V.

      Captain, I respectfully ask a leave of absence for ten days for the following reasons. My mother, who is aged eighty three years, is lying dangerously ill; and her physician announces her recovery as hopeless, and owing to her advanced age, her death may be sudden and unexpected.

>Very Respectfully
>Your Obedient Servant
>Richard W. Davis
>1st Lieutenant,
>Commanding Company F.
>90th P.V.

Lieutenant Richard Davis' application for leave was approved on November 20th. He traveled to Philadelphia to visit his sick mother. It appears that his mother survived. A check of the death records of the City of Philadelphia showed no record of the death of a woman of that name or age, at any time during 1863, 1864, or 1865. Evidently, the visit from her son lifted Mrs. Davis' spirits enough that she recovered from her illness.

Pension File, Henry Mathes

November 22, 1863

Camp near Bealton Station

My Dear Mother.

        I received your welcome letter yesterday, and I was glad to hear that you were all well as this leaves me. You stated in your letter that Fannie was promoted to the 2nd division, secondary. I suppose, when I get home, to find her a school teacher, and I also see that Carrie is getting along first rate at school. I think she will make a smart woman. I am sorry to hear that you have to work so hard. If I was you, I would quit for awhile, for my sake anyhow. It quite surprised me, when I seen in your letter an account of the robbery of Mrs. Kinder, and also of Mrs. Gengenbach. I always thought that Quinn boy was a rascal. Keep Eddie away from him. I see that you have new neighbors. I hope they are as agreeable as the last one. I wrote a letter a few days to Mr. Janney. I expect an answer soon from him.
        I have not yet received the pants, but I expect they will be here soon. Things sent by express do not reach here as soon as those sent by mail. We were paid off a few days ago. There was 4 months due me but I received but two. I sent you $20.00 today by Adams Express. Write to me as soon as you get it. We will be paid again in January. I am sorry to hear of the sickness of David Lentz, and I hope he may be restored to health soon again.
        I have not much news of interest to write. The rebels occasionally make a dash for our pickets, but they generally get well peppered for their trouble. We had quite a rainstorm; it lasted for two days, but the weather is now fine again. Look out that the thieves don't steal anything from you like they did from the others.
        I would like to have your likeness, also, some of the children's. As I am writing, my tent mate is frying

potatoes, and they smell so good that I think I will have to dive in for some. Give my love to Sisters, and Brother, and all inquiring friends and take a good share for yourself. I remain your affectionate son.

                              Henry G. Mathes

P.S. Write as soon as you receive the money.

                                     H. G. M.

Pension File, John Gould,

                                   Dec. 15, 1863

My Dear Mother,

      I wrote a letter a few days ago to you after a box. If you send it to me, I wish you would send me them shirts I drew in the Militia and both pair of them drawers. I got so lousy on this last march, not having any time to wash, that I had to throw away my clothes, keeping only my blouse and a pair of pants on me. I was fairly alive with them. Give my love to all, and don't forget those things is the request of your affectionate son.

                                     John Gould

Please forward to camp near Kelly's Ford, Va.

The march referred to by Private Gould was the Mine Run Campaign. The Army of the Potomac had crossed the Rapidan River late in November 1863 and tried to establish a position which would give the Union troops an advantage in attacking Lee's army. However, the Federal soldiers failed to move quickly enough, and Lee discovered General Meade's intentions. General Lee quickly entrenched his army along Mine Run. General Meade gave General Warren half of the army to make an attack. When Warren examined General Lee's fortifications, he decided that an attack here would produce another Fredericksburg. To his credit, Warren possessed the courage to call off the attack. Meade approved Warren's decision, and the Army of the Potomac trudged back through the rain and mud, crossed the river, and went into winter quarters. By the end of the campaign, it is quite likely that everyone from Private Gould to General Meade was infested with lice.

1864

Pension File, John Stutzman

January 8, 1864
Carver Hospital
Washington, D.C.

Dear Sister,

   ...I tell you I had a poor time down here, a new year. I would have liked to been up home on a new year but I couldn't come. We had a very good dinner that day, but that's nothing if a body can't have no fun besides it. So, I done the best I can do. Further, I let you know that I am going away some place but I don't know where yet...But coming home, I give up to that. I thought once, myself, that I would get home this winter, but now it's all gone to get home. I expect to go to the regiment in a few days, and as quick as I get there, I'll write to you...

   If I was about half dead, I might get one(a furlough). I thought, being we got a new doctor, I would get a furlough, but he thinks I am gaining too fast to go home, so he won't give me one. I'll have to wait till my time is out, then I can come home to stay, that's if I don't get shot in that time, but I hope not. I would like to see Milton once more before I die. Well, I must come to a close by telling you that I am well at present, and I hope that these few lines may find you in the same state of health.

John Stutzman,
No more in Carver Hospital

Pension File, John Dwyer

Culpeper, Virginia
January 16, 1864

Dear John,

Your inquiry of the 8th instant relative to the death of John Dwyer, Company A, of my regiment is at hand. He died at Carver Hospital, Washington D.C. on November 17, 1863 of chronic diarrhea. His final statement papers have been made out today, and will be forwarded to the Adjutant General's Office tomorrow. He was mustered as a substitute for a drafted man July 15, 1863 at Philadelphia and was therefore four months and two days in the service...

I joined the regiment on the 5th inst. They were encamped on Cedar Mountain. On the 5th instant, I was ordered to take three regiments(12th Massachusetts, 88th & 90th P.V.) to garrison Culpeper, where we are comfortably quartered in houses. If you can spare time, I would like you to pay us a visit. There is nothing of interest to write as everything is quiet and dull. Our force is greatly reduced owing to regiments reenlisting and going home. Speaking of reenlisting, the question may be asked you and other members of the Guards why the 90th does not reenlist as a veteran regiment? The order from the War Department will not allow us to reenlist as a veteran regiment. The order from the War Department will not allow any to reenlist except they have served two years and upwards, and three quarters of the regiment must enlist before they will recognize you as a veteran regiment. I have but sixty or seventy of the old men doing duty in the regiment. Last fall they sent me 610 conscripts who are not eligible, therefore, it is impossible for us to become a veteran regiment.

Truly yours,
P. Lyle

The 90th P.V. had a proud history. Twenty years of service as a militia organization in Pennsylvania, had built a strong tradition of service in the regiment. The men had done well in the 90 day service; and once the three year service began, they performed well in battle after battle. Despite this, War Department policy would prevent this proud organization from ever being organized as a Veteran

Volunteer Regiment. The enormous casualties, which the regiment had suffered earlier in war, guaranteed that the unit would not meet the requirements of the War Department relating to the Veteran Regiments.

Colonel Peter Lyle was an excellent officer. He suffered slight wounds in battle on several occasions. However, the Colonel suffered to a much greater extent from periodic bouts of dysentery which caused him to return to the City of Philadelphia on a number of occasions for treatment from his personal physician. In September of 1864, Colonel Lyle went on extended sick leave and did not return to duty before he and the regiment were mustered out on November 26, 1864. At the war's end, Colonel Lyle received a brevet promotion to the rank of Brigadier General. A fitting reward, since he often was called on during his service to command a brigade in both the I and V Corps.

In 1867, Colonel Lyle was elected Sheriff of the City of Philadelphia as a democrat. However, he did not run for reelection and served until 1870. The Colonel remained active in the State Militia, commanding the National Guards Regiment until 1876. Colonel Lyle was in continuous command of the regiment for thirty years, from 1846 to 1876. Peter Lyle died in 1879, after a long career of service to his city, state, and nation.

Pension File, Frederick Lang

                              Headquarters 90th Regiment
                              January 16, 1864

Captain Connors,

        Captain:

                Lieutenant Riley having shown me a letter from you asking for information in the case of Frederick Lang, late of my company. I sent her a letter some time back, but judge it must of been lost by her asking you to write. Lang had every attention paid to him in the division hospital. He died December 23, 1863 near Kelly's Ford, Virginia and his grave marked. We have been on the march so much lately, that I could not get to the hospital to get his effects, but should we remain here, I will attend to it tomorrow or 2 or 3 days at the farthest. I believe he left $15.00 in money. I cannot say, at present, what other property, but all will be sent to his family. I will forward his final statement so his family can get what pay is due. I am sorry that the letter I sent Mrs. Lang, never reached her. I thought that she had been made acquainted with all the facts concerning him, how he died from chronic diarrhea, which he had almost ever since he joined the regiment. Supposing that Mrs. Lang had received my letter explaining how we were situated at the time of his death, and that I could not send his papers, then, for we marched the next day toward Cedar Mountain. As soon as I can get my books out of the wagon and fixed, I will at once fix his case first. I understand that our division hospital is established in this place. If such is the case, I will get his effects collected and forwarded by some of our officers to his family. I feel very sorry for Mrs. Lang, and anything I can do to enable her to get what is due to her late husband. I will be at her service anytime by sending me word, should she need any information, and I will answer.

                              Yours Respectfully
                              Richard W. Davis, 1st Lieutenant
                              Company F, 90th P.V.

Private Frederick Lang had a brief career as a soldier. He had been hired as a substitute in early August of 1863. the $300.00 he had been paid was much too small a sum for the cost of his service. Frederick Lang became ill and died of dysentery on December 23, 1862. Somehow, his wife had not received any official notice of his death.

Pension File, Henry Mathes

February 8, 1864
Camp near Culpeper

My Dear Sister,

    Your welcome letter came to hand on the 5th, and I am glad that you are all well as this leaves me. I am sorry to hear of Charles King's death, but it did not come unexpected. It struck me when you wrote that Joe Budd had reenlisted; he had better come down in my company. We have just returned from a long march to the front and back again...the 2nd Corps had a slight engagement with them but we did not get into it, although we saw the whole of the fight.
    We are now encamped about two miles outside of Culpeper. We are now in log huts, eight of us in one of them and a gay party we are. I have not received a letter from New Jersey for some time. Is Kate yet at his store? There are 3 regiments of our brigade that have reenlisted. They are as follows: the 88th and 11th P.V. and the 97th New York. No man can reenlist who has not served two years in one regiment. You mentioned about sending me the New York Ledger. I am much obliged to you, but I have read all the papers, as some of the boys in the tent take them. It is the general impression in the army that next summer and fall will wind up the rebellion. The rebels are coming into our lines on an average of ten a day. If General Grant only succeed in his undertaking, the Army of the Potomac will do the rest.

I am sorry that we have not been paid off. I would like to send some money to mother. We will be paid off some time in March. How are the children getting along at school? You mentioned about Henry Virdin and John Eldridge getting married. I think it is almost time for me to follow suit.

I see by the papers that there will be a draft on the 10th of March. That will make the big bugs shell out their greenbacks or shoulder a musket. You must excuse my short letters as the fact is news of any interest is very scarce. Give my love to mother, sisters and brothers, Tommy and take a good share for yourself. I remain your affectionate brother.

         Henry Mathes

Private Henry Mathes took some satisfaction in the fact that each time a draft took place, some wealthy citizens had to put out $300.00 to purchase a substitute to take their place in the ranks, if they did not choose to go themselves. The entire substitute and bounty system generated a huge volume of fraud. Many of those who went as substitutes were physically unfit for any kind of service. Others who went as substitutes, or enlisted and took bounty payments, deserted at the first opportunity. These individuals would then enlist in another locale and secure another bounty payment, going through the entire process again and again.

Service Record, Lucas Hoffman

      U.S. Army General Hospital
      Camden Street
      Baltimore, MD February 22, 1864

Baltimore, MD February 22, 1864

Sir

   I have the honor to report that the condition of the within named soldier is such as to warrant his transfer to the "Asylum for Insane" situated at Washington D.C. Having notified the "Adjutant General of the Army" of the fact, I would respectfully request that a guard(of one person) be appointed to conduct him to Washington. Private Lucas Hoffman, Co. H, 90th Penn. Vols.

        Very respectfully
        Your obt. servant

        Z. E. Bliss

           Surgeon U.S. Vols.
           In charge of Hospital

To Col. William H. Chestering, U.S.A.
    A.A.G. VIII Army Corps
    Medical Director

Private Lucas Hoffman of Company H was drafted into the service on July 15, 1863. Immediately after his arrival, Private Hoffman became ill and he was hospitalized. He had suffered sunstroke on August 12, 1863. Then, while a patient in the hospital, he came down with a case of Typhoid Fever on August 31, 1863. The records do not directly connect these illnesses with Hoffman's insanity. However, Private Lucas Hoffman never returned to duty with the 90th, and from the U.S. Army Hospital he was sent to St. Elizabeth's Hospital for the Insane in Washington D.C.

Pension File, William Jones

                                        Tuesday 23rd
                                        Camp Near Culpeper

Dear Sister,

I received your letter of the 6th and was glad to hear from you all. We are encamped two miles above Culpeper Courthouse. We are very comfortable, more than when we were in the church. Victor was here last week and took dinner with us. We had a grand review yesterday. The whole army Corps turned out. It was a pretty sight. We got paid off two weeks ago. I would have wrote before, but thought it unsafe to send money in the mail, for there is so many losses there. I got paid for 2 months. Our next pay will be on the 15th of March. I send you fifteen in this letter. I wish I could send you more, but I was foolish enough to run in debt with the sutler, but I won't do it again. I hope this war will be over this summer; that is the thought with us. No more at present. I have no news to fill up. I am well and wish you all the same. I give my love to all my inquiring friends...Write as soon as you get this, and send me two or three post stamps. A kiss for the young ones; tell them I will send them 5 cents in the next letter but they must make Aunt Maria write as soon as she gets this.

                                        William Jones

From the events William Jones describes in the previous letter and the day and date given, this letter was written in the month of February 1864. Private Jones expressed the belief, actually it was more wishful thinking than real belief; that this summer would see the end of the war. By this point in the conflict most soldiers had seen enough of the horrors of war, they all wanted it over, wanted the killing to end. Perhaps, believing that the next fight would be the last, was the thing that allowed them to keep going. Unfortunately, for the men of the 90th P.V. some of the worst fighting of the war lay just ahead. When General Grant's spring campaign began the 90th would lose 75% of the regiment in the first 3 days fighting at the Wilderness and Spotsylvania.

Pension File, Henry Mathes

Kate Mathes   February 26, 1864
Camp near Culpeper,

My Dear Mother,

       I received your welcome letter on the 21st, and I am glad to hear that you are all well as this leaves me. We had a grand review last week by our Corps Commander. It was a grand sight to see thousands of men marching along the plain. There was a great many persons present from Washington. Amongst them were some ladies (wives of officers). The whole affair passed off very pleasantly. I see by the papers that they intend laying a track on 7th and 9th to run up 9th and down 7th. It will make 9th Street rather noisy than it was.
  One of the boys told me that he seen an account of the resignation of Lieutenant Baker of the 91st P.V. I am glad to hear that the children are getting along so well in school. I would be pleased to get a letter from sister Carrie. I sent you $40.00 by Adams Express. I sent it the day before yesterday, which was on the 24th. Write and let me know if you get it. There is two months more coming to us which will be due on the middle of next month.
  We have had some pretty severe weather lately, but as we do not have much to do at present we are not too much

exposed. Somehow, I do not like this regiment as much as I did the other. The officers seem to be down on us because we are substitutes, but for my part I do not care a snap of my finger for any of them. I think that I can take care of myself without any of their help. When you write let me know how George Rush is getting along. Give my respects to Mrs. Randall and all enquiring friends. Give my love to sisters, and brother, and take a good share for yourself.

                I remain your affectionate son.

                Henry G. Mathes

Service Record, Lucas Hoffman

                U.S Army General Hospital
                Camden Street,
                Baltimore, Maryland
                February 27, 1864

Sir

    Lucas Hoffman, Company H, 90th P.V. was admitted into this hospital February 6, 1864. We were unable to ascertain anything in regard to his previous history. On admission he was in the following condition, very delirious, skin cool, pulse low, and very feeble. All that we were able to get out of him was that he had a pain in the right ear and hypochondriac regions. There was considerable tenderness to pressure in the right region. He would presently get out of bed and endeavor to leave the room, and in being prevented from so doing, would get perfectly furious, striking right and left and requiring several men to manage him. On one occasion he struck and knocked down the lady nurse who had been exceedingly kind and attentive to him. After being in the hospital for 7 or 8 days, he became more quiet and was managed without much difficulty. His condition ,however, varied from day to day at one time being comparatively rational and at another as insane as ever. His appetite was good and he had improved very much in appearance at the time of his leaving the hospital. He was treated with tonics and stimulants, occasionally, an opiate.
    I have the honor to herewith forward the descriptive list of Lucas Hoffman.

Z. E. Bliss
Surgeon U.S. Volunteers

Perhaps, the fate of Lucas Hoffman was the most tragic of all of the soldiers in the 90th P.V. He never fought in any battle, but he became the greatest casualty in the regiment. Hoffman was locked inside his own insanity until the day he died on July 29, 1909. A Hospital review of his case produced the following comments:

"Lucas Hoffman, white male, single admitted to this hospital February 25, 1864 at the age of 25 years. Patient was admitted from the Army General Hospital...Patient was delirious when admitted to the Army General Hospital, was so violent that he had to be restrained, after seven or eight days, he became quiet, and at intervals he seemed lucid. Further than this there is no data at hand...

Patient was mentally deteriorated to a marked degree. He was disoriented. Reason and judgment were poor. His answers to questions were irrelevant and foolish. He sat apart from other patients, was noisy and profane. No delusions or hallucinations are recorded. He had a propensity for stealing everything that was within his reach and in spite of his general mental impairment, he was quite adept at picking pockets. Occasionally, the patient would, without provocation, strike persons near him, there would be no anger apparently accompanying the disorder of conduct."

On another occasion in 1906 when asked who he was, Hoffman replied, "Hannibal", and began laughing to himself. He was locked up in St. Elizabeth's Hospital for the last 46 years of his life. Long after all the other prisoners of war, on both sides, were released and accounted for, Private Lucas Hoffman, Co. H, 90th P.V. remained a prisoner of war, confined in the prison of his madness. After he died in 1909, Lucas Hoffman was buried In Arlington National Cemetery

---

Pension File, William Jones

Camp near Culpeper

Dear Sister,

      I received your letter yesterday. I was glad to hear in George's letter of your getting the money. I got the two papers and the cigar. Victor was here yesterday. His regiment was doing picket two miles west of our camp. The army has not made a general advance yet. I don't want you to send me a box, we expect to leave here every day. We get more grubb here than we know what to do with. Let me know in your next letter what regiment Lizzie Sharps' brother is in. No more at present. Give my love to all inquiring friends. I am well and wish you all the best...

William Jones, 1st

P.S. Send me the tooth brush, a small one, wrap it in newspaper. Here is a quarter for the young ones.

Private William Jones served in the regiment just about 14 months. In the Battle of the Wilderness, he was wounded, but the private recovered from the wound and returned to the ranks during the summer fighting in 1864. William Jones was again a casualty on August 19, 1864 at the battle of Weldon Railroad. Private Jones was one of the prisoners taken by the rebels at that fight. He was sent to a prisoner of war camp in the south where he died on November 18, 1864.

Service Record, John S. Davis

> Camp near Culpeper, Va.
> April 2, 1864

Colonel Peter Lyle

> Commanding 90th Regt. P.V.

> Colonel

I most respectfully ask that a leave of absence be granted me for the space of ten days to enable me to visit Philadelphia upon the following reasons. For nineteen months, I have been on duty, not having applied for or received any leave of absence. The continued painful illness of my wife, and the desire to visit her, and an aged mother of eighty years whose sons are all in the United States service since 1861, and now on duty.
    Also, the necessity of my presence home to prevent me a loss of both money and property. Both the officers of my company are present, and I earnestly I earnestly desire that the above may be granted me.

> John S. Davis, Captain
> Commanding Co. C, 90th Regt. P.V.

Pension File, Thomas Benner

> Camp at Mitchell's Station, Virginia
> April 21, 1864

Dear Father

I received your kind and welcome letter last

evening, and I was happy to hear from you and mother. I was glad to hear that you were both in good health, as I am at this time. Dear Father, Captain Tarr was much mistaken when he told you that I talked too much and that was the cause of my not being promoted. No one is promoted in our regiment until he fills the position of Orderly Sergeant of a company, and that he cannot be until the position is vacant. I have filled the position for nearly a year, yet I did not draw the pay, nor was I the orderly sergeant. I was only 2nd Sergeant, acting orderly. The orderly of my company was acting Commissary Sergeant of the regiment. He filled one man's place for five months, and I filled his. After he returned to the company, he was taken sick and sent to the hospital. I still filled his position until the 19th of September 1863, when he was promoted a 2nd Lieutenant and I was promoted Orderly of the company. When he was promoted, there was not enough of vacancies for me to be promoted to a Lieutenant. Colonel Lyle told me himself, that if there had been one more vacancy, he would have promoted me for I had earned the position, and when he made more promotions, he would make me a Lieutenant.

I am now the Senior Orderly Sergeant of the regiment, and about the 1st of May or June, I will be a Lieutenant. He offered me the Sergeant Majorship of the Regiment, which I refused because I was in command of the company, having lost all my officers at the Battle of Gettysburg. There was no one who was able to attend to the company papers, etc. I knew all about the company from the time it was formed up to the present time, so you will perceive that Captain Tarr is much mistaken, in his knowledge of me and my regiment. Another thing, he had better be careful who he puts under arrest, for the loyalty of a good many officers of the Maryland Brigade is doubted very much, and his loyalty consists considerable in $130.00 per month. I suppose he does not know that Colonel Dick Bowerman of the 4th Maryland Volunteers has offered me a position in his regiment as soon as they are filled up by the draft. A position, which I do not think I will accept, as I will have it before his regiment is filled up. So now I will drop the matter, and let time show which way the wind blows. You may rest assured of one thing, that if I live, the next time you see me I will be a commissioned officer.

Tell Mother she need not feel bad about the way I expressed myself about George or anyone else. I have let all ill feelings drop, and will still continue what I am: a soldier who will raise himself by his own actions. You may rest assured that I will never disgrace myself in a battle. I will either raise myself higher or forever be forgotten, as all soldiers are who die in a glorious cause. My only hope and prayer is that God grant this unnatural war will soon end, and that peace, prosperity, and happiness may once more bless us in a glorious union.

   There is one thing I forgot, and that is when I entered the service I was only 5th Corporal, and in a little over two years, I am Orderly Sergeant, and that in a Regiment that is an old organization. So you will see, that I had to get over the heads of 8 men before I could be what I am. Everything is still about the same here, but I expect a move before long. I will now close. Give my respects to all enquiring friends. Give my love to mother and accept the same for yourself. May God Bless you both and give you many years of prosperity and happiness is the sincere wish of

                          Your ungrateful Son

                          Thomas S. Benner

Write soon.
Direct Sergeant Thomas S. Benner
      Co. A, 90th Regt. P.V.
      Washington, D.C.

   Unfortunately, Sergeant Benner was unable to make peace with his family. The letters he wrote home have this constant contention in them. It appeared that he wanted to put the hostilities to rest, yet, he never quite managed to do so. Unknown to the sergeant or his family, they were running out of time to straighten out their family problems.

Pension File, Henry Mathes

                    Camp near Mitchell's Station, Va.
                    April 30, 1864

My Dear Mother,

I received your welcome letter on the 25th, and I am glad to hear that you are all well as this leaves me. I am sorry to hear that Mrs. Quinn met with such misfortune to lose 2 of her children. We were on picket when I received your letter. We have again moved camp. We moved out of our log houses, and we are now in our shelter tents. I expect it won't be long before we will commence active operations, as everything is in readiness for the coming campaign. Troops are continually arriving. Burnside is expected here with 40,000 men, among them some negro troops. I think if we whip them in the next battle, then this summer will end the war.

You say that Uncle Lewis is engaged to be married. It is as you say, all the fools are not dead yet. I hope that he made a good choice. So Mr. Geokler has commenced Baking business again. Well, he is a queer sort of fellow; he cannot content himself at anything. I suppose that he has plenty of ding bats. I should liked to have seen him. The weather is getting to be very warm down here, from the hill where we are encamped, we can see the rebels plain.

The army places entire confidence in General Grant. If he does as well with the Army of the Potomac, as he did in the western army, I have no doubt but what we will be victorious. We have thrown away our big coats, as we do not need them in this warm weather. Have they commenced to lay the tracks of the 7th and 9th street railway yet, of which there was some talk some time ago? I am glad to hear that the children are getting along well at school. Do you hear anything from Vogels' family yet? How are they getting along? Enclosed I send you $20.00. I had no chance to send it by express, so I send it by mail. I hope you will get it safe. I also received a letter from Miss Benjamin, which I will answer in a few days. Give my love to Sisters and Brother, and take a double helping for yourself. I remain your affectionate son.

Henry Mathes

Private Henry Mathes only served in the regiment for about a year. On June 18, 1864, Mathes was severely wounded in the left leg, while charging the Petersburg trenches with the regiment. The leg was so badly shattered that an army surgeon removed it. Unfortunately, after the amputation, the wound became infected. Gangrene had set in. On July 22, 1864, more than a month after he was wounded, Private Henry Mathes died from the infected wound.

The next five letters, all written by Private John Gould, provide the most detailed account of the "Forty Days", that unbroken period of daily fighting between the Battle of the Wilderness and the crossing of the James River by the Army of the Potomac. Without Private Gould's account, very little would be known about what the men of the 90th P.V. went through in the campaign of 1864.

Pension File, John Gould,

Camp in the field May 12, 1864

My dear Mother,

    I have escaped so far and I am well, but we are still fighting. We are driving them and we have captured a great many prisoners.

                                              John Gould

Pension File, John Gould,

May 21, 1864

My dear Mother,

I have just got back to my own camp again, and thought I would write you again and let you know how I am coming on. I went away from my regiment to get a gun. I had my own gun broke in half with a bullet, and I was picked up by the Provost Guard of the Army and sent to the front on the skirmish line, and I have been with them ever since. I was with Meagher's Irish Brigade when the II Corps made that charge against them, the division of reb prisoners. We charged over there in the morning, about daybreak, and caught them napping. They were bayonetted while they were eating their meals. I was afraid, all the time, that I would be killed while I was with them, and you would not know nothing about it. There was first letters and the papers came for me while I was away. I got the papers, but not the letters. They sent them away again to Fredericksburg. The fighting here is terrible, in fact regular butchering. They send our men right up to their breastworks and the mouth of their cannons on the charge. I have been in four charges. The first one I was in, we lost 142 killed and wounded in five minutes...I suppose the north is in an uproar about this engagement. I wish it was over and I was in old Philadelphia again...

John Gould.

Pension File, John Gould

Camp in front of the enemy

May 25, 1864

Dear Mother,

I wrote you the other day and let you know that I am still in the land of the living. I seen Charlie Drum this morning. He was well and glad to see me. I was glad to see your papers. They were the only ones we had seen since we started on the campaign. When you write to me, send a sheet of paper and an envelope in the letter, for I cannot get any here. Where we are now lying in the rifle pits is about 50 yards from the enemy. I am sick of the business of getting up every day and fighting and no rest. We are capturing a great number of prisoners daily, and I would like to see them take a great deal more than that, already. I want to see this thing ended. My love to Pop and Bell and write soon is a request of your affectionate son.

John Gould

Pension File, John Gould

May 31, 1864

In the entrenchments 14 miles from Richmond,

My Dear Mother,

    I have got a chance to send you another letter this morning, so, I thought I would write one to you. I am still alive and in good health. I saw Charlie Drum again the other day, and he was well. I have wrote to you twice before this, and I have not received any answer yet. Send on the papers as often as you can. We are fighting or skirmishing every day, and I think, up to this time, we have got the best of them, although we have had an awful lot of men killed, wounded, or taken prisoner. Let me know whether you have heard from Uncle Alick or from John Cooper. I think before long they will have to give our army a rest, for they are pretty well worn out with this continual tramping and fighting all the time. We have not got a chance to wash our clothes, and most of us are as lousy as we can be now. We are short of rations too, on account of the wagon train having to fetch the supplies so far to us. I have been two days without a mouthful to eat at a time, but at the time I write this, I was full as a tick. We drew rations last night for three days.

    Colonel Lyle of our regiment is alive and well and has got command of our brigade now. I see that there is a good many reports of him being killed, but this is not so. This country down here in some places is nothing but woods, and in others it is as fine a place as you would like to see. There is plenty of forage, and you can see the boys staggering along under a whole sheep, or a pig, chickens, or something else in the eating line. Give my love to all and write soon and tell Pop and Bell to write to your son.

John Gould

P.S. send me a sheet of paper and an envelope in every letter you write to me, for it is very hard to get any paper or writing materials here.

Pension File, John Gould

June 1, 1864

Camp near Gaines Mill

My Dear Father,

        I was just presented with a sheet of paper and an envelope by the Christian Commission, and thought I would write a letter to you, and let you know how things are going on here with me. Our division is lying here now taking a rest. This is the fourth day we have been here. They say we are waiting for the siege guns to come up and Grant is going to lay siege to the place. The rebels have got a fort here, and the report is that we are undermining it This has been an awful campaign on the men, marching and fighting, and half the time nothing to eat. I received a letter and a paper the other day from you, and I wrote you two letters since.

    I was glad to hear that you were at Cornelius & Baker again. Let me know whether you have got your old position as foreman again, and what Thackard thought of you leaving him.

    I wish this war was over, for the sights a fellow sees and what he has to go through is enough to sicken anyone of a soldiers life. I seen a man the other day that was struck with a shell in his breast, when it exploded and tore the whole top part of his body off. You could see nothing but his legs. His head, arms, and breast was nothing but a lot of mashed bones and torn flesh.

    I seen Charlie Drum several times since I have been here. I also saw Jim and Jake Hammond. I don't think Lee will retreat inside the defenses of Richmond, when he has got thousands of miles of country to move over. It is the general opinion here that he won't go into Richmond and run the risk of being captured, but he will go into North Carolina, and keep the war going from there.

    I spoke in my letter that that tobacco gave me the heartburn. I wish you would get some good tobacco yourself, and send it to me, and as soon as I get paid, I will send $15 or $20 on to you. I wrote also for a Kossuith hat with a little wider brim on than that one I used to wear. Send me a white one instead of the black one that I wrote after; also a fine tooth comb. Give my love to Mother and Belle and all of the children, and write soon to your son.

                 John Gould
                 Co. F, 90th Regt. P.V.
                 Washington, D.C.

Pension file, Thomas Benner

                                   June 8, 1864

Dear Parents,

   I embrace the opportunity of writing these few lines to you, to let you know that I am still living. I have passed all through the different battles we have had, and Thank God, escaped through all without a scratch. We have had some of the hardest fighting to do in this campaign that was ever done.

                                   Thomas Benner

This was the last letter which Thomas Benner wrote to his family. He was killed in action in the attack on Petersburg which the regiment made on June 18, 1864. His death led to controversy after the war about who should get his pension. It turned out that the sergeant had a good reason for using an alias when he enlisted in the regiment. He had two wives and two families. He had left a wife and children in Baltimore, when he left there before the war. In 1862 in

Philadelphia, he married again and had a child with that woman. After his death, both women applied for his pension. The resulting controversy was not resolved until 1867, when Sergeant Benner's pension was awarded to his original family.

Pension File, John Gould

Near Petersburg, June 30, 1864

My Dear Mother,

        I received your letter this morning with fine comb enclosed which I was very happy to get, as I have not had any since I have been on this campaign. I was down to see Charlie Drum yesterday. He is well and looks first rate. I want you to send two shirts like those you made for him. I have got to make out the company pay rolls in a little while, so, I have not got much time to write to you. I am glad to see that you are getting better. If you can't spare the money to get those photographs taken and the album, just now, wait and I will send some to you for we expect to be paid in a few days. Then I want you to have them, right away, and send them on to me. What is Pop going to do in Washington? They say we are going to have a rest here for a little while.

    Our pickets are very friendly with each other. We meet each other half way from the picket lines and trade coffee for Tobacco and exchange papers with each other. I was talking with one the other day when I was on picket. He belonged to the 94th North Carolina. He said he was tired of the war and wished it was over. Give my love to all and write soon, and don't forget to forward them things here your son.

John Gould

P.S. You might go see them fellows out of our army corps if you like. There is one in ward #2 in Nicetown hospital and that James K. Bain, I don't know where he is. He was wounded in the head with a piece of shell. I was lying along side of him when he was hit. The man's name is James Mellor.

J.G.

The two soldiers, Gould asks his parents to go and visit, had far different futures. Private James Bain had been wounded earlier in the war at the Battle of Fredericksburg. He was wounded again on June 19, 1864, suffering a shell wound of the hand. The soldier was then sent back to a hospital in Philadelphia, where he recovered enough to return to the regiment. At the fighting along the Weldon Railroad, the rebels captured a large part of Crawford's Division, including most of the 90th, Private Bain included. James Bain wound up in the Confederate prison camp at Salisbury, North Carolina, where he died on February 17, 1865.

James Mellor travelled a different route than Private Bain. Mellor was wounded in the charge at the Wilderness. At some point, Private Mellor was sent back to a hospital in Philadelphia. He did not, however, remain there very long. On July 1, 1864, Private James Mellor deserted from the hospital. He never again returned to duty with the regiment.

Pennsylvania State Archives, Regimental Records

Washington, D.C. July 1st 1864

To His Excellency

    A. G. Curtin

        Governor of Pennsylvania

            Sir,

                I have the honor to represent that my youngest brother Richard W. Harris, 1st Sergeant Co. C, 90th Regt. P.V., now with his Regiment in front of Petersburg, Va., writes me that he is in command of his company, said company being composed of too few men to warrant a Commissioned Officer being assigned to it. He has been Orderly Sergeant of said company since about the 1st of September 1862, and has frequently had command of it. The previous nominations to you for Commissions in that regiment appear to have been prejudiced, and I would most respectfully urge your Excellency to remember my brother when you next make Commissions in that regiment.

   Richard has been in the service since the rebellion first broke out, having gone out with Colonel Morehead during the three months campaign; and soon being mustered out, again enlisted in the 90th P.V., and has been in the service ever since. He has no high political friends to back him up, so, I offer your Excellency thus, my humble petition in his behalf.

   There are three brothers of us. I, the eldest, age 28, enlisted in May 1862 in Colonel E. D. Baker's California Regt.(71st P.V.) was taken prisoner at Ball's Bluff on October 21st 1861, released Feb. 19th 1862; was through the Peninsula Campaign until ordered back by the Secretary of War as being still on Parole. Immediately after arriving home, I was prostrated with Typhoid Fever, sent to a hospital and my recovery being very slow, I was discharged. I am still unable to take the field, or I should have been out months ago. My second brother, William H., is now a private in Co. H, 15th Pa. Cav.; enlisted in September 1862 and was one of 300 who were in the Battle of Stones River, December 1863. Richard W., the youngest, is the one for whom your Excellency's consideration is now asked. We were all in the service at one time.

   I think I might be pardoned for adding here, that I was

strongly recommended to your Excellency for a Commission in March 1862, by Morton McMichael Esq., L.V. Merrick Esq, and many other prominent Philadelphians. After that I went home in October last, and polled a vote for you for you in 6th Ward Philadelphia.

We are all Philadelphians by birth, and Richard and myself are now citizens of the good old Commonwealth of Pennsylvania.

    I have the honor to be Sir,
     Very Respectfully
      Your obedient servant
       Alva L. Harris
      Chief Clerk Bureau of Deserters
       Provost Marshal Generals Office
        Washington D.C.

After the war ended, the company records of the 90th P.V. were retained by the officers and non-commissioned officers. Over the years, most of the records were lost. I have compiled a list of everyone in the regiment from the Service Records in the National Archives, the Regimental Records in the State Archives, and the regimental roster compiled by Samuel Bates in his History of Pennsylvania Volunteers. In all of these there is no mention of Sergeant Richard Harris. I have no doubt he served in the regiment, but aside from this letter, there is no mention of him anywhere.

Pension File, John Gould

July 10, 1864

Near Petersburg

My Dear Mother,

          I received the package containing one hat and shirt, and as I write this I have got the hat cocked on one side of my head in the latest soldier style. We are building a fort here now, four hundred feet square, and we have to work night and day on it. I have been sick the last week or so, but I am getting better now than I have been. I was down to See Charley two or three times since we laid here, but I heard this morning that his Corps had gone to Pennsylvania. We thought, all along, that our Corps would go, and we are not sure but what we will have to go yet. They, that Charlie's Corps, is going up on a transport. Guess you are in great excitement up there, now, about the rebels. I hope we make a sure thing of it this time, and bag the whole of them. They ought never let such a squad of them as there is to get across the Potomac again.

    This war is an awful thing anyhow. We are getting more men killed than that this whole country is worth. I have seen dead lying in the company in piles. It has been a regular slaughter all through. You must not believe those newspaper stories about the army being in the best of spirits, and all of them having great confidence in Grant; and that they are eager for the war. It is played. The best brigade we have had in our army, are not worth a cent, anymore, and the men all swear they will do no more charging anymore. There has been nothing but charging every time and place we have a fight.

    They told us one night to advance up a hill near where we was laying, and said there was seven lines of battle ahead of ours. We started forward, and the shot and shell seemed to be tearing the whole earth up. It was the awfullest shelling that I ever experienced, and men who have been with the regiment in all the battles of the war, say the same thing. We advanced over this hill, and the first thing we knew, we received a terrible volley from the rebels, and found ourselves fighting on one side of their breastworks and them on the other. We had to use the bayonet most freely to get them, but we did drive them out at last. Now, was that not a nice lie to tell us, there was seven lines ahead of us and there not being one there. Give my love to Pop and Bell and all of the children, and write soon to your son.

                                              John Gould

Like millions of other Americans, in both the North and the South, Private John Gould was wondering if the war was worth what it was costing the country; whether it was worth what it was costing the men who had to do the fighting and killing. The answer to that question was different for each man, depending a great deal on what he was fighting for. For some, the changes the war would be bringing were worth any price they had to pay. For others, nothing was worth the heavy price they and the country had to pay. John Gould had said, "This war is an awful thing"..., but the measure of just how awful was a judgment each man had to make for himself.

Pension File, Edward Steinmetz

Headquarters, Co. B, 90th Regt. P.V. 1st Brigade, 1st Division, V Corps.
                                        Before Petersburg
                                        July 18, 1864

Captain George Monteith

        Assistant Adjutant General

                Captain

                      I would respectfully request that Private Edward Steinmetz of Company B, 90th P.V. who was tried in February last on charges of Desertion, sentence not yet promulgated, be pardoned and released from arrest. That the said Edward Steinmetz has been with the Regiment 10 months since he was arrested, that the prisoners who had been in arrest and those who were tried by court martial were ordered to be armed and to rejoin their regiments, and their future conduct during the campaign would ameliorate their sentences, and in many cases perhaps grant a pardon.

I would state that the actions of Private E. Steinmetz of Company B, during the campaign from the Rapidan to Petersburg, has been that of a good soldier, that he has fought bravely, and is at present doing duty with his company.

Lieutenant John Bowman

Private Edmund Steinmetz enlisted in Company B, 90th P.V. on February 20, 1862. He served with the regiment until December 4, 1862. At that time, he deserted. Steinmetz was listed as a deserter until he returned to the regiment on October 26, 1863. On his return, the soldier was court martialed. At his trial, testimony verified that he had returned voluntarily, without any guard. Private Steinmetz was found guilty of the charge, but his sentence was a light one. He would forfeit $6.00 per month from his pay for 10 months, and he would make good the time lost to the Government.

Edmund Steinmetz's performance in the fighting in the spring and summer of 1864, certainly justified the court martial board's judgment in imposing a light sentence in his case. He continued to do his duty in the ranks, and was captured along the Weldon Railroad on August 19, 1864. He was confined at the prison camp at Salisbury, North Carolina. Private Steinmetz survived in Salisbury and was discharged from the service on June 30, 1865.

Pension File, John H. Stutzman

July 18, 1864

Camp in Fort Grant near Petersburg, Virginia

Dear Sister,

      Your very welcome letter came to hand last evening, and I was very glad to hear that you was well. We get our mail in the night. I was on guard in the fort. We are still working, yet, it is so, now, we can use it. We have one battery in four pieces, twelve pound battery. General Warren is here most every day. Sometimes, the work don't do to suit him, he commence to cuss the men. Last night, they expected an attack on our lines, but they didn't come. I expect that as soon as this fort gets done, there will be a big artillery duel.

We do picket duty and fatigue duty, so we hain't got much rest at the present time, but when it gets done then we will have some. Our pickets and the rebel pickets trades papers and gives coffee or tobacco. Here the other day two of our boys was talking to some of the rebs and they took them, and about half a hour there was a Rebel Major belonging to the Washington Battery, and one of our fellows snatched him and brought him into our lines. They still think that they are going to have their independence.

I would like to know how they are making out in Maryland. I think they will get the worst of the bargain going up there. Sherman is running them pretty hard in Georgia, and if he licks them down there, it won't last long anymore. I would like to see it over now. They hain't much fighting here now. Shelling is kept up at regular intervals. We are going to have some large guns in this fort when it's done. It will be a hot place in here, for they hain't a great ways away from us.

The picket lines is so close that they can talk to each other but no firing. We have some big mortar guns. They don't like them. The shells go up in the air and make a turn, and come right down on them in their breastworks. They have them; but theirs are not as good as ours, so, we have the best of them. Well, that's about all I know about the war this time. Cousin Isaac was over here to see me and he got his letter. I left him read my letter, and he said that his letter was wrote better than mine. I hope that we will lay in this fort till my time is out, that's a little over four months. I haven't seen action for sometime...

You want to know about the rain. We haven't had any rain for nearly two months. Dry and awful hot here.

John Stutzman

Corporal John Stutzman of Company B saw a great deal of action in the spring and summer of 1864. He was a casualty in the Wilderness and again in the Battle for the Weldon railroad. Stutzman suffered a gunshot wound in the charge in the Wilderness. He recovered and returned to the ranks. Three months later at the Weldon Railroad, Corporal Stutzman was taken prisoner. He died in the Confederate prison camp at Salisbury, North Carolina on November 30, 1864. The 90th P.V. had 82 men die in Southern prison camps. Of these, 37 died in the Salisbury camp, 21 others died in Andersonville, Georgia. The remainder were spread among other, smaller prisoner of war locations.

An artist's rendition of the stockade at Andersonville. As the prisoner of war camps, both North and South, became overcrowded, they became death camps. More than 13,000 Union soldiers died in Andersonville. Twenty one men from the 90th P.V. died there. The 90th lost 82 men who died as Confederate prisoners of war.

Pennsylvania State Archives, Regimental Records

                        Cincinnati, Ohio 24 July 1864

To His Excellency Governor Curtin.

   May it please your excellency--My husband, Abram Nash Cooper was Corporal in Co. G, 90th Regiment Pen. Vet. Vol, the last account I have had of him was from his Lieut. Col. Wm. Leech, saying that he had been wounded at Spotsylvania Court House, May 8th 1864 and left on the field. Since then, I applyed for information to the War Department at Washington. My answer was Missing in Action. I would pray Your Excellency to inform me whether or not you have any information on his fate. I have no means to support myself and child, and would earnestly pray your early attention.

                        Yours respectfully

                        Althea Cooper.

On May 8, 1864, the 90th P.V. took part in the attack made by Robinson's Division at Laurel Hill. Despite a valiant effort, Robinson's men were repulsed and forced to retreat. The men of the 90th P.V. were the last to be driven away from the Confederate lines. As Lieutenant John Harris of Company G and his men were advancing on the rebel line, Corporal Abraham Cooper was shot and fell to the ground. Later, as the regiment was forced to retreat, Harris passed the wounded Cooper. He stopped and spoke to the man. The Corporal was shot through the left part of his chest. The bullet passed through causing a fatal wound. The Lieutenant tried to ease the soldier as much as possible, but he could not remain with the dying man long, as the rebels held possession of the field. As a result, Cooper was left on the field dying, and his body was not recovered to be given a proper burial.

Service Record, Richard W. Davis,

August 5, 1864

To Major General Halleck,

        Chief of Staff,

                General,

                      I have the honor to make application for a leave of abscence(for a few days) to visit Philadelphia, in consequence of the dangerous illness of my wife and child. I, this morning received a telegram that, if I wished to see them alive, I must come immediately. Having been wounded in the knee in the late campaign of Lt. General Grant and sent to this hospital, I remain still unfit for duty and a few days granted in the present condition of my wound, will not be a loss to the government of my service in the field. At the same time you will be granting an everlasting blessing on my family. I, as a husband and a father, respectfully ask that my petition may be granted that I may be with them, that time they have to remain in this world.

                                    Very Respectfully,
                                    Your Obedient Servant

                                    Richard W. Davis
                                    1st Lieutenant, 90th P.V.

This was approved by General Halleck on August 6, 1864 through an order sent to the Officer in Charge at Officers Hospital at Annapolis, Maryland. The General authorized the hospital commander to approve leave for Lieutenant Davis.

Pension File, Henry Snyder

Near Petersburg
August 17, 1864

Dear Parents,

I take the present opportunity to write a few lines to inform you that I am well, and hope that these few lines will find you all the same. I have not received a letter from you for about two weeks, so I have given up looking for any, and thought that I would write and tell you how I am getting along, alive or dead. We have left the fort. We was relieved by colored troops and under marching orders to move at a minutes notice to what point we don't know. It is now raining, although we are comfortably fixed and have plenty to eat. We was payed off several days ago. I gave Lewis Labar $20.00 for him to express home with him. So, Mrs. Labar will get it...Have you sent that shirt or not? Send it as soon as you can, for I want them bad. I can't wear government shirts, they are too coarse. You may think things is too dear when we have to pay $1.50 for a small watermellon. All the money I spend is for good use for things to eat. I will close with my love to all. Good bye, write soon from your son.

Sergeant Henry C. Snyder

It is getting too dark to write and the mail goes out at midnight. If we do not move, I will write a long letter tomorrow.

This is the last letter we got from our dear son. It was wrote on the 17th and he was killed on the 18th.

Sergeant Henry C. Snyder was killed in action during the first day of fighting along the Weldon Railroad, August 18, 1864.

General Warren, Commander of the V Army Corps, here directs the construction of fortifications along the Weldon Railroad, during the fighting there.

Pension File, Isaac Paxson

                            Richmond, August 22, 1864

Dear Mother

         It is with much pleasure I write to you to let you know that I am a prisoner of war and well, and when these few lines reach you, I hope they may find you the same. Mother, I cannot write much, but I will just write enough to let you know that I am here, well. I must stop. Do not write until I tell you to, so goodbye.

                            From your affectionate son

                            I. V. Paxson

Private Isaac Paxson had been drafted into the regiment on September 15, 1863, and had served with the regiment all through the campaign in the Wilderness and on through the Petersburg fighting. In the Battle for the Weldon Railroad, Private Paxson was taken prisoner along with most of the regiment. Six weeks later Isaac Paxson was dead. He died of fever in the Salisbury prison camp on October 29, 1864.

Pension File, Henry Snyder

                            Camp on the Weldon Railroad
                            August 28, 1864

Mr. S.W. Brodhead,

Dear Sir,

Your favor of the 22nd was placed in my hands by Colonel P. Lyle. I immediately set to work to meet the wishes of Mr. Snyder. I rode up to headquarters to get permission to send the body of Sergeant Henry Snyder home, which was refused. An order from the War Department forbids taking any body up until after the 25th.

Sergeant Henry Snyder was buried by his comrades, and a headboard marks his resting place. You will please tell Mr. Snyder that his son proved himself a brave and good soldier. He was well liked by his officers and, had the respect of the regiment. Had he been spared a short time, he would have been promoted to Lieutenant. He died as a good soldier ought to die, with his face to the enemy. He did not suffer much after he was hit, but a few moments, and he was dead.

We were contending for the Weldon Railroad, which we now hold. The rebs have four times tried to take it from us, and the loss on both sides will amount to over 6,000 men killed, wounded, and taken prisoners.

Lieutenant Colonel and Major with several line officers were taken prisoner. We now number 55 men and 5 officers for duty...Though it be slow, we are still making ground, and our campaign will yet come out all right. If we had as strong an army as we had when we commenced this campaign, we could end the war this fall. Why do not the good men of the country come out, and not send us all the cowards and scoundrels that you can purchase with a few dollars? They are not men. They are things. You at home think our army large, that is not the fact. So far as fighting goes, three dollar men never go into the fight. They skulk, and run, and play sick and everything possible that they can do to get clear of their duty as soldiers and men. You may not know me by name but your son does. Give him my regards, also the rest of the boys of Company K to yourself and brother. If I get out of this war alive, I intend to pay your county a visit, but until this job is properly finished and honorably settled, I will have to forgo my visit.

Lieutenant J. A. Harris
Company G, 90th Regt. P.V.

Pennsylvania State Archives, Regimental Records

Armory Infantry Corps National Guard,

Philadelphia, September 1st, 1864

To The Family and Relatives

of

CAPTAIN WILBUR T. MYERS

90th Regiment, P.V., National Guards

 At a meeting of the Infantry Corps National Guards, held as above, the following PREAMBLE and RESOLUTIONS were unanimously adopted, as reported by a committee appointed to draft Resolutions expressive of the feelings of the Corps.
 Whereas, it has pleased a Divine providence to remove from the scenes of earth, our esteemed friend and brother, CAPTAIN WILBUR T. MYERS, 90th Regt. P.V., (National Guards,) one noted for many endearing qualities of heart and mind, and respected by all for his manly virtues, and whilst we bow submissively before the Divine mandate of Him who "giveth and taketh away;" whilst we respect and Reverence the dispensation made by the all wise Disposer of everything human, we feel, that it becomes us, in this hour of affliction, to give a proper expression of our feelings, for the great loss we are called upon to sustain.
 Resolved, that regretting as we do, the necessity which compels us to know, that he is removed from us; yet we are consoled with the truth that his memory survives him, that the patriotism and bravery evinced by him upon the many battlefields of this cursed rebellion, live and are appreciated; that old memories, old associations and old ties, cannot be forgotten. Agreeable in manners, gentlemanly in principle, honest and candid in decision, and possessing in a great degree that noble passion, the noblest that can animate a man in the character of a citizen, viz: Patriotism, we feel that his loss is, not only to us, but to his family and relatives, irreparable. A brave and cool soldier, a true and tried friend, with a noble and generous heart.
 Resolved, That the Corps tender the heartfelt feelings of condolence to the family and relatives of our late comrade in their affliction.
 Resolved, That the meeting room be draped, and the Corps attend the funeral of our late companion in arms, and pay the last sad tribute of respect to the memory of the deceased, by wearing the usual badge of mourning for thirty days.
 Resolved, That a copy of these Resolutions be transmitted

to the family of our departed comrade, and also printed for members of the Corps.

                                          Edward W. Ferry,
                                          John H. Crawford,
                                          P. H. Jacobus

Personal Papers, Nicholas Guyger

                                          October 6, 1864

To Abraham Lincoln
President of the United States,

                          I take the liberty of directing your attention to my especial case. I am an exile from Richmond, Virginia being forced to leave in a very short space of time on account of my Union proclivities, being ordered to do so, or have my head shaved & imprisoned or possible death. I enlisted in the National Guards, 90th Regiment P.V., as a teamster. The above regiment was in camp some six months during which time I was forced to get work to support my family, and I also received notice that the above regiment had all the teamsters they wanted.
    Consequently, I paid no more attention to it, and I was never arrested until about six weeks ago. I was arrested by Captain Moran after the time of service had expired, and was and am confined in the barracks, 5th and Buttonwood Sts. as a prisoner or deserter. I never received any clothing nor any money or anything from the said regiment, nor was ever mustered in the said regiment nor any other. I am here confined and my family starving for bread, as they have no other means of support. If I am not released soon, my family will have to go to the poor house or to beggary. Also, I am afflicted with the kidney disease so that I am not able to scarcely support my family at the very lightest work I can do. Also, I have one son now in the service. I implore you to have me released, if possible. If I had no family, I would not care so much about it, or if I had means to support my family. Hoping that your excellency will not think that I am asking too much, you will excuse me for taking the liberty of writing to you in regard to my affairs. If you think the above worthy of answering, you will do so by directing your letter to the S.W. corner 13th & Race St.,

Philadelphia.

> Very respectfully, your
> most obedient servant
>
> Nicholas Guyger

Nicholas Guyger never served a day as a soldier in the 90th P.V. However, his enlistment on November 4, 1861 led directly to his death. The story he told to an investigator assigned to his case differed greatly from what he wrote to President Lincoln. Guyger and some friends went out drinking in November 1861. They got drunk and enlisted in the army. Guyger enlisted in the 90th P.V. as a teamster, but later claimed that he had not enlisted. He continued to make this claim, despite being told by his friends on several different occasions that he had enlisted. Private Guyger never took the trouble to find out if his friends were correct or not. He remained in Philadelphia until he was arrested there on September 8, 1864.

After his arrest, Guyger was sent to Alexandria, Virginia. He was, for a time, held in Forrest Hall prison in Washington, D.C. On December 6, 1864, it was determined that Nicholas Guyger had officially enlisted in the 90th P.V. A short time later, he was transferred to a hospital in City Point, Virginia. Guyger died there on January 29, 1865 of Tuberculosis, without ever being brought to trial.

Pension File, Peter Westerman

> Headquarters, 90th P.V.
> Fort Dushane, Virginia
> October 15, 1864

Charles Grindlock,

    You will do me and the company a favor if you go to Peter Westerman's mother, and tell her he is dead. He was taken prisoner on the 19th of August and died in or near Richmond. George Saxer of our company was taken the same time, but has since been paroled, and it was through him that we received the information. We are having a fine time just now. Have been in this fort about two weeks and, no doubt, will stay until next spring. I hope so, anyhow. There are none left in the company that came out with but, Morris and myself, but six in all.

> Yours respectfully,
> Corporal John Rau,
> Company C, 90th P.V.

Since joining the regiment on January 14, 1862, Corporal John Rau had seen a lot of fighting, a lot of killing, and more than a few good men die. He had been shot twice himself, once at Gettysburg, and a second time along the Weldon railroad. His company, at one time, had consisted of a hundred men. Now, there were only six.

Private Peter Westerman, the subject of Rau's letter, had enlisted in the 90th on November 15, 1861 and was assigned to Company C. Like Corporal Rau, Westerman served throughout the war. He survived a wound suffered at the Battle of Fredericksburg and returned to duty.

Private Westerman was charged with desertion as a result of falling out of the regiment during General Burnside's famous mud march. In what was a ludicrous administrative decision, the high command of the Army of the Potomac decided to Court Martial thousands of men. Private Westerman was among them. He was found guilty of being absent without leave and sentenced to forfeit four months pay and to serve four months at hard labor.

When he returned to duty, Private Westerman continued to be a good soldier and do his duty. He was captured along with about 120 others in the regiment at the Weldon Railroad. Westerman died less than a month later at the Confederate prison camp in Salisbury, North Carolina.

Pennsylvania State Archives, Regimental Records

                       Headquarters. Co. F, 90th P.V.
                       October 25, 1864

Dear Mrs. Street

    I received your letter inquiring about your son, John Gould of my company. I am sorry to inform you that he was taken prisoner on the Weldon railroad on the 21st of August. I have not heard anything of him since, but suppose he is safe within the enemy's lines. Some of our men are at Annapolis, MD, who were taken with him, if you direct to

I. Sigafoos, he might give you some information about your son. I enclose a receipt for $15.00 sent by your son by Adams Express. I sincerely hope your son may soon be released and return safely home to you. Respectfully.

       Richard W. Davis
       1st Lieutenant, Co. F, 90th
       Regt. P.V.

At the time Lieutenant Davis wrote this letter to Catherine Street, John Gould's mother, the soldier was a prisoner of the Confederacy. However, after his capture at the Weldon Railroad, Private John Gould was sent to the Prison camp at Florence, South Carolina. He died in that place on January 29, 1865.

Service Record, Edward Jenkins, letter to General Couch

Major General Couch   November 2, 1864

    Dear sir, I was at your office on Wednesday last. You were absent but I saw one of your aids, who promised to write to me on your return, but I received no answer. The object of my visit was to see you in regard to my son, Edward Jenkins, Company B, 90th P.V., who was court martialed before Captain Clarke. I wish to know whether you would not cause him to be discharged, as his term of enlistment has expired, on condition that he joins another regiment. By doing this, you will confer a great favor on me, as he is the only support I have.

       Mrs. Christine Jenkins

Records of Assistant Adjutant General, National Archives, RG #94 , Court Martial File, Private Edward Jenkins

Charge: Conduct prejudicial to good order and military discipline

Specification: In this that the said Edward Jenkins, Private Company B, 90th regiment P.V. while confined in the guard house of the U.S. General Hospital, Christian Street, Phila. did abstract from the pocket of fellow prisoner William H. Johnson, a contract nurse, a pocket book containing about 24 dollars and a promissory note or notes for about $200.00 while the said William Johnson was asleep.
This in the Guard House of the U.S. General Hospital, Christian Street, Phila., PA, on or about the 8th day of August, 1864.

Charge: Desertion

Specification: In this that the said Edward Jenkins, Private, Company B, 90th Regiment P.V., did escape between the bars of the window of the Guard House of the U.S. General Hospital, Christian Street, Philadelphia, PA, on or about August 8, 1864 and did remain absent till the 22nd day of August 1864 when he was arrested.

Edward Jenkins pleaded guilty to everything except the 2nd charge. The court found Jenkins guilty of both charges and both specifications. The sentence imposed was to be dishonorably discharged from the service, lose all pay due, and to be sent to a military prison for five years of hard labor. His mother's plea saved him from prison.

Records of Assistant Adjutant General, Court Martial File,

Edward Jenkins

Special order 309	War Department
	Adjutant General's Office
	Washington, November 15, 1864

The sentence of the General Court Martial as promulgated in General order #56, Headquarters Department of the Susquehanna of October 15, 1864 in the case of Private Edward Jenkins, Company B, 90th P.V. now supposed to be with that regiment, is remitted.

By order of the President of the United States,
E.D. Townsend

Assistant Adjutant General

Unfortunately, this was not the end of Edward Jenkins' criminal career. After the war ended, he was arrested and convicted of various crimes in Philadelphia and Trenton. He served jail terms in both cities. His mother was successful in obtaining his early release from both places. Jenkins repaid her by robbing his grandmother's house while the rest of the family went to his father's funeral. After committing this crime, he disappeared from Philadelphia. Later, he applied for a pension from the Government, but was rejected because of his criminal activities.

Pennsylvania State Archives, Regimental Records

Philadelphia November 31, 1864

Dear Sir

Will you be kind enough to let me know if John Gould belonging to Company F, 90th Regiment P.V., who was taken prisoner on the 19th of August at the battle on the Weldon Railroad is dead or still living? You will greatly oblige his anxious Mother.

Catherine Street

P.S. Please direct to William J. Street, care of Cornelius & Co., No. 710 Chestnut Street, Philadelphia, Pa.

Personal Papers, Corporal David H. Deahl, Letter from sister

Philadelphia December 8, 1864

Dear Sir,

My brother, Corporal David H. Deahl of Colonel Lyle's 90th Regiment, Company H, was taken prisoner the 5th of May. We have heard nothing of him since, although we have written everywhere. We were told to go to the Sanitary Commission, and they said to write to you. If you will be so kind as to answer this, and let us know whether you can give us any information about him. His mother and all would be a thousand times obliged to you.

Please direct to Mrs. Sallie Conway
122 Callowhill Street
Philadelphia

Corporal David Deahl had enlisted in the 90th P.V. on June 30, 1863. He took part in the ill fated charge made by the regiment near the end of the first day of fighting in the Wilderness. In the five minute charge, half of the regiment was killed, wounded, or captured. Corporal Deahl was one of the wounded who could not be brought off the battlefield. He was captured and confined until December 11, 1864, when he was paroled. Ten days later, December 21, 1864, Corporal David Deahl died of chronic diarrhea.

Service Record, Captain John S. Davis, letter of Eleanor Davis

December 10, 1864

To Major Breck
Respected Sir,

    Excuse the liberty I have taken in writing to you. My only child is very sick with the scarlet fever and I would like my husband to get home for a few days to see him. I have telegraphed twice and also sent a doctors certificate, but all to no purpose. My child is very sick, and I would like my husband to see him. It is the only one left out of five, and if anything serious happens to him, it would be a terrible blow to my husband. Part of his regiment has come home. The others have been consolidated into the 11th Penna. Vols. My husband and three other officers have been left in charge of them. His name is Captain John S. Davis, Company C, 90th Regiment Penna. Vols. He has held his commission three years from the 3rd of last September. I was advised to write to you, for you might probably have it in your power to do something for him. If you will oblige me by doing what you can towards getting him home, you will have the thanks and prayers of a distressed wife and mother.

                I remain yours very respectfully

                Mrs. Eleanor W. Davis
                No. 863 North 9th St.

Captain John Davis received the furlough and went home to visit his son. Apparently, his visit had the desired effect on the child. A search of Philadelphia death records for 1864 do not show the death of any child with the surname of Davis.

1865

Personal Papers, John Reed

February 1, 1865,

Mr. Governor Curtin,

          I take this opportunity of calling your attention to my case being that I now have been in confinement fourteen months at Fort Jefferson, Florida. My time in my judgment is not out yet. I should be very glad, if possible, to be returned back to my regiment, for my confinement has been very unpleasant. Besides; I think I have been punished amply for my crime, being the first offense I have committed. This is my second enlistment, besides all this, I have a poor widowed mother who is most depending on me for support.

    What can I do after going in 1861, then again in 1863, and now for my first crime, to be sent to Tortugas for three years...I appeal to you for assistance to get returned to duty again. I wish to go to my regiment and do my duty as a soldier. I am sorry for what I have done, and hope I shall have the pleasure of meeting you, a fellow soldier on the battlefield.

    I hope you will do all you can for me and let me hear from you soon and you will oblige me.

                                        John Reed
                                        Private, Company H
                                        90th Regiment P.V.

Private John Reed had been drafted into Company H of the 90th P.V. on September 25, 1863. He had previous service in Company I of the 3rd Delaware Infantry and had been honorably discharged from that regiment. Private Reed wanted no parts of the army on his second hitch. He deserted one day short of a month. The soldier left camp on October 24, 1863 but was apprehended a short time later. John Reed was Court Martialed for desertion, found guilty, and sentenced to three years at hard labor. He was confined at Fort Jefferson in the Dry Tortugas, a most unpleasant place. It is not surprising Reed asked Governor Curtin to help him get back to his regiment. Unhappily for John Reed, Andrew Curtin did not assist him in returning to his regiment. However, Reed did not serve his full sentence. Andrew Johnson pardoned most Federal Military prisoners and John Reed was among them. He was discharged from the service and from prison on July 1, 1865.

The Watson Case

All the letters in this section refer to a Promotion that went drastically wrong. In early 1863, Colonel Peter Lyle recommended twenty promotions of non-commissioned and commissioned officers. 1st Lieutenant George Watson's name was not included in the list. Watson believed he was entitled to a promotion. Colonel Lyle disagreed. Major Alfred Sellers and several Philadelphia politicians interceded with Governor Curtin, and the governor issued a Captain's Commission for George Watson as Captain of Company H.

When this commission arrived at the Army of the Potomac, Colonel Lyle refused to present it to Watson. The Colonel then appealed to the governor to withdraw the offending commission. These letters detail the controversy surrounding this political promotion until Lieutenant Watson suffered a crippling wound in the charge at the Wilderness, and the controversy disappeared, at least temporarily. Even after George Watson was wounded and had his leg amputated, he continued to pursue the promotion which he believed was justly his. The officers, who were originally recommended by Colonel Lyle, began to write letters to the governor in support of their Colonel. A considerable amount of hard feelings were generated within the regiment as a result of this case. The matter of Watson's promotion was not finally settled until 26 years after Colonel Peter Lyle made his initial recommendation for promotions.

I have not included every letter which was written in the Watson case. I have chosen instead to use those which provide the clearest understanding of the events involved in the controversy.

Pennsylvania State Archives, Regimental Records

>   Headquarters 90th Regt. Penn. Vol.
>   Camp near Belle Plain, Virginia.
>   January 9, 1863.

To his Excellency

    Andrew Curtin,

Governor of the Commonwealth of Pennsylvania

        Sir;

            I beg leave to make the following nominations for your confirmation of Officers and Non-Commissioned Officers for promotion for efficiency in the field and for gallant and meritorious conduct in all the battles in which the Regiment has been engaged since they entered the service.
To wit,

Cedar Mountain	August 9, 1862
Rappahannock Station	August 20, 22, 23, 1862
Thoroughfare Gap	August 28, 1862
Groveton or Bull Run	August 30, 1862
Chantilly	September 1, 1862
South Mountain	September 14, 1862

Antietam	September 16 & 17, 1862
Fredericksburg	December 12, 13, 14, 15, 1862
First Lieutenant	William P. Davis, of Co. A to be Captain Of Co H., vice Captain Rush dropped from the rolls to date August 29, 1862.
First Lieutenant	Francis A. Chadwick of Co. I, to be Captain of Co. K, vice Captain Belsinger resigned to date August 1, 1862.
Second Lieutenant	William S. Ellis, of Co. H, to be 1st Lieutenant of Co. A, vice Davis promoted to date August 29, 1862.
Second Lieutenant	Samuel J. Moore, Co. B, to be 1st Lieutenant of Co. B, vice Samuel B. Roney promoted September 6, 1862, to Regiment Quartermaster.
Second Lieutenant	William H. Hewlings, of Co C, to be 1st Lieutenant of Co. E, vice E. W. Ferry, resigned to date January 3, 1863.
Second Lieutenant	James P. Meade of Co. G, to be 1st Lieutenant of Co. K, vice F. A. Chadwick promoted to date August 1, 1862.
Second Lieutenant	John F. Reilly, of Co. F, to be 1st Lieutenant of Co. K, vice Charles W. Duke, killed at the Battle of Fredericksburg to date December 14, 1862.
Sergeant Major	Charles Ricketts, to be 2nd Lieutenant of Co. B, vice Moore promoted to date September 6, 1862.
Quartermaster Sergeant	Jesse W. Super, to be 2nd Lieutenant of Co. C, vice Hewlings, promoted to date January 3, 1863.
First Sergeant	John A. Griffin, to be 2nd Lieutenant of Co. E, vice William E. Lindsley, dropped from the rolls, to date January 1, 1863.
First Sergeant	David F. Barry, to be 2nd Lieutenant of Co. F, vice Reilly promoted to date December 14, 1862.
First Sergeant	Benjamin F. Bond, to be 2nd Lieutenant of Co. G, vice Meade promoted to date August 1, 1862.

First Sergeant	Hillery Beyer, to be 2nd Lieutenant of Co. H, vice Ellis, promoted to date August 29, 1862.
First Sergeant	Alfred Ballinger, to be 2nd Lieutenant Co, I, vice Peter H. Zell, resigned to date December 12, 1862.
First Lieutenant	Nathan Raymond, to be Captain of Co. d, vice John A. Gorgas, resigned on Surgeon's Certificate of disability to date March 8, 1863.
Second Lieutenant	John H. Harris of Co. K, to be 1st Lieutenant Co. G, vice 1st Lieutenant James Moore, promoted to be Captain and Asst. Q. Master, U.S. Vols., to date February 26, 1863.
Second Lieutenant	Richard W. Davis, of Co. D, to be 1st Lieutenant Co. F, vice Raymond promoted to date March 9, 1863.
Sergeant Major	James S. Bonsall of Co. K, to be 2nd Lieutenant of Co. F, vice John T. Reilly promoted in place of Sergeant David Barry recommended for promotion January 9, 1863, he having since been discharged on account of wounds received in battle
First Sergeant	George Jewell of Co. D, to be 2nd Lieutenant of Co. K, vice Harris promoted to date February 27, 1863.
First Sergeant	Henry Bockius, of Co I, to be 2nd Lieutenant of Co. D, vice Davis promoted to date March 10, 1863.

   Hoping the above nominations will meet with your approval, I must respectfully ask that you will cause the commissions of the above named officers to be issued in order that they may be mustered and enter upon their duties at once. They have all been officiating in their several capacities as above recommended for promotion, in the place of officers absent wounded. They are good soldiers and well fitted for, as be assured sir, I would not recommend them or anyone else, unless I had a perfect knowledge of them and their acts. I would also further ask that the names of the aforesaid Battles be inscribed upon our tattered Flag.

With my best wishes for your health

I remain your Obedient Servant

Peter Lyle, Colonel 90th Regt. P.V.
Commdg. 2nd Brigade 2nd Division
I Army Corps.

Pennsylvania State Archives, Regimental Records

Philadelphia, January 12, 1863

To Hon. Andrew G. Curtin

Governor State of Pennsylvania

Respected Sir,

Through the Kindness of Mr. Richard Wildy Esq.(member, State Legislature) who has favored me with the accompanying letter, I take the liberty of addressing you.

I have the honor to be attached to the Pennsylvania Volunteers the 90th(2nd Regiment "National Guards", State Militia) and am mow confined to my bed from wounds received at Fredericksburg, 13th ultimo.

I have received information of a promotion of Officers and Privates in our Regiments, though not from an official source, but if such is correct, I feel it my duty to solemnly protest against the injustice done to Lieutenant George W. Watson commanding Co. H.

You are no doubt aware, that it is customary for the Field Officers of a regiment to consult and canvass the merit and qualifications of those entitled to promotion. As vacancies have occurred from time to time and no promotions, it, at times, has somewhat dampened the ardor of the soldiers. At last, I have the misfortune to be absent from my command, then, apparently <u>then</u>, the opportunity is embraced to make promotions.

The injustice shewn me, is nothing. To Lieutenant Watson, it is everything. He considers his prospects blasted. May I claim your patience a little longer?

I have been identified with the State Militia since April 1854, in the service of my country since April 1861, and claim to know of the merits and qualifications of the Lieutenant in question. He, ranking second Senior First

Lieutenant in the regiment, had command of his company in every engagement in which the regiment has participated, off duty but <u>one</u> day since the date of his commission, September 3, 1861 and recruited more men for the Regiment than any officer in it(and with less expense to the Government) and above all performed his duties admirably with credit to himself and his country. In the official report of the part taken by the Regiment in the Battle of Antietam, received the commendation of his commander.

Aside from the military qualifications of Lieutenant George W. Watson, he has other noble traits which stamp him as a true patriot. He has ably replied to the many constant expressions of opposition to the Administration, thereby rendering himself "no doubt unpopular with his superiors." Perhaps you can imagine his position. I enclose a few brief lines of his letter.

If in the event his promotion has been neglected by Colonel Lyle or Lieutenant Colonel William A. Leech, who is now in command, I trust you will consider the case.

If you would do me the honor to reply and inform me of those recommended and their rank, I shall never miss the opportunity to reciprocate the favor.

Very Respectfully

Your friend

A. J. Sellers
Major 90th Regt. P.V.
Box 1075 Philadelphia, Pa.

Pennsylvania State Archives, Regimental Records,

Headquarters Co. H, 90th P.V.
Belle Plain Virginia
February 20th, 1863

His Excellency Andrew G. Curtin

       Governor Commonwealth Pennsylvania

Respected Sir

       I have received information that Major A. J. Sellers of 90th Regt. P.V.(now at home in Philadelphia from wounds received at Battle of Fredericksburg,) has addressed letters on the 13th inst. and the 3rd inst., to your Excellency in regard to a great and grievous injustice done to me. His action in my case was as generous as it was unsolicited.

And thus having most excellent, and holding the axiom as good "An injustice to the humblest individual is an injury to the state," will therefore proceed to state my grievance.

I have the honor to be engaged in the service of my state and country as 1st Lieutenant of Co. H, 90th P.V., Colonel Peter Lyle. My commission dating from September 3, 1861. I was also in the service on three months call, and have been identified with the State Militia since 1854 or 1855. When entering on my present term of service, I left a business in Philadelphia that I was successfully carrying on and recruited more men than any officer in the regiment, using largely of my personal means. Up to the present time I have been but one day off duty, then sick.

I have participated in every battle(eight in number) in which my regiment has taken part, and in the official report of the part taken by the Regiment in the Battle of Antietam, received the commendation of my commander, being then in command of my company and as also at four preceding battles, and more that have occurred since. The command having devolved on me since August 29, 1862. I rank second senior 1st Lieutenant in the regiment. Judge then of my deep mortification and indignation when about 30th ult., the following was read before the Regiment. This being the reading and first promotion of fourteen made by Colonel Lyle commanding Brigade. I copy verbatim.

                    Headquarters 90th P.V.
                    January 4, 1863

General Orders #

II. The following promotions for efficiency in the field and for gallant and meritorious conduct in all the Battles in which the Regt. has been engaged from Cedar Mountain, August 9, 1862 to the Battle of Fredericksburg, December 13, 1862 are hereby promulgated to the Regiment.

This Lieutenant of Co. A, promoted over me(1st Lieutenant of Co. H) had been absent sick from the regiment since the day before Cedar Mountain Battle and did not rejoin us until a few days before Battle of Fredericksburg which last was the only Battle he ever participated in. Also according to Army rule Lieutenant William P. Davis ranks fifth or sixth while I am as before stated second senior 1st Lieutenant in the Regiment. I will defy any person to say aught against my conduct or efficiency as an officer, but suppose Major Sellers will satisfy you on that point, or inquiry can be instituted.

I have at all times opposed those who make party predominant over patriotism, and advocated a firm and determined support of the Administration as the only means of crushing the rebellion. I have been very open in this matter and have, perhaps, given offense to my superior in rank, for in no other way can I account for my unpopularity in that quarter.

Thanking you for patience thus far, and most earnestly praying that you may give attention, to my case in securing to me my right of promotion. Or failure of which, to secure for me an Honorable discharge from the service, in case of which last, I design when levies of men are again made, to enter the service of my country again. In conclusion I would state that considerable attention in the Regiment, and among my friends, is attracted to my case and should it be understood in the Army that <u>rights</u> are <u>not</u> <u>guaranteed</u>, and services in the field are not recognized, then much will be done toward demoralization.

And now leaving my case in your hands believing that justice will be obtained me I beg to subscribe myself

Most Respectfully Yours etc.
Lieutenant George W. Watson
90th Regiment, P.V.

Pennsylvania State Archives, Regimental Records

Headquarters 90th Regt. Penna. Vols.
In Camp Lower Belle Plain, Virginia
March 19, 1863.

To His Excellency

Andrew Curtin

Governor of the Commonwealth of Penna.

Sir,

We, the undersigned officers of the 90th

P.V., having been recently promoted and assigned to duty in accordance with General Order #1 from these headquarters, having learned that parties have represented that our promotions were based on political principles, and deeming it our duty to defend our Colonel from false accusations, would respectfully state that politics have never been broached in the regiment, and further that Colonel Peter Lyle is not acquainted with the political feelings of more than one or two of us; and that but four of us, of the fourteen promotions, have ever in any manner being connected with the Democratic Party.

Captain William P. Davis

Captain Francis P. Chadwick

1st Lt. William S. Ellis

1st Lt. Samuel W. Moore

1st Lt. J. T. Riley

2nd Lt. Benjamin F. Bond

2nd Lt. Alfred Ballinger

2nd Lt. Charles Ricketts

2nd Lt. William Hewlings

2nd Lt. Jesse W. Super

2nd Lt. Hilary Beyer

2nd Lt. John A. Griffin

Pennsylvania State Archives, Regimental Records

Headquarters Co. H, 90th Regt. P.V.
Bell Plain, Virginia, March 21, 1863

His Excellency, A. G. Curtin,

Governor Commonwealth, Pennsylvania

Respected Sir:--

I had occasion, a short time ago, to call your attention to a gross injustice done myself, in appointing 1st Lieutenant William P. Davis, of another company, over me, 1st Lieutenant of Co. H, in violation of your Excellency's printed order, No. 17, and the modification thereto in General Order No. 22, issued May 15, 1862. I would again respectfully call your attention to the fact of having mainly, and with my personal means, recruited the company, and without assistance of the officers of other companies in the regiment. That I have been constantly on duty with my company, and in all battles (eight in number), and in command of it in the principal battles in which our regiment took part—or since August 29, 1862. The Lieutenant who is appointed over me by the Colonel has been absent sick from the regiment since August 8, 1862, until a short time before the Battle of Fredericksburg, which was the only engagement in which he had participated. Our Commissions bear the same date—the date of my muster preceding his. The order promulgating the promotions (falsely, as I have shown), explicitly states, are made for gallant and meritorious conduct in all the battles in which the regiment has been engaged, thereby reflecting upon me in a discreditable and shameful manner, and blasting to my reputation, inducing many inquiries from my friends in Philadelphia and elsewhere, to which I am at a loss to give answers. You recollect the above facts as briefly stated being brought, accompanied with proper credentials, to your knowledge, through postal communication, of an officer in the regiment who had been constantly on duty and was cognizant of all the facts, and a committee of my friends calling upon you, while in Philadelphia among whom was said officer—and I subsequently, sending you a communication on the same subject. The result was my rights were guaranteed, and services in the field recognized by your causing a commission to be made out in my name for the vacancy above me in my company. I, about this time, having a short leave of absence granted, made a visit to Harrisburg and tendered you in person my heart felt thanks for interest in my behalf. I felt inspired with new energy to do battle for my government.

What I desire to complain of is, that my commission which arrived here two weeks ago, is yet withheld from me by Col. P. Lyle, and I understand that he will endeavor to obtain from your Excellency some special privilege for the establishment of a precedent in his favor in regard to the manner of promotions. Knowing the righteousness of yourself, and my cause, I now leave the matter at your disposal.

Pennsylvania State Archives, Regimental Records

                              Camp of the 90th P.V
                              King George County, Virginia
                              April 27, 1863

His Excellency A. G. Curtin

Governor Commonwealth of Pennsylvania

Respected Sir

        I would respectfully call your Excellency's attention to the grievous wrong done me by the palpable violation of your authority as at present occurring in the Regiment to which I am attached as 1st Lieutenant. You will please recollect my establishing my claim to the vacant Captaincy of my company by reason of the Army and of seniority of muster, and also as according to your order No. 22, May 15, besides having earned the position in every battle with my company in which the Regiment had been...
    The 1st Lieutenant of another company whom Colonel P. Lyle sought to promote over me, having none of these claims and on the facts being brought to your notice, Your Excellency graciously sent a Captain's Commission in my name to the Regiment which reached here on or about the 9th of March. I now complain that this commission has been unjustly with held from me by Colonel Lyle and his abettor Lieutenant Colonel Leech, they at this time retaining the junior Lieutenant in command over me and my company.
    As at present situated I find myself in an unenviable and undeserved position, yet reposing perfect confidence in the justness of my cause, and your ability to enforce your orders and in view of the consolidation of the regiment...I respectfully appeal to you to give my case your early attention. That I may obtain justice, and in return I can only offer a life of long gratitude.

                                      With great respect

                                        Yours truly

                        Yours With Great Right, George W. Watson,

                        1st Lieutenant, Co. H, 90th P.V.

                              Lieutenant George W. Watson

                              90th Regiment P.V.

Pennsylvania State Archives, Regimental Records

Samuel B. Thomas A.D.C.
State of Pa., Executive Military Department
Harrisburg, September 4, 1863

Captain George W. Watson
Co. A, 90th P.V.
via Washington D.C.

Captain: I am instructed by his excellency Governor Curtin to request that upon the furlough which has been applied for being granted you, you will report to these headquarters, his excellency being desirous of seeing you in reference to the subject of your promotion, from which you were lately commissioned.

                              Very Respectfully
                              Your Obedient Servant

                              Samuel B. Thomas
                              Aide De Camp

Service Record, George Watson

                              September 5, 1863

General Meade

    I desire to see Captain George Watson of Co. H, 90th Regiment Penna. Vols. as soon as possible and would be much obliged if you can grant him the necessary leave of absence without the delay of an application through the regular military channels.

                    I am General
                    with much respect
                    Your Obedient Servant

                    A. G. Curtin

Service Record, George Watson

                    Headquarters Army of the
                    Potomac

Special Orders #202

Leave of absence is hereby granted to the following named officer.

   Captain George H. Watson, 90th P.V. for eight days.

                    by command

                    Major General George Meade
                    September 11, 1863

Service Record, George Watson

Headquarters, 90th Penna Vols.
Rappahannock Station, Va.

                              September 12, 1863

There is no such officer as Captain George W. Watson in this regiment. There is one 1st Lieutenant George W. Watson of Co. H. who is now in arrest against whom charges have been preferred. A copy of these papers are respectfully returned for information. The original papers being held at this headquarters for answer.

Lieutenant Colonel William Leech.

Service Record, George Watson

                    Headquarters Army of the Potomac
                    September 18, 1863,

I have the honor to inform you that in conformity to your request of the 5th Inst. I directed that eight days leave of absence be granted to Captain George Watson of 90th Regiment Penna. Vols. I have since been advised that this officer is under arrest and awaiting trial by Court Martial, under these circumstances I have deemed it my duty to revoke the order.

                    Major General George Meade.

Pennsylvania State Archives, Regimental Records

                Headquarters 90th Regiment Penna. Vols.
                Camp Near Culpeper, Virginia March 20, 1864

Colonel Samuel B. Thomas,

        Aid-de-Camp,

                To His Excellency Governor Curtin,

                                      Col.,

                                              Your communication of February 3rd, together with Commissions, and received while the regiment was at the front, on the Rapidan. In regard to your inquiry about Lieutenant Watson, I would beg leave to state that I did not know, until some eighteen or twenty days ago, that the charges against him had been withdrawn, as there was no record left in the office.
    They were withdrawn on the 12th of December; Major Sellers who since resigned at that time being in command of the regiment, and by him handed over to Watson. Immediately ascertaining that the charges had been withdrawn, I called on Lieutenant Watson, for the Charges, and to know if he

accepted the Captaincy of E Company, and if I should write for his commission. He asked for a day to consider the matter. On the third day afterwards, he called on me and declined to accept it, as he said it would be backing out on his friends at home, as they had got the position for him and that he had nothing to do with it. Stating at the same time that he would rather keep his position as 1st lieutenant of H Company, than take the Captaincy of E, but that he would rather get out of the Service, and asked my opinion whether it could be done. I answered that the orders were that resignations could only be accepted on Surgeon's Certificate of Disability. I have since then endeavored to bring about a reconciliation but without effect.

I respectfully ask that you will issue his Commission as Captain of E Company, that I may officially tender it to him, and also all the other Commissions which have been dependant on his case.

Hoping that the above explanation will prove satisfactory, I respectfully enclose the Commission of the officers of H Company, they not being in that line of promotion excepting Beyer, which reads Berger, that being a clerical error.

Say to his Excellency that in the early part of last month, I addressed a communication to the Secretary of War requesting that the drafted men in the regiment be temporarily transferred to some Pennsylvania regiment not eligible to reenlist, in order that the old regiment proper might reenlist as a Veteran Organization; the Officers and Men being willing so to do, providing they could keep their present organization. Under existing orders it requires three-fourths of the whole number to reenlist before they can become a veteran regiment, and it is absolutely necessary for these men to be transferred as they are not eligible; to prevent them counting against those who are.

It was forwarded approved through all the different headquarters until it reached Headquarters, Army of the Potomac, when it was returned with the following endorsement:

Headquarters Army of the Potomac, February 15, 1864

Respectfully returned to the Commanding Officer I Corps. The War Department having proscribed in General Orders under what circumstances regts. can be sent home to reorganize and recruit refuse to make exceptions to such orders and the Commanding General declines to forward further applications.

By Command of Major General Meade

You will perceive by the above endorsement that General Meade refuses to forward to the Secretary of War, this or any other, communication on this subject, and if I send it direct to the Secretary of War, I would be put under arrest for not sending it through the proper channels.

With my best wishes for your health,

I am, Colonel

Yours Very Respectfully

P. Lyle Colonel

Pennsylvania State Archives, Regimental Records

Headquarters 90th Regiment(National Guards)P.V.
Second Brigade 2nd Division I Army Corps
Near Guilford Station Virginia
June 23, 1864.

Major Thomas M. Vincent

Assistant Adjutant General, U.S.A.

Washington D.C.

Major:

In reply to the within communication of Lieutenant Watson of my regiment, I would respectfully present the following Statement.

My regiment is an old organization, the officers being in Commission before the breaking out of the present Rebellion. Upon the call of the President for 75,000 troops, the Regiment was ordered into the service by his Excellency Governor Curtin and the officers were mustered upon their old Commissions, at the expiration of the three months service when the Regiment returned to Philadelphia there were many new regiments organizing. Four hundred and fifty of my command immediately received positions from Colonels down to non commissioned-in both Regulars and Volunteer Service, which left but few of the original command to reorganize with. On the third of September, 1861, I was authorized by the Secretary of War and Governor Curtin to reorganize the regiment for the War. And was instructed by the Governor to make promotions from non-commissioned officers to fill the vacancies of those who had gone into other regiments, send the names to him, and they were commissioned according to seniority as they stood in the old organization. During the time the regiment was reorganizing I received an order from the Adjutant General of the State directing that all promotions of Line Officers should be by seniority in Regiment, and not by company. Upon which order I induced many to enlist making Warrant Officers of them so that they would be in line for promotion.

On the 9th of January 1863 I sent the names to the Governor of Fourteen Commissioned and Non-Commissioned officers for promotion to fill vacancies, from which I never received answers until the early part of March, when to my surprise a commission as Captain of Co. H came for Lieutenant Watson(who had not been recommended) in place of Lieutenant Davis senior 1st Lieutenant I had recommended. Lieutenant Watson being fifth in line of promotion. One for 2nd Lieutenant Ellis as 1st Lieutenant of Company H, he being senior 2nd Lieutenant of the regiment which commission should have been 1st Lieutenant of Company A in place of Lieutenant Davis, who was recommended on account of seniority for Captain of Company H, and a 2nd Lieutenant commission for one Berger which should have been Beyer, these were the only commissions out of the Fourteen that I received. I have every reason to believe that when Lieutenant Watson went home upon two days leave, he visited Harrisburg with his friends and made false representations to the Governor, or this commission would never have been issued. Anxious to have the Officers commissioned, and prevent them from disgrace of being oversloughed, on the 20th of March I obtained leave of absence for ten days for the purpose of visiting Harrisburg to see the Governor, but arriving in Philadelphia, I learned that he had left the same night for the Army of the Potomac. I left the matter in Colonel Ruff's hands, to make proper explanation to the Governor when he returned. About the last of May, I received the commissions of all the Officers with the exception of those mentioned above. I would earnestly request that the Commission of Lieutenant Watson as Captain and Lieutenant Ellis as 1st Lieutenant of Co. H. be annulled and commissions issued to Lieutenant Ellis as 1st Lieutenant of Co. A. and Lieutenant Davis as Captain of Co. H., he being a member of the organization for the last eighteen years, also one to Sergeant Hillary Beyer as 2nd Lieutenant of Co. H instead of Berger, which is a clerical error. As to withholding the commission from Lieutenant Watson, it was

Lieutenant Hillary Beyer, he was awarded the Congressional Medal of Honor for his bravery in assisting the wounded men of the regiment at the battle of Antietam. His promtion was one of twenty which were delayed due to the promotion of George Watson.

done with his consent, at the time he wrote the within letter he informed me he would write to the Governor declining the commission. As to recruiting the company at his private expenses it was not so. Transportation was furnished for all Officers recruiting, and the transportation and subsistence for all recruits. There was no recruiting done for any particular Company it was for the Regiment, whilst the Officers of some companies were kept recruiting, the officers of others were kept in camp instructing the recruits as their Military Knowledge excluded those who were recruiting.

Lieutenant Watson's commission, as already stated has been retained with his consent. The other commissions have been delivered and returned by the several officers(although they have been acting in their various capacities, and have been mustered for pay but not mustered for rank for want of Commissions) because of this attempt to override merit as well as the organization of the Regiment.

The within paper was mislaid and found upon the 12th of June the day before we marched from White Oak Church, since then, this is the only opportunity I have had to make a reply.

   I have the honor Major to be

     Very respectfully Your Obedient Servant

     P. Lyle Colonel

       Comdg. 90th Regt. Penna. Vol.

Pennsylvania State Archives, Regimental Records

   Headquarters 1st Brigade 3rd Division V Army Corps
   Near Petersburg Virginia July 4, 1864.

To His Excellency Andrew G. Curtin,

   Governor of the Commonwealth of Pennsylvania,

       Governor,

          I have the

honor to enclose a list of nominations of Officers in my regiment for promotion, and desire to make some explanation in regard to them. The vacancy exists in E Company in consequence of Lieutenant George Watson's declining to accept the commission tendered him. On the 6th of May, I received a communication from Colonel Samuel B. Thomas, A.D.C. dated Harrisburg April 29th, 1864 and enclosing a Captains commission for 1st Lieutenant. Watson in H. Company, in place of Captain William P. Davis, whom I had recommended but who has never yet received his Commission.

Unfortunately, Lieutenant Watson was seriously wounded in the charge made by the regiment on the 5th of May 1864, (the first days battle in the Wilderness) and was then taken prisoner by the rebels, which of course prevented me from complying with his request. He was afterwards seen by Dr. Hayes, Surgeon of the Regiment in the rebel hospital, with his right leg amputated above the knee, and we have since received letters from him confirming Dr. Hayes statement. As the nature of his wound will prevent his being mustered in as a Captain, I would respectfully ask that a Captain's Commission be issued to Captain William P. Davis(and all others depending on this case, as some of these officers have not, nor cannot receive any pay until they receive their commissions) who has served with great gallantry throughout the present campaign, in command of the Company, and who was originally nominated for the vacancy in January 1863.

I beg leave to offer the following reasons for not recommending the following named officers.(although in line of promotion).

    1st Lieutenant James P. Mead has been detached from his regiment for the past eighteen months, and has used every exertion to keep himself away from his company and regiment. At the time he was detached he was acting Regimental Quartermaster; he has never settled his accounts, and I have been unable to get him to do so. Besides being absent from his company he has not seen the same amount of service that the other officers have.

    1st Lieutenant Benjamin F Bond Jr. is, and has been for a long time absent sick, and manages to keep himself so; and has done but very little duty with the Regiment since his promotion.

2nd Lieutenant James S. Bonsall has not acted with as much credit to himself or the Regiment as would justify me in recommending him for a higher position.

I have the honor to be

Very Respectfully

Your Obedient Servant

P. Lyle

Colonel 90th Penna. Vols.

Commdg 1st brigade.

Pennsylvania State Archives, Regimental Records

Philadelphia Pa. February 9, 1866

To His Excellency A. G. Curtin

Governor of Pennsylvania

Your Excellency will I know allow as sufficient apology for not presenting the matter herein contained to your attention sooner when I state that during the latter part of the campaign closed I was badly wounded losing my right leg at the thigh, and have been incarcerated in Rebel prisons for a number of months, been prostrated within extreme sickness, and lately have undergone a second amputation of my mutilated limb from which I am present suffering. It is with regret that I now feel compelled to trespass upon your Excellency's valuable time but requesting attention to a matter wherein there is a gross disrespect done yourself and a violation of your authority as well as Army Orders and Regulations. In the matter of a Captains Commission which you have twice decided I was entitled to by forwarding it that number of times to my Regt.(90th) to be given to me, but in violation of every right withheld by Peter Lyle the late Colonel, I have already fully substantiated my claim. 1st in accordance with orders issued

216

at Harrisburg governing promotions, 2nd my seniority of muster in the Regt. in accordance with your orders and Army orders and regulations, 3rd By reason of having expended of my time and means in recruiting my company, beside I claim to have well earned the promotion by long service in the field and in command of my company, and by extreme suffering.

I had forwarded on several occasions complaints of Colonel Lyle's conduct, to higher authority in the Army, these would be delayed as long as possible, once I was placed under arrest for forwarding over the head of the Commandant of my Regt. On my last communication forwarded Colonel Lyle placed the endorsement "that he had not my commission in his possession" in consequence thereof it was returned by General Warren with the endorsement "that it was a matter between the Governor of Pennsylvania and myself". On the last occasion of the commission reaching the regiment, I made a formal demand for it but was met by equivocation, whereupon I decided to at once, prefer charges against my Colonel, unhappily for me we received orders to cross the Rapidan.

I was placed in command of the color company and while charging the enemy, I was badly wounded and taken prisoner, as before alluded to, finally reached home about the time of my expiration of term of service in an extremely debilitated condition and was honorably discharged. Thus by my misfortune I was prevented from Court Martialing Colonel Lyle, of this he now takes advantage, for on my lately appealing to him for my commission, I was met with a peremptory refusal.

For sometime before and during the time I was wounded and a prisoner, Colonel Lyle had assigned a junior Lieutenant, William P. Davis to the command of my company(H) who was entered on the rolls and received pay as its Captain in which capacity he certified on honor to its correctness etc. in the usual manner. Now, Colonel Lyle informs me that the other officers are depending on the result of my commission, I wish it directly understood, that such is not the case, as my promotion cannot conflict with any other Officer than the Lieutenant William P. Davis aforesaid whom the Colonel recommended for H. But whose claim has so justly been discountenanced. At present, the Captaincy of Co. E is vacant and was long before I was wounded; and if Colonel Lyle had complied with the orders of your Excellency and recommended this junior Lieutenant William P. Davis for Captaincy of E. instead of pursuing an unworthy course there would of been no difficulty in the matter. He still further had the effrontery to inform me that he would endeavor to obtain from your Excellency a commission for me for

Captaincy of Co. E. This I totally disclaim and would respectfully ask you not to grant it, and if possible, secure for me the withheld commission which has been so much anxiety to me and to which I alone am entitled. Colonel Lyle, as near as I can ascertain, evidently endeavors to puzzle and confuse those who are not familiar with this affair. He will speak of seniority ascending to an old Militia organization, then of seniority dating from a three months Regiment; but facts will not bear him out. I have been a member, since 1854, of the militia organization he commanded, and have yet to comprehend that while in the service of the U.S. laws made by Militia supersede Army laws. This, however, is but a subterfuge as well as the assertion that promotions were recommended by him in accordance with seniority in the three months Regiment(which I was also connected with), for of those who went out as officers of the 90th, some at no time belonged to the militia organization, others who during the three months service were enlisted men in very many instances got positions over those who had been commissioned. One who went as a Captain was not out with the three months Regiment. Colonel Lyle thus uses worse than sophistry to bolster his action and has gone so far as to exult in his success.

I have extended this to a grater length than intended presuming on your well deserved reputation of being, "the soldier's friend," and thanking you for the stand taken in my behalf against oppression and wrong, and wishing your Excellency long life and happiness I have the honor to subscribe myself

    Yours obediently

      George W. Watson
      Late 90th P.V

    Residence No. 12 S. 10th St.

Pension File, George Watson

George W. Watson,

Captain, 90th P.V.

Dated Adjutant General's Office March 22, 1889 of this officer as of the grade named above to date from 1st day of September 1862.

Headquarters of the Army, Adjutant General's Office, Washington, Special Order#67

By direction of the Secretary of War under the act approved June 3, 1884 the act ammendatory thereof approved February 3, 1887 to complete the records. The muster into service of George W. Watson as Captain, 90th Pa. Vols. Inf., March 3, 1863 by paragraph 9 Special Orders#280, series of 1863 from this office is amended to take effect September 1, 1862, and he is mustered for pay in said grade during the period embraced between the aforesaid dates.

by command of
Major General John Schofield

It seems from the final outcome that, while Colonel Lyle won the battle over this promotion, George Watson outlasted the Colonel; and he eventually won the war.

My Dear Brother & Sister

Private Frank Jennings joined the 90th P.V. on February 15, 1862 and he was assigned to Company A. He enlisted in the army immediately after the failure of his marriage. Initially, Jennings expressed the hope that he would die in battle. However, shortly after joining up, his instinct for survival began to operate. Jennings served in the 90th throughout the war, winning promotion to Corporal and Sergeant. Late in 1864, Sergeant Jennings reenlisted for the remainder of the war. Consequently, he was with the regiment along the Weldon Railroad when they met with disaster there.

On August 19, 1864, the rebels turned the Union flank and swept down the line behind Crawford's Division of the V Corps. Mahone's Division then swept through the Federal lines from the rear, capturing several of Crawford's Brigades almost entirely. The 90th P.V. lost about 120 officers and men as prisoners, Sergeant Frank Jennings was among them. After being captured, Frank Jennings final destination was the Confederate Prison camp at Salisbury, North Carolina. Jennings, however, survived that terrible place. He was exchanged and survived the war.

This letter to his sister, written after the war, gives

a good general history of when and where the 90th fought. There are a few factual errors, but it is very accurate otherwise. Most of the errors in this letter consist of the casualty figures which Frank Jennings lists; almost all of these are incorrect. Aside from this, Jennings letter is both accurate and informative.

U.S. Army Military History Institute, Civil War Times Illustrated Collection, Frank Jennings 90th & 11th P.V.

Montreal, January 7, 1867

My dear brother & sister,

                I scarce know how to commence this letter, however, as everything has a beginning so must this. I suppose Father gave you an outline of my past 5 years existence, so I will try and make you better acquainted with it.
   I was married on the 21st of September 1861. We lived very happily together for two months or so, when Alice (that is my wife) began to get indolent, in fact would not pretend to do anything. I remonstrated with her again and again but to no purpose. I endured it as long as I could, and made up my mind to part. I was like a great many young fellows in the States, got married and scarce had a dollar to commence with, but where there is a will there is a way, so I started work in good earnest, working early and late, and in three months had saved nearly $100.00. We lived together four months when she went home to her father on a visit. My intention was to go after her in a week or two. Father said she should not come there again, so I looked the matter over and concluded she had better stay home, as she was working quite contrary to myself. I was working 14 and 16 hours per day and trying my best to get along, and Alice not lifting her finger to do anything, and as saucy as a highwayman in the bargain.
   One week after I enlisted in the Philadelphia National Guards, or 90th Regiment Pennsylvania Volunteers. I have not seen Alice since. Father and myself went to see her folks at

Providence, Rhode Island. They were very kind to us, and did not blame me for treating her as I had. Alice were confined with a little girl in the following August. I would give anything to have the dear little soul. The trouble is I can't find out where Alice is. In fact, her mother knew nothing of her whereabouts, only that she left there with a man whom report says she is married to. I have applied for a divorce. In fact, it has hung about since September 65. I can't say when I shall get it. I should have been divorced long before this, the trouble is these...such fellows to keep their cases in hand, I suppose...thinks I have plenty of money for every whip-stretch...for $10.00 or so. I have come to the conclusion not to send any more money until the case is settled.

As I said before, I enlisted. It was on the 15th of February '62. I knew but one man in the regiment. We left Philadelphia March 31st and passed into Virginia. When I enlisted, I fully expected to get killed, or I should not have enlisted, as I was very unhappy indeed, not caring what became of me. There had been but one or two battles fought up to this time(that is of any consequences). We soon started on the march; and advanced to Bull Run and the Shenandoah Valley, where the rebel Jackson was with 20,000 men. As we neared Front Royal, Jackson took to the mountains and escaped us. We marched back to Bull Run, through Warrenton and Culpeper, within a few miles of Cedar Mountain, where our advanced guard were skirmishing with the enemy. General Pope was in command of all the forces at this time, that is the Army of Virginia as we were called, about 60,000 strong. McClellan was in command of the Army of the Potomac, which was at Richmond. General Pope addressed us in a few brief remarks, telling us he expected great things of us, etc. We then started double quick for the scene of conflict and reached the battlefield about sunset. We fully expected to have a good fight but the enemy decamped, leaving but a mere skirmish line, who kept up a steady fire till midnight, when they decamped also. We captured about 200 besides their killed and wounded. We lost but few(that is our regiment).

The next day, we started in pursuit, in fact for a week, and found them on the south side of the Rapidan River waiting for us. Not having pontoons, we could not cross, so we endeavored to make a flank movement, but instead of flanking them, they flanked us, and we were obliged to fall back to the Rappahannock River which they reached almost as soon as us. Our artillery kept them at bay so that they could not cross. I think it was at this point we received news that McClellan was falling back from Richmond so we were obliged to do the same, Jackson gaining ground considerably. At Thoroughfare Gap our division general received orders to hold Longstreet(?) in check at all hazards, we being in he rear of the army. Leaving Longstreet at the Gap to check us while he[Jackson] passed on to Bull Run to intercept Pope. We did so and lost about 100. We reached Bull Run the next morning; this was September 29th '62[August]. The men at this time were in a destitute condition, nearly all being barefooted and ragged to say nothing of dirt and vermin. Our food on the retreat were chiefly corn and anything we could lay our hands on. Our supplies being in advance of the army it was impossible to get any rations. As we reached Bull Run, we were issued rations and ordered to...and advance. As we was advancing, I saw to my right and noticed some men on a hill. I enquired what troops they were and I learned they were General Fitz John Porter's Corps. I thought at the time that it was very singular that they should put us in the fight in the condition we were in and marching several hundred miles, having very little rest. The fact of the matter was this: Mr. Porter was afraid General Pope would get too much praise if he gained a victory, McClellan being his(Porter's) favorite, who he expected to be there to command both armies, so that he would not put his Corps in the engagement. The consequence was that we were defeated. Mr. Porter was cashiered and dismissed from the service.

Our regiment had a good position on a high bluff. We must have killed or wounded several hundreds. The first volley we fired, scores fell. They fell back, and rallied, and advanced again, the same results followed, when we saw three lines of battle advancing on us. We kept them at bay as long as we could(we having no support). Some few of us, getting excited, advanced to the edge of the hill to get a better shot at them, when, lo and behold, they were almost in reach of us. Our brigade, being flanked, were obliged to retire. So, we took to our heels and made tracks for the regiment. I thought, for me, I should have been captured or killed. I think dozens of bullets whizzed past my head as I was running. About a mile from the battlefield, I heard a poor fellow calling for water. I thought I had some in my canteen. I took hold of it as it hung by my side and found it was empty. I told the poor fellow, I would get him some, as a stream of water was close at hand. I took my canteen off and were about filling it, when I found a hole through it. I then remembered, in the beginning of the engagement, I felt something strike my leg, I thought at the time I was hit; but seeing no blood, nor feeling any pain, I came to the conclusion I was mistaken. At the same time, I heard a

Corporal of our company cry out he was wounded, I suppose that the bullet that passed through my canteen, struck this poor corporal on the leg. The same poor fellow's bowels were blown out with a cannon ball in the first days engagement at the Battle of the Wilderness. We lost in this engagement (Bull Run) 126 men.

Our next engagement were at Chantilly situated between Fairfax Court House and Washington D.C., where we lost but few, this time was about a week after Bull Run. We then heard the advanced guard of the enemy had crossed the Potomac River into Maryland. We started in pursuit. We marched through Washington on Saturday (midnight), and continued marching...days and found the enemy at South Mountain, routing them and killing and wounding several thousands. We lost 56 men (our regiment) (I am only giving our own regiment's killed and wounded). The enemy fell back to Antietam, where we gained a glorious victory. I was not in this engagement (Antietam), as I had a gathering on my foot through being barefooted. The enemy, then, recrossed the Potomac, and we rested two or three weeks to recruit and draw clothing.

Our next engagement was at Fredericksburg, Virginia, where we received a severe thrashing, and soon after the battle we were beaten at Chancellorsville, losing in both engagements about 80 men...and I was promoted to Corporal. We then made another advance into Maryland and Pennsylvania, and found the enemy at Gettysburg, Pennsylvania; our Corps (which is the 1st) being on the advance. This was July 1st, '63. I never saw the men more willing to fight than they were at Gettysburg. Our Corps consisted of 7,000 men, commanded by General Reynolds, who I am very sorry to say was killed in the beginning of the engagement. The enemy in our front was commanded by General Ewell, 40,000 strong. As soon as we reached the battlefield our company was ordered to the skirmish line on the right flank. Our regiment was the right of the Corps, our company the right of the regiment. We fought them till a division of the XI Corps was sent to take position where the skirmish line was so that we joined the regiment. Well, in fact there were only 6 of us that came in and joined the regiment and the balance of 11 men lay out on the ground till the enemy drove us, when they too joined the regiment. As I said before, 6 of us joined the regiment and as soon as we reached it, our brigade was ordered to advance We fought them for hours, when they flanked the Division of the IX Corps and got in our rear, so that we had to escape the best way we could. The 2nd and 3rd days, we made up our defeat by the greatest victory of the war, our loss was 100 men killed wounded and prisoners. On the 4th day, I was taken sick and had to be sent to the hospital, where I remained for 3 months. I forgot to mention that I came very near losing my legs. It was the night of the 3rd. Our division was ordered to the left to support the III Corps. We started by the left flank on double quick for a mile or so, when we were ordered to quick time, that is steady marching. The artillery on both sides were firing very rapidly; shot and shell flying over our heads like hail. A cannon ball whizzed past my legs between the 1st sergeant of the next company and myself. If I had been 4 or 5 inches ahead of the spot I was then, I should most assuredly have had both of my legs taken off. In fact the officer by my side who was in command of the company thought I was struck for a certainty. He caught me, as I was almost falling, the force of the ball so close to me almost taking me off my feet. I can tell you that it scared me for a few moments.

After I returned to the regiment from the hospital I was promoted to Sergeant of the Company, and the following Spring reenlisted for 3 more years. At the Battle of Petersburg, I was promoted to 1st Sergeant of the Company, the 1st Sergeant getting killed in the charge we made. I was close by him when the order was given to charge. The Sergeant, being rather corpulent, could not keep up with us, and one of their rifle balls passed through his heart, killing him instantly. He was a good soldier and a clever fellow. He left a wife and 2 children to mourn his loss. I should have mentioned our regiment received 700 casualties at the Battle of Gettysburg.

In the Battle of the Wilderness,...River Anna and several at Petersburg we lost 200 men. At a place called...Church I was struck with a piece of shell, about 2 inches from the ankle. We were in a wood and were ordered to lie there. When the artillery opened on both sides, a shell struck in the tree I was lying under, a piece glancing my leg and drawing blood. It did not pain much.

On the 18th of August we were ordered to the Weldon Railroad. a distance of about 10 miles, which we reached in the afternoon. We had not the faintest idea of getting into an engagement. As we neared the railroad, we saw the artillery getting into position and as soon as ready commenced firing. The Johnnys, or rebs as we call them, replied very quickly, and very soon it became general. The skirmishers also commenced, and we were ordered to their support. The enemy drove them in, when we were ordered to advance, and soon reached in sight of them, when they opened on us. Of course, we returned the compliment, and kept it up till darkness fell and put a stop to it, neither side losing ground. We then put up breastworks, which took us nearly all night. We lost a great many that day; I never heard exactly how many. All the time we were fighting, it rained very hard, in fact all that night and the next day. It was afternoon the following day before the battle was resumed; and when it did commence, it was terrible. We fired nearly 100 rounds of cartridges. At about 5:00 o'clock, things looked very favorable on our side, and we fully expected to gain a glorious victory, but the brigade on our right giving way, the enemy got in our rear, and captured nearly the whole of our division. We were marched to the rear of Petersburg where we remained two days and nights.

The 3rd day we were taken in the cars to Richmond and confined to Libby prison. We had not room to lie down. The next day, we received the first rations since our captivity. We all felt mighty hungry and devoured the small piece of bread and meat like so many ravenous wolves. The jailer told us to hand our valuables in to an officer who was for that duty, with our names, company and regiment, that we would receive them on the day of parole. I came to the conclusion to keep mine, so I took the caps off the buttons of my jacket and folded each note in as small a compass as I could, and place one in each and then

In the Spring Campaign of 1864, the use of fortifications changed the way the war was being fought. The defenders of trenches had a great advantge over an attacking line. The shovel becme as important as the rifle during this period.

put the caps on so that when we were searched, no money was found upon me. I had $300.00 in green backs, quite a nice little sum for them devils to get a hold of. My money saved my life, for we could buy anything the market afforded ...I have paid as high as $5.00 for two small loves of bread. It seems incredible, but it is a fact, and one that I shall long remember.

We were kept in Libby 8 days, and then sent to Belle Island where there was plenty of good water to drink and wash with(river water). It was excellent in comparison with the water at Libby which was...,and we could scarce drink it. Our rations each day were 1/4 lb. bread... and a pint of soup, beans, or rice not half enough to subsist on. The soup I could not eat at first it being covered with maggots from the beans and rice. I was at last obliged to come to it and thankful to get it. The most of the time I was a prisoner of war, I kept two others of my company, that is as long as my money lasted. After that. we were obliged to look out for ourselves. We had tolerable good quarters for prisoners, one large camp tent to 16 men, just room to lie down.

After being at Belle Island 7 weeks, we were shipped in the cars to Salisbury, North Carolina. It was extremely cold the night we reached there, in fact, freezing very hard. We were obliged to lie out for six weeks, without any covering but the sky. Sometimes, it would rain for 3 or 4 days, and then, start freezing which would make it very uncomfortable, indeed. I have been wet through to the skin for a week at a time. I have often wondered how I lived through it. Our daily allowance of food was very poor, 1/4 lb. cornbread, a small piece of meat, if they had it to give us, and pint of soup (one bean to a quart of water) and as much wood as two men could carry to keep us warm. The bread was shocking stuff: cob all ground up together, and as hard as a bullet (heavy victuals as Uncle Paul used to say). Several times we were kept 3 and 4 days without anything to eat. After we were there a week or two, the men began to die very rapidly. I have known as high as 70 in one day, the most through starvation, some by disease contracted through exposure, and some through their own negligence, not keeping themselves clean.

In fact, none of us could keep ourselves very clean as we had no soap, but a little wood ashes which would help considerably to take some of the dirt off. Every morning, I would get up and take a wash and then a walk, for an hour or two, up and down what we called the park. By this time the rations would be ready for issue. After breakfast, dinner and supper, which we all took together, I went to skirmishing, that is take off shirt and pants and hunt for vermin. I have killed over a hundred at a time. This I did 2 or 3 times every day. It makes me scratch when I think of it. I have seen men with thousands and thousands of these vermin on them. Hundreds died through these loathsome creatures.

I forgot to mention the kind of place we were confined in. I should think it was three or four acres square with a fence around it 12 or 14 feet high. Six feet from the fence there was a ditch 10 feet deep and the same width. We were not allowed to get within 6 feet of it in daytime and double the distance at night. I have seen a poor fellow shot for stepping too near it. On the outside of the fence was a path for the guards to walk their beats on. They were about 10 yards apart during the day, and at night an extra guard was placed about 10 paces further out. At each corner of the fence was a piece of artillery loaded with canister.

Some three or four hundred men thought they could make a break and escape, which they tried, and about one hundred were killed through it. Two of our regiment were killed. I knew nothing of it till the firing commenced. About 40 grape shot passed through our tent, which made us lie close to the ground. Not one escaped. Several of the guards in the prison, who were guarding different points were killed.

At the time we entered this prison, there was between 10,000 and 11,000 of us. Out of this, 5,216 died in the 5 months we was there, and a great many killed. This I got from the head steward of the hospital, so that it is correct. The dead were taken out in a cart expressly for that purpose, driven by a negro. They were thrown in the cart, as though they were logs of wood, 10 or 12 in the cart at once, and were buried about 1/4 mile from the prison in a long ditch, piled on top of one another.

We heard, almost every day, from the guards or the Rebel officers that we were to be paroled. At first, we believed it but hearing it so often it got stale, and we paid little attention to it. After my money was all spent, I had to find another way to get extra rations. Every afternoon we were counted off in hundreds, and a sergeant appointed to see after the rations for us. I would get counted in the squad I belonged to, and evade the guards, and run into another squad and get counted again, so that instead of one ration; I got two which would keep me tolerably well.

It would take me a week to write you all I have seen and endured in a Rebel prison. Thank Fortune, I kept in good health and spirits; that was half the battle.

At last, we were told we were to be paroled for a

certainty. Of course we thought it was a hoax, but no, in a day or two we saw plainly it was fact. The cooks and bakers were working all day and night, and on 22nd February, 1865 we were let loose like a drove of sheep and marched to Raleigh N. C., about 50 miles. It took us several days to travel it and we stopped there several days to get our parole papers made out. We then took the cars for Wilmington, the place of exchange which we reached about noon March 3rd. It was near a large wood. There were the Rebel officers and pickets and ours talking together. The Rebel officers called two of their men and our officers called two of ours. The 4 guards made a gateway two on each side facing each other. We were then ordered out of the cars and fell in two ranks. The command was given, "Right Face," and, "undouble files," as we neared the 4 guards we had to pass through. As soon as we were all through, we gave, "three cheers and a tiger," for the stars and stripes, and marched about two miles where a collation was waiting for us, which we did ample justice to.

We then marched to Wilmington, and slept there all night. I slept in a Baptist Church. The next morning, we were shipped to Annapolis, Maryland reaching there on the 10th. This the general depot for parole prisoners. On the 13th I received a furlough for 30 days and went home. Father, Mother, and all of them had given me up for dead. I can tell you, I startled them when I walked in the house.--such another time, I never saw. While home, poor Abe Lincoln was brutally assassinated. Almost every house was draped in mourning and remained so for weeks. People in the street were actually crying, and now he is dead and gone. He is looked upon by some as a tyrant.

At the expiration of my furlough, I went back to Annapolis. While there, General Lee surrendered and orders were issued from the Government to discharge all parole prisoners. The Commanding Officer of the camp, thinking he would have his hands full in making out our discharge papers, sent us immediately to our regiments. Our regiment --time being up while I was a prisoner--were discharged. What there were left, the reenlisted and substitutes, were transferred to the 11th Pennsylvania Volunteers, so I had to report to that regiment, as I was a reenlisted man. As luck would have it there was no vacancy for me, which I was glad of as I did not care about having 70 or 80 strange men under me. So I did the duty of Sergeant Major to oblige the Colonel. If I had refused, he could not have done anything with me, as I was not exchanged. Of course, when I returned to the Regiment I expected to be discharged immediately. Not seeing or hearing anything to that effect,

I began to make enquiries and made it my business to go to Division Headquarters and state my case to the monitoring officer. He told me to go back to my regiment and make out my papers, and he would muster me out of the service. I did so and was discharged that afternoon. The camp was all alive, when I made it known to the men who were prisoners with me. In a few days, they were all discharged in a body.

The next morning I started for home a citizen instead of a soldier.

After being home a short time, I took a notion to go to college to learn bookkeeping, etc. So I went to Lowell's Commercial College, New York, and graduated in 4 months, receiving a diploma and a splendid recommendation from the Principal. It was useless to try to get a situation as bookkeeper, as so many discharge soldiers were home who were practical bookkeepers, so I worked a little at home, and last September came here to work for Joe(Clara's husband), who is in the file business, does all the work for the Grand Trunk R.R. Co. of Canada, and also the grinding and polishing of the works here. I am learning the grinding and polishing, get $7.00 per week, $2.50 I pay for board so I have enough to make me comfortable. I like it first rate, so far.

And now, my dear Brother & Sister, I must say I am extremely glad to hear from you. I have read it again and again and wish it was ten times longer. I have been going to write for months, but like you, it was neglected. Not that I never think of you, for scarce a day passes but what I think of you and wish I could drop in on you by surprise. I shan't say but what I may take a notion to pay you a visit, but when, I can't say. I had partly made up my mind to go to England, after I was discharged but thought as you did not write, you were in difficulties again. Nothing would give me more pleasure than to see Annie and the children. I often laugh to myself when I think of calling Annie "Sister" before she was married, but, God knows, I am proud to call her such. And now in regards to dear Sally, who I hope has gone to a happier world. To tell the truth, it quite unmanned me when Father wrote to me and said she was dead. Thousands and thousands of times, have I thought of her and said to myself, if I had only gotten myself a wife with a disposition like poor dear Sally's, I should now be happy, for poor Sally had the sweetest disposition of any person I know. Her likeness I shall take special care of. I look at it very; often and wish I could see her, once more, in reality. Poor dear Sally, I shall never forget her.

I was surprised to find you looking so old, though,it is you to a T. Father sent Annie's photograph for me to...

I think it is an excellent picture of her. Please send me one, when you answer this. Also Willie's, Johnnie's, and Frank's; and do not forget to send me George's and wife and likewise Mr. and Mrs. Guy's, as I am all anxiety to have them in my possession. I have often thought of Annie's aunt (Mrs. Nash), is she married again? How is Aunt Mary and Marchant, Aunt Lydia and Uncle Paul, and what has become of Cousin Lydia and Rhuben? Give my kind love to them all. When you write, which I hope will be very soon, don't forget to mention what house it is you live in, as I cannot make out where it is situated. I shall not say anything about the folks home as I suppose Father has. Joe and Clara send their kind love to you. They have only one child living—Joshua is 11 years of age the 6th of last September. Hope you are all enjoying the best of health, I am right well and comfortable. Give Annie and the children a kiss for me. If I was there I would save you the trouble. Tell Willie, Johnnie, Frank, and Polly to be good children and learn all they can at school, and always obey their Father and mother in everything they tell them and that I should very much love to see them.

On Christmas day, I ran against George Weight. I knew him as soon as I laid eyes on him. He did not know me. He is doing very well. He desired to be remembered to you.

As you said in yours, I intended to send you a long letter. I don't think you will be disappointed. I hope you will send me a long letter and not neglect it as before. All your letters I will answer immediately.
    With my kindest love to you all
        I remain
    My dear brother and Sister,
      Your ever affectionate brother,
        Frank Jennings.

P.S. Address
   No. 178 St. Joseph Street,
     Montreal, Canada East,
Care of Joseph Tildsley, File Manufacturer.

    Please enquire if Jane Rodman is in Montreal or what place she is in. As we always understood that she was in Montreal...Is James Rodman still at Rungerford & how is he getting along?

The Fate of Charles Ricketts

Charles Ricketts served in the 19th P.V. as a private, and he later enlisted in the 90th P.V. on March 10, 1862 as Sergeant Major of the regiment. Ricketts continued to move up through the ranks until he achieved the rank of 1st Lieutenant in December 1863. He must have been an outstanding soldier. He was promoted several times and, in the latter part of the war, was assigned to the staff of General Warren, Commander of the V Corps. Lieutenant Ricketts served in that position until he was mustered out of the service on October 31, 1864.

After the war, Charles Ricketts worked for the Pennsylvania Railroad. His first marriage, which occurred in the late 1860's, ended in divorce. Both parties made accusations of adultery against the other. Ricketts married his second wife, Helen, on December 13, 1874 in Jersey City, New Jersey. After the wedding, Charles was transferred to Philadelphia. He and Helen lived together for about a year before Charles lost his job. This took place about the time his son, George, was born in September of 1875. Shortly afterwards, his wife took their newborn son and moved into her fathers house. She later described Charles: "He had become badly dissipated and spent all his money on himself, when he had it, so my father refused to let him live with us."

It is unknown if Charles Ricketts had an alcohol problem during the war. If he did, he was able to either control it or conceal it. It is possible the problem developed as a result of the war. Perhaps Charles Ricketts was one of those men who performed well in wartime, and later could not adjust to a quiet peacetime existence. The fact is that by 1875, Charles Ricketts was a hopeless alcoholic.

The letters which Charles wrote to his wife show that he was a man held desperately in the grip of alcohol. He was one of those men fighting a terrible battle inside himself for control of his life. Charles Ricketts was torn between who he was, and who he wanted to be. He made promise after promise to his wife in an effort to reconcile with her. He then proceeded to break every promise. All his efforts failed. Helen Ricketts never lived with her husband again. Charles continued to write to her until November 1876. She never responded to his pleas.

Sometime in September or October 1875, after Helen left him, Charles Ricketts made a suicide attempt. One newspaper described it as follows:

" A sad case. a man shoots himself. Depression of Spirits is the cause.
Late last evening a man went into a saloon on Merrick Street, above Chestnut, West of Broad, and walking into the yard he held a pistol to his mouth and discharged one of the

loads. Reserve Officer Steeple found him lying apparently dead and bleeding at the mouth. He was taken to the hospital, and gave his name as Charles Ricketts, and residence as 1121 Callowhill Street. He stated that he had been a conductor on the Pennsylvania railroad, but that he was discharged on the 9th inst.

Further, that his wife had been confined the following day, and that being without employment, he found himself unable to support his family. Under depression of spirits from that cause he had procured the pistol, and sought to end his life and his troubles at the same time. An effort was made at the hospital to find the ball, but it was not successful."

The old soldier had fallen very low. He even failed at suicide.

Pension Files, Court Papers filed in the appeal contain copies of the following letters, Charles Ricketts

October 25, 1875

Dear Helen
    I wish no longer to be an inmate of your father's house. I cannot and will not be the ridicule for the family. I have some **pride** left, and God willing I shall have something to do very shortly. I will send you some money this week so please have my valise ready when I send for it(which will be done this week.) Pardon me, darling, if I offend you; I cannot help it. May God bless you and the baby is the fervent wish of

                            Your Husband.

Pension File, Charles Ricketts

November 8, 1875

Dear, dear Helen:
              At last I have obtained employment. Will go to work tomorrow at Brady & Co.'s mill #161-163, Allen St., above Shackamaxon. Please send by bearer my old

coat, pants, some socks and the old heavy boots. Darling, I hope shortly to have you to myself and take care of our little family. I can hardly bear the idea of remaining from you much longer. How is our little George? May God bless you all.

>Your loving but nearly broken hearted
>Charlie.

Pension File, Charles Ricketts

November 24, 1875

My darling wife:
>My whole ambition is to have you and the baby with me, and rest assured, darling, I am trying my very best to accomplish it. X X X X Give my love to all and hoping I will be able to accomplish my object Believe me,

>Your loving husband

God Bless you and the baby.

Pension File, Charles Ricketts

January 2, 1876

Dear Helen:
>I cannot imagine why you have never asked me to call again or even asked me to see George (asleep or awake). Do you hate me or are you influenced by outside talk? I do not know what will become of me, I am nearly crazy to think that my only, should be friend, has discarded me.

>Yours,
>Charlie.

Pension File, Charles Ricketts

May 2, 1876

    My dear dear wife:

                      I cannot stand your silence any longer. I have written you and have sent verbal messages by Emily, Frank, and John and yet no reply. Unless I hear from you within 24 hours I shall never hear from you again. Everybody and everything is against me. I have called to see you and not been allowed to see you or the baby. I go on the new road from here to New York tomorrow night. I may return and may not. I cannot account for your long silence unless you wish to get rid of me entirely. God knows I love you sincerely and was it in my power I would have you with me. I cannot write anymore my feelings overcome me.

                                      Your still loving
                                              Husband.

Pension File, Charles Ricketts

Atlantic City, New Jersey
July 5, 1876

    Mrs. Ricketts,
        Madam:

                Should you hear of a thing called Charles Ricketts being found drowned, you can imagine it to be the head clerk of the Mansion House
    There is no danger of the said Charles Ricketts drowning himself with rum or salt water

                                              Respectfully,

                                              Chas. Ricketts,

I sincerely hope the baby is well.

Pension File, Charles Ricketts

Philadelphia
August 28, 1876

Dear dear Helen:

    Once again and only once will, I ask you to sympathize with me. I saw your father this morning and when told by him it was your wish not to see me, I could hardly realize it. In fact, I cannot believe it, for darling, believe me, I never willfully did you a wrong, and God knows I never intended nor intend you any. On the contrary, could I do you any service within my power, I would sincerely be only too glad. Rest Assured, I shall never attempt to cross the threshold of your father's house, but I should love dearly to see you and George.
 Do not think me the beast you have, but let me hear one cheering word from you, and I pledge you my word as a man everything will be well. I cannot and will not entertain the idea that you hate me, even should you, I shall return love for hate.
 Let me hear from you, darling and believe me.

          Your

            Charlie.

Pension File, Charles Ricketts

November 21, 1876

Dear Helen:

    You cannot imagine my surprise when I was told on Wednesday last of the death and burial of your father. I should call on you but the fear of having the door closed, in my face, prevents me. I seldom have time even to read the papers, for as soon as I get home I am asleep, being on the road about 20 hours out of 24, running freight on the N.Y. Div. P.R.R.
 It is much harder work than on passenger train, but better pay. I dare not touch rum for two reasons: viz., for fear of falling off while running over the roofs of the cars and if Joe Hawk (Warren Hawk's brother) smells liquor on you, it is a discharge.
 Should anything serious happen to either yourself or

George, please oblige me by having word sent to No. 740 N. 37th St.

                                      Yours respectfully,

                                      Charlie.

Chris Baker was a Philadelphia man who was a friend of Charles Ricketts. He had lived and worked in the Orient from 1867 to 1876. He returned to Philadelphia in 1876 to visit the Centennial Exhibition in that city. During his visit to Philadelphia, Baker often ran into Ricketts in various saloons, which they both frequented. They were soon making plans to go to the Orient together to find work. At some point in late 1876 or early 1877, the two men met and traveled around town, saying goodbye to their friends and acquaintances, visiting at least one saloon in the process.

Baker claimed he last saw Charles Ricketts at 9:00 P.M. near 9th and Arch Sts., and they had agreed to meet at the railroad station at 6:30 the next morning to leave for New York. Baker also remembered that Ricketts was carrying several hundred dollars in a money belt, on the night he was last seen. The next morning at the train station, Ricketts did not appear and Baker left for New York. However, Baker did send a message to Ricketts from New York, telling Charlie that he should take the train overland to San

Francisco, and Baker would wait for him there. Baker claimed that he waited in California for two weeks, but Ricketts never arrived and Baker left for China without him.

John Black, a saloon keeper, claimed to have spent time with Ricketts and Baker on the night they were leaving for China. Black believed that Charles Ricketts really cared for his wife but simply could not control his drinking. The fate of Charles Ricketts is unknown. He was never again seen by anyone who knew him. In late 1907, Helen Ricketts obtained a pension as a survivor of Lieutenant Charles Ricketts. She had first filed this claim in 1890, but it was rejected three times because she could show no evidence that Charles was dead. Finally, on appeal, the claim was approved.

Recovering the Body of the "Perfect Soldier"

As the fighting near Chantilly ended, Major General Phil Kearny rode through the darkened woods, and as the lightning flashed and the thunder rolled, he rode out to reconnoiter and stumbled directly into the Confederate lines. There was a shouted demand for surrender. Kearny, with his sword in his one arm and the reins of his horse between his teeth; wheeled his horse around and tried to break away. A Confederate officer nearby shouted, "You are crazy, man, you can't get ten feet, don't be foolish." Kearny threw himself down on his horse's neck as it turned, riding low to avoid being hit. A volley was fired by the Confederate infantry line and Phil Kearny fell from the saddle, dead.

The word spread quickly among the Confederate troops that a high ranking Yankee general had been killed. Within a short time, Stonewall Jackson arrived on the scene. Instantly recognizing Kearny, Stonewall said, "My God boys, you know who you have killed? You have shot the most gallant officer in the United States Army. This is Phil Kearny, who lost his arm in the Mexican War."

Arrangements were made to move the body, first to Confederate Headquarters, then to the Stuart House, Chantilly Mansion at Ox Hill. General Lee ordered the body guarded and sent a communication to General Hooker notifying him that Kearny's body would be sent through the lines the following morning with an escort. The first troops to meet that escort were from the 90th P.V.

Philadelphia Weekly Tribune, December 25, 1879, letter from David Weaver Published January 3, 1880

...On the day of the Battle of Chantilly the Federal army was being drawn into the defenses around Washington. Our regiment (the Ninetieth Pennsylvania Volunteers) after leaving Centreville, and when at Ball's Cross Roads turned to the left and went up the Little Falls or River turnpike, where we halted in the woods. The regiment was detached to relieve the Twenty First New York Volunteers. It then commenced raining. By the time we reached our position the thunder, lightning, and rain were so terrific that both armies ceased fighting, but held their relative positions. We remained upon picket; the night was very cold, and not being allowed fire, the men suffered severely. The next morning, the sun came out bright and warm. We fully expected the battle to be renewed, but our army was steadily moving toward Washington, while the enemy were coming into Maryland. The Chantilly battle was a feint to cover their crossing. About 9:00 A.M. Major Sellers and myself saw an ambulance coming down the turnpike preceded by a mounted officer with a white handkerchief attached to a stick. We ran to the foot of the hill when the officer halted and announced himself as Major Early of General Lee's staff, and that he had the body of General Kearny, who was killed the night before. We, at first, thought he had made a mistake, and we asked if it was not General Stevens--he being the only general we had then heard of as killed.

I knew Kearny when he was Captain of the First Dragoons, in Mexico, where he had an arm taken off, and looking in the ambulance, saw that it was he. We then placed a sergeant as the driver in charge, who delivered the body to General Ricketts, our division commander, from whom, no doubt the Fifty Seventh Pennsylvania Volunteers received and escorted it to Washington.

Major Early remained some time awaiting the receipt for the body, when suddenly, the Major looking toward their lines, bid us goodday and rode away saying the receipt could follow, which it did shortly after. If Major Early is still alive, I think he will corroborate the above statement.

                                      Lieutenant David P. Weaver
                                      90th Regt. P.V.

Major General Phillip Kearney was killed in action at the Battle of Chantilly on September 1, 1862. He was one of the most aggressive Generals in the Army of the Potomac. His spirit and courage would be sorely missed. When his body was returned by General Lee's order, Major Sellers and Lieutenant Weaver of the 90th P.V. were the officers who took custody of it.

Winfield Scott had described Kearny as the "bravest man I ever saw", also calling him "the perfect soldier." When pompous John Pope heard of Kearny's death, he made his most astute observation of the war saying, "Its the kind of death he would have wanted." It was just that, a soldier's death for "the perfect soldier."

242

Letters to the National Tribune

The National Tribune was the Veterans Newspaper of the Civil War Union soldiers. The letters written to, and published in, the Tribune provide a colorful source of eyewitness information. Despite being written long after the shooting stopped, these documents provide many colorful personal experiences of soldiers, which stood out in their memories many years later. One good example of how well their memories held up, is the escape from Libby prison told in this section. All the important details in the two soldier's letters are the same except for the discrepancy in Corporal Quayle's name. The letters of the Tribune, if read critically, are a valuable source of information.

Private Rufus Northrup enlisted in Company A, 90th P.V. on February 18, 1862. He was among the troops in the 90th who were taken prisoner in the retreat through the town of Gettysburg after the first day of fighting along Seminary Ridge. He, most likely, was among the troops which General Lee paroled after the battle, which were considered to have been "illegally paroled" by the U.S. Army afterwards. No exchange of prisoners was ever made on these men.

LETTER 1.   NATIONAL TRIBUNE, VOLUME XXIX, NO.61, PAGE 61
December 30, 1909

BOOZE MADE TIGERS RECKLESS
RUFUS NORTHROP, CO. A, 90TH P.V

   The recent accounts of the fierce charge of the Louisiana Tigers at the Cemetery brings to my mind an incident that occurred at the time the First Corps was falling back thru the town. They were closely followed by the Johnnies, who were firing up the street and picking off those who had halted for a moment to get a drink. I managed to get as far as the public square by hugging closely to the houses without getting hit, but was gobbled up soon after, along with my Lieutenant and tentmate. The Johnnies had swung around the town and corralled about 2500 prisoners. As they approached, I saw they were under guard, and I was invited by one of the guards to, "Drop that 'er gun and fall in." I dropped my old Harpers Ferry with my last cartridge in it and joined the procession. Scotty, an old Regular of our company, was trying to dodge the sniping, and was so hard pressed that he took refuge in a church which was used as a hospital. He secreted himself in the belfry, where he could see what was going on in the street without being detected. He tied a piece of white muslin on his arm to pass for a nurse in case they discovered him, but he was not disturbed, and remained there until the return of our forces. He said he saw the Tigers stack arms in the street, and could see them diving in and out of cellars looking for things to eat and drink, and judging from the symptoms, they found something stronger than milk. When they broke stacks to make the charge, many of the rear rank men, who had to reach for their guns, were very unsteady, and some lost their balance. This may explain in part their savage recklessness in charging up to the mouth of our guns.

                        Rufus A. Northrup, Co. A, 90th P.V.
                        Westminster, Maryland

LETTER #2 NATIONAL TRIBUNE, VOLUME XXIV, NO. 50, PAGE 6.
October 21, 1904

GOING INTO GETTYSBURG
RUFUS P. NORTHRUP, CO A, 90TH P.V.

    The evening of the last day of June, the First Corps went into camp about midway between Emmittsburg and Gettysburg. General Reynolds taking up his quarters for the night at a house, now a Post office, which stands at a corner where a by road leads off from the pike. Here, the corps filed off to the right, going into camp in an old peach orchard but a short distance from the pike. There had not been, up to this time, a hint of any trouble ahead, and the boys thought more of securing a supply of the fine wheat bread and fresh cherry pie just out of the oven, supplied by the thrifty farmer's wives, than they did of the enemy. Our march through Maryland had been a regular picnic, compared to conditions we left in desolated Virginia, and when we struck "God's country" once more, we felt like "Caddy" of Company B, who used to say(whenever there were indications of "trouble") "Say Boys, I ain't got nothing against the rebs; have you?"
    But our fancied security received a sudden jolt as we filed out onto the pike in the early morning, headed toward Gettysburg, and heard the deep detonations of Devin's guns. We congratulated ourselves that the firing must be fully 20 miles away, but we were soon disabused of this fancy when an orderly flew past us to the rear, and we were ordered to give way to let two batteries past going at a break neck pace—one battery of steel guns, the other brass "Napoleons". They rattled over the little covered bridge which spans Marsh Creek, shaking it to its very foundation and giving no heed to the "$5 penalty for driving faster than a walk!"
    We immediately fell in and followed at a double-quick in the wake of the batteries. As we approached Gettysburg, we noticed many of the residents along the pike leaving by the crossroads, their families stowed away in front of their wagons, with what goods and chattels they could pack in a big bundle in the rear.
    As we came in sight of the town, we passed at the gateway of a farmhouse, a very aged man, his hair long and silvery, and hanging down well over his shoulders. His voice was tremulous and he tottered on his cane, being supported on the other side by his granddaughter, a blooming lass of 14 or 15 years. As we hurried by, the old man exhorted us in beseeching, tremulous tones: "Whip em boys, this time, If you don't whip em now, you'll never whip em." The boys replied with a "Bully for the old man," and a "hip hip for the girl" as we quickened our pace to take up our position,

where our monument now marks the extreme right of the first days fighting, which position we held late in the day, until the XI Corps gave way, and we were flanked and forced to fall back.

The first intimation we had of the seriousness of the engagement was when we turned off the pike into the field very near the little stone house where General Reynolds died. As his white haired boyish orderly dashed by us with a strange expression in his face that we read as bad news. One of the boys asked, "What's the matter orderly?" and we could just catch as he passed, "General Reynolds is very badly wounded."

I had often recalled to mind, in later years, the old man and the fair girl whom we passed that day, and when I joined the boys on the field to dedicate our monuments, while riding over the battlefield with my wife and an old tentmate, who has just answered the last roll call, I inquired of the colored driver if he could tell me who he was. His reply was prompt: "Yes indeed: That was old Mr. Rogers. He owned that farm, and he stayed right thar in the house all through the fight, and the girl she stayed there too, nursing the wounded and cooking for the 1st Mass. boys who fought all over the old man's farm. The girl, she's married now, and lives out west, and when the 1st Mass. Boys put up their monument, they sent for her and they called her out on the platform and pinned a beautiful diamond pin on her." "Is the old man dead?" I queried. "Yes, he's dead long ago and they say he cried for joy when he heard the rebs had retreated."

I afterwards wrote one of the Battlefield Commissioners to verify the story of the colored driver, and obtained the girl's address, wrote her and received a very cordial, modest reply, expressing much pleasure at hearing from one of the boys who met her at the gate on that eventful morn!

        Rufus P. Northrup, Co. A, 90th P.V.
        Harrisonburg, Virginia

LETTER #3 NATIONAL TRIBUNE, VOLUME XXXI, NO. 12, PAGE 3.
March 28, 1911

RUFUS G. NORTHRUP, CO A, 90TH P.V.
GOODBYE HOECAKE

  I was taken prisoner by the rebels with my tentmate when

the I Corps fell back through the town on the afternoon of the first day's fighting at Gettysburg along with about 2500 others. They marched us over back of Seminary Ridge, and rounded us up in a field through which a sluggish stream ran; Marsh Creek, I think. We were packed together a la Andersonville and most of us were without rations. The water in the stream was muddy and bore marks of the fighting further up. The field was off the main road and a short distance up a lane, which led to a low, one story, unpainted house, where there was a spring. At first we were allowed to go in squads under guard for water, but the men began to rush to get in the water squad, and the Johnnies, fearing a general break, shut down, and we were without a drop of water to drink or cook with.

The wounded men were quartered on the opposite side of the lane, and were allowed after water without a guard. Sutton, my tentmate, was an old Californian of the days of '49, and came East to take his brother's place, who had been wounded.

The Johnnies issued to us, on the evening of the second day, a bit of bacon and a handful of flour. Sutton said if I could get some water, he would show me how they made hoecake in California. I took our canteens, and watched the guard turn his back, when I slipped over among the wounded and limped down to the spring. The front yard was littered with bandages from bedding. Evidently the Johnnies had used it temporarily to care for their wounded. The spring was nearly dry, but I filled my canteens with an old broken spoon, and had just gotten them filled when a rebel Sergeant bore down on me. He hailed me with, "What are you doin' down hyer?" "After water, Sarge. Have a swig?" He took a long pull and escorted me back without a word, and when I got in, the men grabbed my canteens and helped themselves, but I managed to save enough to mix the batter. Sutton had fried out the bacon for shortening, found an old broken crock to mix the batter. A flat shale rock and a couple of pieces of rails completed the outfit. The batter was poured on the stone while the crowd stood around and watched Sutton manipulate the savory cake. He had turned it several times, and it was taking on a tempting rich brown(my, but it smelled good), when suddenly there was an explosion, and when the dust had cleared away all that was left of our California cake was little pieces of dough and bits of stone. The crowd let up a yell, and poor Sutton turned sadly away, remarking that swearing could not do the subject justice.

Rufus P. Northrup, Co. A, 90th P.V.
Westminster, Maryland

Private John Stulen joined the regiment in Philadelphia on October 8, 1861. Although wounded at Fredericksburg, he recovered from the wound and served with the regiment throughout the remainder of its term of service. Private Stulen was mustered out of the service on October 20, 1864, just about a month before the remainder of the regiment was discharged. He lived a long life, surviving until 1908.

LETTER #4, NATIONAL TRIBUNE, VOLUME XXIX, NO. 7, PAGE 6.
December 17, 1908

PRIVATE JOHN STULEN, CO. H, 90TH P.V
BRAVE OLD DICK COULTER

It was with much regret that I learned of the death of Gen. Dick Coulter. During the existence of the I Corps, our regiment, the 90th Pa., and the 11th Pa., Col. Coulter's regiment saw much of each other while in Gen. Baxter's Brigade, and we boys of the 90th took quite a fancy to Gen. Coulter. I remember him a soldier with a determined spirit. While a man of strong language, he was always ready for a fight; a brave officer without any frills. It may be of interest to some who are still living to learn how Gen. Coulter came to be wounded at the Battle of Spotsylvania, May 10, 1864. On that day the II Corps had a very hard and hot engagement with the enemy in the morning. We, after a hot march, arrived in the afternoon and took our position in the line of battle. The losses had been very heavy on both sides, and we had taken many prisoners. The dead still lay on the field where they fell, including many artillery horses, and the stench was horrible. The rebels were strongly intrenched in our front, and the musketry and cannonading was very brisk. During the engagement, I noticed an officer coming toward us alone, with his scabbard dragging along the ground. He evidently had dismounted his horse in the rear, and left it in charge of his orderly, and as he came near, say about 300 feet from our line of battle, I could hear him shout: "Give them Hell, boys!" I looked back, and thru the smoke recognized General Coulter, who had come out alone to encourage us, at great risk, as it was afterwards proved. A short time afterwards, on looking back, I saw him fall. I quickly laid my gun on the ground and ran towards him. He was lying on the ground, severely wounded, in a very exposed location. The rebel yells, at that moment, seemed to be getting closer. I partly carried him, partly dragged him, a short distance to a safer location. While trying to make him as comfortable as possible, I stooped down and asked him if I could do anything more for him. He said, "No," and immediately added, "I have an Aunt at home praying for me." It was only a short time after that when some staff officers came and had him carried off the field, and I returned to the_ position I had left. I don't think it was more than 20 minutes from the time he was wounded until he was taken away. I felt so sure that he was dying when I left him that I told our boys when I went back that Coulter was killed. It was no doubt owing to smoke and the noise that others did not notice the General and see him fall.

John Stulen, Co. H, 90th P.V.
Pittsburgh, Pennsylvania

LETTER #5 NATIONAL TRIBUNE, VOLUME XI, NO. 8, PAGE 6.
May 11, 1891

JOHN MCGOWAN
DOES ANY ONE REMEMBER THE CIRCUMSTANCES

I escaped from Libby Prison about Sept. 9, 1862. There were 24 prisoners of war exchanged from the floor I was on in Libby Prison on that date to make up some 300 prisoners of war off Belle Isle, and these exchanged prisoners were halted in front of the prison until the 24 exchanged soldiers joined them. My friend James Quail,[Corporal William Quayle] was among the 24 men to be exchanged. We agreed that I should answer his name in the event of it being called about the 12th or 13th on the roll of the 24 to be exchanged. Of course, if I failed to get out of the front door, I was to give myself up. When Ross opened his book to call the roll, he looked around at the anxious and hungry faces, and told us if anyone attempted to answer anyone's name but his own, he would have him placed in a cell during the war. This little devil commenced to call the roll, and, as a lucky chance, James Quail was called the 13th name, and I answered and passed down stairs. I made the first in the fourth file, four in each file. Major Turner, the prison keeper, was standing about two feet from me, with the 24 men in front of his office ready to move out. Ross came up to Turner, flurried and excited, with my friend Quail by the collar, and insisted that there was something wrong and that he wanted to count us over again. While they were talking, I gave the order in a loud voice, to "Foreward March!" Thinking it was from someone in authority, we started for the street. Turner pulled Ross aside and told Quail to take his place, and we marched out of Libby prison, and joined the paroled prisoners in front of the Island, and took up our weary march to Aikens Landing, on the James River. There we found the same number of rebel prisoners of war to be exchanged for the paroled men off the Island and the 24 from Libby. An Illinois Captain had charge of the rebel prisoners. The name of the flag-of-truce boat was the Causic; she had been the old "Eastern City." I concealed myself on this boat until about 12 o'clock that night. When she had left the wharf I reported to the Illinois Captain, and he treated me very kindly. I reported again at Fortress Monroe, Virginia and from there was sent to Alexandria, Virginia. The flag-of-truce boat took the paroled prisoners to Fort Lafayette for clothing. I reported again to the Assistant Provost Marshal at Alexandria, Virginia. His name was Lieutenant McMasters. He sent me to Washington, D.C. From there I went to Baltimore and was sick for a long time. When well enough, I was sent to the Northwest by Secretary of War Stanton. I enlisted May 27, 1861 in Colonel John Kenly's 1st Maryland. I was honorably discharged July 1864, in Baltimore, Maryland. I write this record of my escape hoping that there may be some poor prisoner who will recall the circumstance of at the above date, so I can get the testimony of his personal knowledge of the fact.

John McGowan, 1st Maryland

Corporal William Quayle was a member of the 90th P.V. who had also been a member of the old National Guards state

Militia Regiment. He had served in Baltimore in 1861 with the 19th P.V. Quayle had enlisted in the 90th on September 17, 1861. At the Battle of Rappahannock Station on August 23, 1862, the rebels captured Corporal Quayle on the retreat from the Rappahannock River. He was confined in Libby until September 9, 1862 when he assisted in Jack McGowan's escape. Corporal Quayle continued to serve with the regiment until his muster out on September 17, 1864. After the war, he survived until 1914.

LETTER #6, NATIONAL TRIBUNE, VOLUME XI, NO. 8, PAGE 7
September 24, 1891

CORPORAL WILLIAM H. QUAYLE, CO D, 90TH P.V.
THE MAN WHO HELPED JOHN McGOWAN OUT OF LIBBY

In your paper of May 14, 1891, I notice a communication from John McGowan, 3233 N Street, N.W., Georgetown, D.C., in relation to his escape from Libby Prison, Virginia about September 9, 1862, through the assistance of his friend James Quail. His account is correct in the main, but how he gets his friend's name James Quail I cannot tell, but then it is many years since then and memory does not always serve faithfully. I am the party who aided him to escape. My name is William H. Quayle, and I was a Corporal of Co. D, 90th Pa. I have often wondered what became of Jack McGowan, as I then called him. While I did not know, after he answered to my name and had gone down the stairs to liberty, how he felt, I do know my own feeling at the time, for we had been notified that anyone caught aiding another to escape would be kept a close prisoner for the balance of the war, or worse. Comrade McGowan was a prisoner at Libby when I got there. If I remember correctly, he had made his escape once, had been recaptured, and belonging, as he did to a loyal Maryland regiment, and a hard fighting one at that, he was particularly obnoxious to the Confederates. Per consequence, he was good for a long captivity, with Belle Island or

Andersonville in prospective. Jack was very ill, and I felt certain a dead man if he remained there but a few months longer, hence my offer to aid him in making his escape, and its success.

After Jack had passed down the stairs I called the guard and asked him to call the officer or Mr. Ross. Mr. Ross came. I asked him how it was my name had not been called on the list, as it had been called the day before. He then asked me my name, company and regiment, which I gave. He said it was called and had been checked and somebody had answered to it. Well, I replied, there's my name and here am I. I was standing away over there by the window, which may account for my not hearing it. "Well," Ross replied "there is something wrong here. I'll go downstairs and see. You remain here." My only hope for poor Jack then, was that he may have gotten safely out into the street and gone up about the head of the line with the prisoners from Belle Island as it had been arranged that he should do. After what seemed an age to me, Ross returned to the foot of the stairs and called to the guard to pass me down. He did not take me by the collar as Jack thinks, but placed his hand on my shoulder as we walked toward the entrance to the street and remarked that he really ought to keep me in Castle Thunder on bread and water until after the war, and would but that Captain Turner wanted to look at me and seemed to think that I was honest. We walked up to where Captain Turner stood. He gave me a long searching look. I looked him squarely and honestly in the face in return, and he ordered Ross to let me go, and told me to take my place in line, and you bet I got there quick. I have never seen or heard from McGowan since until I accidentally saw his communication in your paper.

William H. Quayle, Co. D, 90th P.V.
1186 Pacific Ave, Dallas, Texas.

LETTER #7, NATIONAL TRIBUNE, VOLUME XXIX, NO 25, PAGE 6.

PRIVATE JOHN STULEN, CO H, 90TH P.V.
OPENING THE BATTLE

A PENNSYLVANIA BOY RUNS IN THE ENEMY PICKET LINE IN THE WILDERNESS

No doubt it is very interesting to many comrades to read

the articles in the National Tribune, giving account of their observations and experience without unnecessary laudation. It is almost a fact that the children of this generation know very little of the civil war and what it stood for, and I think we are excusable if we allow our thoughts to wander back 44 or more years to events that came directly under our observation.

Many of you of the I Corps, which camped in winter quarters around Culpeper during the winter of 1864, will remember our surprise when the general order was read consolidating the I Corps with the V Corps and thereby losing our identity, which we prized so much. Also, the excitement caused by the news that General Grant was to be our commander. We had heard of his victories in other fields, but would he pan out against General Lee? Would we cross the Rapidan, fight a battle and then cross back again, as we had done so often before? Such were the nightly talks around our campfires. We did not despair, however, but rather seemed pleased at the change and glad of the opportunity to show our new commander that we could fight as good if not better than his Western troops.

DETAILED AS ORDERLY

Several months before going into winter quarters, an order came to our Colonel from Brigade headquarters for a detail of two privates from the 90th to serve temporarily as Orderlies at General Henry Baxter's headquarters. It resulted in Jack Bowen of Co. A, and myself being chosen and ordered to report to the Brigade Quartermaster who furnished us with a horse each, a sword and the necessary equipment, and we were changed from the infantry to the cavalry service, but retained our Infantry uniform.

I may add here that my tentmate, Bowen, now holds a responsible position in the United States Mint at Philadelphia. I felt pleased and looked upon my position as a promotion, though the pay remained the same: $13 a month.

It is needless to say that we were kept busy day and night. Our many visits to different headquarters gave us an opportunity to see many Generals and their staffs, including General Grant.

As the 1st of May drew near, the active preparations that had been going on all winter in supplying and reinforcing the army began to show results. When we began to move out on the 4th of May, the V Corps, recruited up to its full quota, began its march, first the cavalry, then the infantry and artillery.

It was a beautiful and inspiring sight as we marched on

our way to Germanna Ford to cross over the Rapidan, all in fine spirits to do and to die to save the nation and its flag. In the carnage that followed day after day many thousands of them did find a patriot's grave in a shallow dug hole, with a piece of cracker box and a lead pencil mark for a tombstone.

We marched out on the Plank Road for a considerable distance. Later in the afternoon, we passed General Alexander Hays. He was sitting on a log surrounded by his staff, who were listening to what he was saying. He had a stick in his hand, scratching on the ground, no doubt explaining to them the line of battle. He was killed the next day. He was a general much beloved by his troops.

As night came on, we were forbidden making any campfires, and the troops were ordered to lie on their arms. Shortly after daybreak the next morning, May 5, a staff officer from General Robinson's headquarters rode up to General Baxter, saluted, and I heard him say, "The general directs that you advance your picket line until you find the enemy." General Baxter called a staff officer, and repeated the order verbally to him, and I, as his orderly, started off with him. At first we rode at a brisk pace, but after we had gone into the woods a short distance, our progress was slow. The fallen trees and the underbrush was so dense that we could only see a few feet ahead. The place was well named a Wilderness. Many times, I came near losing the staff officer, and I finally did lose him, and after trying my best to find him I gave it up. I felt ashamed of myself; it would not do to go back and report that I had got lost, so I determined to find our picket line, and give the order if they had not already received it. I had no compass, but I made up my mind to go straight ahead and trust to luck. I pushed on through the thick underbrush, horse and rider getting many scratches. Now and then I would halt and listen, revolver in hand, but could not hear a sound.

I must have gone about a mile or more, when all of a sudden a head popped out from a tree about 20 feet in my front and called out, "What regiment you going to?" We both fired at each other before he finished speaking, for we knew instinctively that we were enemies. The flash of his gun coming so close to my horse's face caused him, fortunately for me, to wheel around and go to the rear. Our shots started the rebel picket line to firing, but the underbrush hid me from view, and my horse took me faster to the rear than I came. I had not located our picket line, and as the rebels did not get any reply, they soon ceased firing. You can readily realize how this shooting would put our picket line on edge and make them very alert. After going about a half a mile I came to a small clearing, at the edge of which I saw our picket line. I put spurs to my horse, stood up in the stirrups and shouted to them not to shoot. Many of them had already raised their guns to fire. During the excitement, the Officer of the picket came up, and I made a satisfactory explanation, and told him what order General Baxter gave, and told him that I had found the rebel pickets, and explained where it was. Going further to the rear, I noticed that our battle line was close up to our skirmish line, ready to commence the fight, which became quite lively a short time afterwards, and more desperate as the day advanced. I believe that I am well within the truth when I say through this adventure I was the means of starting the Battle of the Wilderness in front of the V Corps, and which continued all that day and the next.

GENERAL WADSWORTH

On the morning of the 6th we passed that distinguished looking General Wadsworth, with that familiar cap on which he always wore. His staff and troops were waiting for the order to go forward into the bloody contest raging in their front. They did go in, and New York lost a famous general and the idol of his troops. Those who were there know that it was only by the sound in many places that you could tell how close you were to the enemy, owing to the dense undergrowth and smoke, and it was an easy matter for one or the other to be taken prisoner. As we were shifting our position, my chum Bowen was captured with the Brigade Headquarters flag, but succeeded in keeping it from capture, and is the proud possessor of it. His capture broke up the combination, and in making the change back to cavalry orderlies, I was ordered to return to my regiment; presto chango, I again shouldered a musket.

I certainly owe much to that Confederate soldier who by his good military training saved me from capture.

About this time we became satisfied that General Grant did not intend to make any backward movement, as our fighting continued day after day, and always moved forward, in spite of unparalleled difficulties. For that indomitable pluck of General Grant became in evidence, and General Lee had found his match.

John Stulen, Co. H, 90th P.V.
Pittsburgh, Pa.

The Slowest Mail of All

Captain George Watson made this written statement to be read before the Survivors Association of the 90th P.V. It seems it was the practice of the association to read a paper, detailing a soldier's wartime service, before the association at each monthly meeting. Unfortunately, none of the other papers read have survived to this day.

It might be argued that this statement is technically not a letter, and should not be included in a book consisting mainly of letters. However, since Captain Watson had enough of a sense of history to place this statement in his pension file in 1891, I believe it should be included here. I think that George Watson placed this item in his pension file because he expected that someone, eventually, would search that file while researching the history of the 90th P.V. In 1993, when I was researching the regiment, that is exactly what happened. When I came across the statement, it was almost as if the good Captain had mailed it directly to me. Of course, delivery was slow, but I got it just the same. He placed it where he knew someone would find it and make use of it. I include it for these reasons, and, of course, for its obvious research and historical value.

Captain George Watson's Account of His Mutilation in Battle, Captivity, and Suffering as a Prisoner of War, Together with Incidents in connection therewith.

Commending and desiring to aid in what I understand is the custom of members of the 90th Regiment P.V. Survivors Association, of reading, or having read, at its meetings their individual experiences and reminiscences of the time when we were engaged in battling against the attempted dismemberment of our government and the perpetuation of slavery. In accordance with this custom I beg to offer the following account of my capture and imprisonment as a prisoner of war and incidents connected therewith.

My statement commences with the Battle of the Wilderness, May 5th 1864, and includes my subsequent martyrdom of near six months with some account of my sufferings then and immediately thereafter through having been badly mutilated and captured at the said battle:

After we of the command (Lyle's Brigade, Robinson's Division), of which the 90th formed a part, had moved well to the front...and were lying on the ground in an edge of woods, with the artillery and small arms shot of the enemy mostly passing over us. I crept forward and peering through the bushes saw that at least four pieces of artillery were planted against us on the crest of an elevation of ground in front; to reach which a gentle descent and then a quicker ascent of cleared surface would have to be passed over. Accordingly, when the order to advance, or charge, was given, I was impressed with the necessity of allowing the enemy as little time as possible to get off discharges against us, and said to our brave color bearer, Sergeant

Carter, that "Speed was our greatest safety." This had so much effect that Carter was soon leading the line at the apex of a formation somewhat like an inverted letter V. The enemy during our progress toward them got off several discharges of artillery, but probably in consequence of our down hill course and they not depressing muzzles sufficiently,...the missiles did not seem to strike our line, although I saw plainly that one of these guns was immediately in front of the command.

When nearing the enemy and having yet to climb the quick ascent of ground in front, I threw my sword in its scabbard and drew revolver for the purpose of capturing the aforementioned piece of artillery in front. At this moment was to be seen the infantry of the enemy pressing forward and firing as it halted in line. I was struck twice, one shot going through my right thigh and badly fracturing the bone, the other striking my sheathed sword, bending it and the metal scabbard and bruising my hip. I was thus thrown to the ground and on attempting to rise, fell again with my broke leg under me. I then found that our thin unsupported battle line was being driven back under a murderous fire leaving many killed and wounded. (I have since been informed that we lost 85 men inside of five minutes).

The heavy firing soon ceased. Then the dead, dying, and wounded were my only companions. I laid thus on the battle field forty eight hours, during which time several matters claimed my attention. The first was to check by external pressure, my loss of blood. I did this by making a handkerchief tourniquet in the manner taught many of us in a lecture at the hall, by a medical gentleman, at the time of starting on our three months service. If any of you remember the surgeon referred to, and if he is now living, I would like to have him thanked for his valuable advice which I used as stated, as also in several previous cases for the benefit of others.

The night of the 5th of May soon spread its pall over the battlefield. Then came the sounds of prayers and singing as if a Methodist camp meeting was in progress on the Confederate side. The ceasing of this was followed by prowlers spreading over the field robbing the dead and the helpless. While two or three were robbing a comrade near me, I hastily placed my watch and pocketbook, the latter containing a few dollars, under my back, and with pocket screw driver and wrench, took my revolver apart and scattered the pieces within easy reach, thinking to obtain them again in case of rescue and being taken, as I hoped to our lines. Exhausted by exertion and loss of blood, I fell asleep from which I was awakened by the aforesaid prowlers who disclosed by their conversation that they thought me dead. I endeavored to persuade them that I had no valuables for the reason that marauders had taken all. After verifying this, as they thought, by a search of my pockets, I was not further molested during the night.

The next day was one of some anxiety as to the probable fate of myself and others on the field. This was increased by the pickets or sharpshooters, on both sides firing over us and an occasional shot striking among us. A wounded companion near me was thus struck, and it is fair to presume that others were also. I called to one "Johnny Reb," firing screened by the trunk of a tree some distance in front, and asked him to change his position as he was drawing fire on a line with me. He responded with a hearty assent, and I was gratified to see him take another tree to my right.

One of the 90th, a Swede by birth, who had been left wounded on the field, had crawled over to me on this day and on my solicitation, procured some water from a near ditch. He also obtained the straps and inside wooden frame of a knapsack; from these I endeavored to bind my shattered leg and taking the stock of a gun, I made an effort during the night to get off the field, but had to desist because of the unbearable torture.

With this exception this night on the field was like the first; the force in front having evidently moved away, there was not so much praying to be heard and less preying, in the other sense of the word, on the victims of the battle. The stillness late on the second night seemed to be broken by the near hooting and distant responses of the owls, and with thought of the oft quoted sayings in this connection, I well remember how dismal and weird the sounds seemed.

At early dawn of the next day, 7th of May, I was startled by a trumpet signal which was followed by a line of skirmishers emerging from the woods in front and passing, after alignment, quickly over the field in the direction of what was then, or had been, our line. Almost immediately there was a fusillade of small arms soon mingled with artillery firing. One shot of the latter violently plowed the ground and throwed quite a weight of earth over myself and others. This firing soon ended. I saw no more of the skirmishers who having been evidently sent out to ascertain the position of our side, had, I thought, struck the rear guard.

Following the just related exciting episode were visits to the field of seeming camp followers, who, I suppose had been kept away by the previous flying shot. These commenced looking for things having any value, but by lying on the ground with my pockets turned inside out, I was not disturbed. As the day advanced I saw ambulances taking up the wounded until finally I was reached. I was thus jolted over rough ground and tortured for a distance of what seemed to me near a mile, until under a clump of trees an improvised operating table, attended by Confederate surgeons and assistants was arrived at. Now a hasty and torturing examination was made and the verdict arrived at that my mutilated leg must come off at the thigh. A sponge charged with ether was used, the tortuous cutting commenced before I had become unconscious. After this I knew no more until I found myself on the ground nearby and in sight of the work of surgery still going on; the amount of it being attested to by the blood bespattered surgeons and their helpers, and the quantity of arms and legs in a heap nearby. I must have shortly thereafter again become unconscious, for I knew nothing until the next morning at daybreak when I found myself with seven others, each with an arm or a leg off, under a shelter formed by the outer covering of a tent. This shelter was soon after removed, at which time there was a bustle of moving which ended, so far as I could see, in none being left but the hundreds of mutilated covering the ground.

Some of those whose wounds were not extremely severe could move about, and in answer to the appeals of the extremely helpless would give them water, and in other ways try to alleviate distress, but such help was inadequate to the task, and great suffering prevailed which was increased by the delirium of a few, who going about aimlessly, would tramp upon, fall over, and otherwise injure others. Many incidents of the horrors of this hospital in the woods occur to my mind but they cannot be told here without greatly lengthening this statement.

During the time when taken off the field and being operated upon, my haversack, cap, and the boot on my only remaining leg, was stolen from me. I had by hiding as before stated, and afterwards in the lining of my coat, been able to retain my watch, memorandum book, and a few dollars.

Seeing on the third day after, an empty barrel and a man wounded in one arm doing some work with a hatchet nearby, I by the offer of two dollars, induced him to make a bedstead for me with crotched stakes, saplings, and the staves of said barrel, in the usual way in the army. Later I procured a small coarse blanket through the same means. All my money was now expended, but the bedstead procured with it, greatly alleviated my discomfort, especially during the heavy rains which prevailed about that time. I had caused a sapling growing close to the foot of my bed, to be bent over it and the blanket stretched over this, done duty as a leaky shelter. For several days in the beginning of this open air hospital, I received no food, then was brought to me a small piece of fat bacon. I saved this, for in my weak condition, I had but little appetite. The next day, getting a couple of crackers, I made my first meal since the battle five days before.

About this time, I discovered that a Confederate surgeon was in charge of us. He informed me that there was about 800 wounded at that place, many of whom were sick, and he was without medicine and appliances. This gentleman, however, did a great amount of good in organizing squads of the least wounded and dividing off and assigning the care of the helpless to them, as also the duty of daily burying the dead. I saw one of the party, earlier assigned to this last mentioned duty, go past me one day with my amputated leg, which I recognized by the boot on it, and carried an amputated arm in his other hand, to a pit dug near by for the burial of the pile of limbs. From my elevated position on my extemporized bedstead, I could overlook the wounded gathered thick about me; death was making sad havoc among them. Groans and shrieks prevailed, sometimes proceeding from the delirious. Many of the poor fellows were wallowing in the black mud, soaked by the heavy downpour of rain. I can describe only the horrible as occurring at this time. During the several weeks of sojourn in these woods there was no change of the bandages first put on by the operating surgeons and with flies abounding, I will leave to the imagination the filling up of the sickening picture outlined above. Where was our "Sanitary Commission?" Could they not get through the lines to us?...I have no doubt that this excellent commission was doing good work elsewhere but having more than it could attend to, we were not reached.

Of the 800 mutilated companions, the number was constantly being reduced by death, and in many cases, by deserting to our lines. The Confederate surgeon informed me that he had succeeded in having Federal Surgeons and prisoners assigned to help him but, they had all left. Commenting on this to one of my wounded companions who was assisting the others, he informed me of a secret scheme for all who were able to march to desert in a body. They had been gathering up arms and ammunition from the battlefield, cleaning up and hiding these, and would leave prepared to resist arrest. Accordingly a few nights after, a body of my companions, organized and with officers in command, marched through the woods and near where I was lying, and then took the road. Those who could use guns had them, while others carried ammunition and other articles. Very early the next morning a company of mounted guerrillas passed in pursuit. These returned a couple of days after; one of them stating that they had gotten sight of the "yanks" who showed fight and were too many for them, so they gave up the chase.

After this for several days we did not get our extremely small allowance of corn bread and bacon and were told as a reason that the escaping men had broken into the storehouse and taken everything. The kind Surgeon in Charge(George B. Moffett, 49th Virginia Infantry) after this occurrence, had those of us left brought together in a smaller space. In this way I came in closer companionship with several brother officers. One of these could do a limited amount of walking with crutches, bargained with a greatly distorted rheumatic cripple, a resident in the neighborhood, to be taken for $20.00 near to or within our lines. This was accomplished the next night by the said cripple bringing his miserable old horse and ramshackle wagon near enough to reach, when with a hand pressure and a whispered goodbye, my companion was off. The same cripple helped others to get away in a like manner, who were able to pay. I, after much haggling, sold my watch to this man for a small amount of Confederate money and some food of an inferior kind, such as boiled garden greens. Poor as it was, I was glad to get it.

The month of June had now set in, and we began to despair of being soon exchanged. At this time there was a report current among us of the approach of Union Cavalry. We had been hoping that information given by those deserting would cause our rescue. There was evidently some grounds for this rumor, for on the 5th of June, Confederate ambulances arrived, and we were taken to Orange Courthouse Railroad Station, and the next day to Gordonsville. Some of the buildings here contained Confederate wounded and sick. Again was reported the near approach of our cavalry. Then, all the nurses and others, including the Confederate hospital convalescents, were armed, organized, and sent out to repel attack. These returned a day or two after and reported that our forces had turned off on another route, and thus was our hope of rescue disappointed.

After this I was taken, along with many others wounded, to Lynchburg. We were quartered in a room assigned to officers in a large tobacco warehouse surrounded by a cordon of sentinels. At this time my stump of a limb was greatly inflamed by the shaking caused by rough travel I had undergone. Some of the others with me were in, more or less, the same condition. I had now a rest that extended over a greater portion of my captivity. Those who have been prisoners of war know the many methods of passing time; the most frequent being the picking over of garments. We had plenty of this as the building seemed to be infested with vermin: cots, walls, and everywhere. The food consisted of a very scant allowance of corn bread and bacon. To this was added, on the Wednesday of each week, a small amount of broth made by thickening with flour the water in which mutton had been boiled. Sometimes, some of us were fortunate enough to get a bone or a small piece of meat.

My craving for more food was incessant and induced dreams when asleep of being at feasts with inability to get enough. One day it occurred to my mind that a boyhood acquaintance, George Gamble, who learned copper smithing with former sheriff George Magee in Philadelphia, had emigrated to the town I was then in. I, at once, decided to try and ascertain if he was then in Lynchburg, and if so to communicate with him. This was not easy to accomplish as the one or two who were sometimes sent into the room to do work were forbidden to hold conversation with us, and one of them had been severely whipped a few days before for violating this rule. However, by watching my chance I whispered to one of these colored men and gave him my name and the name and calling of my friend on a piece of paper, with promise of reward if successful in finding him. A few nights after, I was startled by seeing, by a light from the sky, a head poke up alongside of me, and the hurried information was given me by the negro that he had found my friend Gamble who would try to see me.

After the lapse of several days, two Confederate soldiers came in having Gamble with them, who explained that on account of the refusal of the Surgeon in Charge, he had been unable to see me sooner, but a change of surgeon and renewed application had given him this success. Our interview ended by his giving me $200.00 of Confederate money for my pencilled promissory note, on a leaf torn from my much prized memorandum book, for $100.00. The visit was afterwards repeated and a like amount obtained in a like manner. I found that my friend had escaped service in the field by being detailed in the locomotive works in the city. I am glad to here record that my promises to pay were afterwards redeemed at a large profit to my benefactor.

With the Confederate money thus obtained I was enabled, through a colored woman having access to the hospital, to buy greatly needed food in place of dry corn bread, as I was then attacked with a disorder of the bowels, which prevailed like an epidemic among my companions. I bought at this time a pair of crutches and the money also enabled me to help others, and the care thus bestowed diverted attention from my own sufferings. Captain A. G. Happer, of the 11th P.V., badly wounded and at times delirious, occupied a cot next to mine and thus became subject to my care. Captain Henry C.

Kenner, 4th U. S. Cavalry, admitted to the hospital September 5, 1864, wounded left breast. This officer lingered about three days in great agony and then died.

Before this took place he had, in consequence of my attention to him, informed me of having considerable money sewed up in the waistband of his drawers; that he expected to die, and wanted me to have it. When the attendants, under the direction of the surgeon were about removing the body, I told them about the money and the gift, with the result of seeing the surgeon quickly appropriate it. I later, when at home, wrote to the address in New York this officer gave me, but never received any acknowledgment. Our number was occasionally augmented by new arrivals. The stories and adventures told by many of these and those previously with us, together with the daily occurring incidents, would fill a book. One wounded officer brought in, on finding the hard fare he had to put up with, and the opportunity by having money to buy better food, told us of having secreted his money, $600.00, in his canteen, and had, along with his companions, to throw it on a pile of canteens collecting for the use of the enemy.

Our quarters were twice changed during my involuntary sojourn in Lynchburg. I was not aware of the purpose of this, but it gave a little variety to the dull living. On an occasion of this kind, one of the white hospital attendants asked me what ground was last occupied by the portion of the army I belonged to. On my stating between Culpeper and the Rapidan River and near the latter, he asked me whether I knew of a certain house there, to which I answered that near the place he described the reserve pickets were kept when I was last on that duty. The women living in the house had baked flour and cooked other rations supplied by me, and with her children we had partook of the meals together. Judging by his questioning, that he was acquainted with the family, I proceeded to tell him of a circumstance that came partly under my notice of the woman losing her cow and finding it at the headquarters of a regiment, and on being disputed or bantered to prove her property, she said, "Let this cow loose and if it don't follow me it is not mine." On this being done, she called out,"Sukey, Sukey," and with sun bonnet in hand started on a hard run, with the cow, first in a trot and then in a gallop, after her, much to the amusement and delight of the many who had assembled and witnessed the performance. I then found I was talking to the husband of the woman and I had given him the latest news of his wife and children. He was greatly pleased and bestowed extra attention on me afterward.

All through my captivity, rumors were rife of an exchange

of prisoners soon to take place; these seemed at least to be born of "The hope, that deferred maketh the heart sick," until finally one day several wagons drove up to our hospital and prison, into which we were hastily bundled and driven to a building near the railroad depot and there placed in an extremely crowded room, in which the night was very uncomfortably spent. The next day, we were placed on passenger cars, the first of this kind of conveyance I had traveled in since a prisoner. I now ascertained that we were speeding for Richmond. During this journey, I found myself among a group of rebel officers some of whom seemed disposed to be sociable and plied me with questions as to my opinion as to the ultimate of the war. I reminded them that I was not in a position to discuss such questions, but if they wanted my honest opinion I had no objection to stating it but perhaps, through not being in accord, I might anger them with serious consequences to myself. One chivalrous young officer insisted that I should be heard and protected, whereupon I told them of having only a few months previous been to my home, on leave from the army, and found nothing in the section visited but industry and thrift. The north was living as if the war was a business for life, that with the exception of a few croakers, always to be found, there was a united sentiment and determination to prevent the dismemberment of the government and setting up of another in which the barbarism of slavery was to be incorporated. At this juncture I was interrupted...by a typical southerner with long hair and a slouch hat, who, I thought saw a safe opportunity to display himself as a bully who would knife a man. It had spread through the car with exaggeration attached, what the "Yank" was saying. The young officer, aided by others, reiterated in great part what I really had said with his promise of protection, to which he added his comments and sentiments, all of which tended to allay the excitement, which soon, thereafter, subsided.

At the commencement of the journey to Richmond, I had been separated from all my companions. It was dark when the train entered the city and having to go some distance at the depot over a cross plank walk and open cracks of same, with my crutches, which I was not used to, I had great trouble. Several of the crippled in the procession we formed had bad tumbles. Obeying an order given me, I got into one of the wagons outside of the depot, and was taken to the second story of a building and into a room surrounded by cots, many of which I saw were occupied by negroes. I was assigned to a hard cot next to a negro from whom emanated the, to me, well known, stench of gangrene in his wounds. I was nauseated by this proximity, but being very tired was, nevertheless, soon asleep. It had been daylight a little while the next morning when I awoke and found a man whose face I knew and who called me by name, stating that he had been waiting for me to awaken. I could only remember him as a member of the 90th, and the account of himself was that he had been taken prisoner in battle and since detailed, by Confederate authority, where I found him, as assistant to the doctor and as nurse. I wish I could recall this man's name, as he was very kind to me in having me removed to another cot away from the great stench before referred to, and in procuring me a cup of thickened broth, which I was glad to get as I had not eaten anything for two days. I was visited later by a seeming official who asked me if I was an officer of colored troops, to which I, of course, gave a negative reply and mentioned with some pride that I had entered into the service of the United States before colored troops were thought of or organized. I then gave him the number of my regiment, what state it was from, etc. After this gentleman had left me I pondered over the circumstances and the thought occurred to me that I had mentioned the day before on the train, in reply to a question, that at the time of being wounded, I was in command of the Color Company of my regiment, only through a misunderstanding of the word "color" and the word having been taken for colored, could I account for having been taken to a negro hospital.

In a short time after my conversation with the aforesaid official, I was taken out of the building and carried on a hospital stretcher on the shoulders of four blacks, through the streets of Richmond, for a considerable distance, to the famous "Libby Prison." Here, in a short time after, I met our comrade Jacob M. Davis, who was then Major of our regiment. Long before this, I was entirely out of funds and...presented an extremely dilapidated appearance. Happily for me, comrade Davis was only influenced by looks to consider and determine that I needed care, and to my dying day I shall ever feel the liveliest gratitude to him for his unremitting care and sharing with me, equal with himself. The food he was able to procure only at high prices. This good treatment was continued during our sojourn together at "Libby," then, after on the flag of truce boat during our conveyance-again under the old flag-to our lines, and then, finally, at Annapolis, Maryland where, October 9, 1864, we parted for that time.

I want Colonel Davis to write, for our the 90th Association, his experience met with, and incidents noted before, during, and after our meeting at "Libby Prison," therefore, I have not trenched in this upon what I consider

An artist depicts the suffering of several Union prisoners confined in Libby Prison in Richmond. This was one of several places where Lt. George Watson was confined

his prerogative, further than to state only, in this particular, what I conceive, his well known modesty would be in the way of stating.

I remained at the Annapolis hospital. The nice clean beds, well kept wards, good food and attendance was a great contrast to my experience of the previous...five months. I was suffering with my mutilated limb in a bad condition, and a continued disorder of the bowels. Thus sick, weak, and ragged, I craved to see the familiar faces, and be with those in sympathy with me to a greater amount. Accordingly, against the advice of my then medical attendant, I applied for and received a hospital discharge, then went to Washington, D.C. and after considerable distress, in consequence of my condition, and being referred to officials apart from each other, I received some pay due me, purchased clothing, and started homeward for Philadelphia. I remember being very sick on the train, and the kind sympathy and assistance of some ladies, in having seats turned and being well disposed on them, with their shawls about me, and at the change of cars in Baltimore, the conductor carried me like an infant from one car to the other. Home was at last reached. Soon, thereafter, my term of service expired and I was discharged from the army, and had to depend on other resource for a living, determined not to be a burden, in the least, in any direction.

After a short lapse of time, Dr. Hays Agnew was called in and decided that it would be needful for me to undergo a second amputation. Before and after this time Doctor James W. White, lately deceased, manager of the dental depot, 12th & Chestnut Sts., gratuitously gave me constant and valuable attention, that I might arrive at a condition to be able to undergo the operation decided upon. This was performed after several months had elapsed by cutting off a portion of my thigh and taking dead bone therefrom nearly to my hip. My condition was no doubt by the exposure, lack of proper sustenance, care, and the rough travel and consequent shaking up I had undergone, whereby healing was prevented during the early part of my captivity in rebeldom. I have left out much that could be stated in this connection, having lengthened my statement as much probably as the patience of my comrades, who are to hear it read, will allow. I will now close with my kind regards to all my fellow members of the 90th Regiment P.V., Survivors Association for whom it is written.

George Watson

Washington D. C., October 19, 1891

Antietam
By John L. Candelet
Sergeant, Company E
90th Pennsylvania Volunteers

Scarce had the gloom of night by daylight been dispelled,
When pickets firing,
Tells the foe arise.
There, aroused from slumber we are now compelled,
To Fall in Line.
The shock of war to bear,
Each man jumps to his post.
Each, now shows he fears not.
Shirks not, when his duty calls.

The soldier survives on his musket
and makes a firm resolve as on his face he falls.
And now the din of battle has begun its roar,
Swift flies the whistling ball and hissing shell.
Our comrade falls, alas, to rise no more
While thundering cannon sounds his dying knell.

Undismayed, our column rushes on
And hurls destruction on the frightened foe.
Though death claims many a father or a son,
Our ghastly wounds are talebearers as we go.
Crash go the shells,
Swift grape shot upon its way
And groups of men are seen to bleed and die,
But still undaunted,
We still seek the fury.

Determined that the rebel hordes shall fly.
Close Up Your Ranks and Forward, is the cry.
Onward, with overwhelming fury now we press.
The foe now wavers, Now, they turn and fly,
The blood of slaughter, comrades cry redress.
The field is ours
The foe in terror now has fled.
Three heartful cheers are given for Uncle Sam
But many a Union Patriot here has bled
Upon the gory field of Antietam.

Sources

The source of each letter used in this book is listed with the individual letters. The vast majority of the general information about individual soldiers of the 90th comes mostly from four sources:

The Service Records of the regiment, RG98, National Archives.
The Pension Files of the regiment, RG15, National Archives.
The General Court Martial Files of the regiment, RG94, National Archives.
The Regimental Records, 90th P.V., State Archives of Pennsylvania

In addition the following works provided information:

Advance The Colors, Richard A. Sauers, 1991, Capitol Preservation Committee, Harrisburg, Pa.

Campaigns of the Civil War, Chancellorsville & Gettysburg, Major General Abner Doubleday, New York, 1882, Charles Scribner's Sons,

General Phillip Kearny: Battle Soldier of Five Wars, Thomas Kearny, New York, 1937.

History of Pennsylvania Volunteers, Samuel Bates, 1865, Harrisburg,

History Second Regiment field Artillery, Colonel Hamilton D Turner, Commanding Officer, Philadelphia 1914.

History of 12th Massachusetts Regiment, Lt. Col. Benjamin F. Cook, 12th Webster Regiment Association, Boston, 1882.

Life in Southern Prisons, From the Diary of Corporal Charles Smedley, Ladies & Gentlemen's Fulton Aid Society, Lancaster, 1867.

Military Medal of Honor Legion of the United States, Brevet Major General St. Clair Mulholland, 1905.

Mayors of Baltimore, Wilbur F. Coyle, Baltimore Municipal Journal, 1919.

The Nineteenth of April 1861, George W. Brown, Baltimore, 1887, Copyright N. Murray.

Official Records Of The Union & Confederate Armies, Series 1, United States Government, 128 Volumes.

"Operations of the Army of the Potomac May 7-11, 1864," **Papers of the Military Historical Society of Massachusetts**, Brevet Brigadier General Charles l. Pierson, 1905, Boston, The Military Historical Society of Massachusetts.

Philadelphia In The Civil War, 1861-1865, Frank H. Taylor, Philadelphia, 1913, City of Philadelphia.

Survivors Association Publication, Suvivors of the 90th Pa. Volunteers, Gettysburg, 1888-89, Compiled by A. J. Sellers, published by the Survivors' Association, John W. Clarks' Sons, Book-binders, 7th & Commerce Sts., Phila.

The 39th Regiment, Massachusett's Volunteers, 1862-1865, Alfred S. Roe, Regimental Veterans Association, Worcester, Massachusetts, 1914.

Government Records

NARS, Record Group 59 State Department Records

NARS, Record Group 94, Microfilm Publication 594, Roll 177

NARS, Record Group 94, Records Relating to Congressional Medal of Honor Winners.

Private Records

Military Order Of The Loyal Legion of The United States, Archives item #654. Record of Major Alfred Sellers, 90th Pennsylvania Volunteers.

Records of the Grand Army of the Republic, G.A.R. Anna M. Ross Post #94.

Diaries

Account of the Trip of the 90th Regiment(National Guards) P.V. Down to Dixieland, Diary of Lieutenant Samuel B. Moore, Company B, 90th P.V. Antietam National Military Park.

War Diary, John D. Vautier, USAMHI

Newspapers

Baltimore American.

Baltimore Republican.

Philadelphia Evening Bulletin,

Philadelphia Inquirer.

Notes

I have chosen not to use formal footnotes within the body of the text, since I have used only a very limited amount of quoted material outside of the letters themselves. Instead, all quotations are listed below by their page number in the text.

Page 9, **History of Pennsylvania Volunteers**, Samuel Bates, 1865, Harrisburg, Volume 1, page 176.

Page 10. **Official Records of the Union and Confederate Armies**, United States Government, Series 1, Volume II, page 138–139.

Page 10, **Maryland in the Civil War**, Harold R. Manakee, Maryland Historical Society, Page 37–38.

Page 14, Baltimore American, June 28, 1861.

Page 14, **Official Records**, Series 1, Volume II, Page 156.

Page 112, National Archives & Records service, Record Group 15, Pension File, Samuel Mellor, Statement of Samuel Jackaway.

Page 135, War Diary of John Vautier, United States Army Military History Institute, Carlsile PA. Page 200.

Page 156, National Archives & Records Service, Records of St. Elizabeth's Hospital, Case File#1280, Private Lucas Hoffman.

Page 233, NARS, RG#15, Pension File, Charles Ricketts, 234, undated, unattributed newspaper clipping.

Page 240, **General Phillip kearny, Battle Soldier of Five Wars**, Thomas kearny, New York, 1937, New York, Page 387–388.

Index

Active duty, 89
Adams' Express, 40, 143, 154, 188
Adjutant General's Office, 129 147, 152
Advance guard, 69
Aiken's Landing, VA, 250
Alexandria General Hospital, 85, 90, 91
Alexandria, VA, 30, 49, 53, 54, 66, 70, 82, 86, 93, 127, 185, 250
Allebach, Joseph. 25
Ambulances, 260
Ammunition Train, stampede, 71
Amputation, 112, 162
Ancient & Honorable Artillery Company, 5
Anderson, Private Samuel, 32
Andersonville Prison, 68, 175
Annapolis Hospital, 267
Annapolis, MD, 187, 229, 256
Antietam, Battle of, 21–22, 55, 82, 103–104, 198; artillery fire at, 269; casualties 90th P.V., 105; East Woods,104 fighting 90th, P.V., 105; near Cornfield, 104; retreat 90th P.V., 105; promotion of Major Sellers at, 122
Appointment of Doctors, 89
Aquia Creek, VA, 29, 30, 45, 46, 48, 53, 57, 94
Arlington National Cemetery, 157
Army of Virginia, 74–75
Army of the Potomac, 22, 23, 124, 125, 129, 138, 145, 150, 161, 187, 209, 210
Arrest for desertion, 47
Arrest of soldiers, 87
Artillery fire, 49, 63, 71, 82, 85, 113, 114, 116, 117, 259; casualties of, 112
Artillery pieces captured, 142
Artillery salute, President Lincoln, 106
Artillery shell, 20 LB., 117
Ashby, Colonel Turner, 63
Atlantic City, N.J., 236
Bad weather, 54, 57, 58, 62, 92, 154, 175
Baggage Train, stampede of, 71
Bain, Private James K., 168
Baker, Christopher, 238–239
Baker, Colonel Edward, 169
Baker, Lieutenant, 154
Ballinger, Captain Alfred, 204; LT, 199

Balloon train, 31
Ball's Bluff, Battle of, 169
Balls Cross Roads, VA, 199
Baltimore, MD, 6, 15, 16, 18, 19, 27, 28, 29, 35, 58, 102, 103, 152, 167, 250, 251, 268; burning of railroad bridges 8; Chief of Police, 8, 9; Police Board of, 10; Riot, 7, 9, 10
Band music in camp, 119
Banks Ford, VA, 114
Banks, General Nathaniel, 8, 9, 14, 15, 29, 49, 56, 57, 85, 101
Barbarous foes, 65
Barber, Private Herman, 132, 133–134, 136–137, See also Von Heinecke, Private
Barry, Lieutenant David F., 198
Bartin, Sam, 28
Battalion Drill, 119
Battle Flag Inscriptions, 199
Baxter's Brigade, 124
Baxter, General Henry, 114, 254
Baxter, Major D.W.C., 17
Bayonets, 59
Bealton Station, VA, 140, 142, 143
Belinger, Doctor, 93
Bellas, Private John, 141, 142; wounded, 141; killed, 141
Belle Plain, VA, 36, 103, 107, 110, 197, 203, 204
Bellman's Regiment, 45
Benner, Sergeant Thomas, 101, 102, 158, 160; mistakenly reported killed, 101; promotions, 102; also see Gibney, Sergeant Thomas
Berks Co., PA, 25
Bethesda Church, Battle of, 21
Beyer, Lieutenant Hillary, 198, 204, 210, 212
Bigamy, 167
Bird, Lieutenant Christian, 17
Black Horse Cavalry, 64
Black, John, 239
Bliss, Dr. Z.E., 152, 156
Blue Mountains, 54
Blue Reserves, 126
Blue Ridge Mountains, 49
Bockius, Lieutenant Henry, 199
Bond, Lieutenant Benjamin F., 198, 201, 215
Bonsall, Lieutenant James, 199; not promoted, 216
Bonsall, H.W., 25
Boots, wearing out, 62
Boston, MASS, 5
Bounty men, 131

274

Bounty payments, 108, 151
Bowen, Private John, 253, 255; captured with flag, 255
Bowerman, Colonel Richard, 159
Bradford, A. W., Governor of MD, 102
Brandy's Station, VA, 140
Bread & water, 88
Breastworks, 117; attacks on, 163 171
Breck, Major, 192
Brevet promotions, 122, 148
Breyer, Sergeant Charles, 91
Brigade Review, 80
Brigade, rumors of breaking up, 110
Brodhead, Senator Charles, PA, 111
Brooks Station, VA, 50
Brutality, 88
Buck and ball, 124
Bucktails' Regiment, 114
Bull Run, Battle of, 16, 21, 44, 55, 61, 64, 72, 73, 81, 82, 83, 84, 139, 197, 223, 224; battlefield, 64, 73, 83; casualties, 81, 224
Burial of dead, 73
Buried dead, 64
Burnside, General Ambrose, 84, 96, 161, 187
Buying food, 90
Byrne, Private Sylvester, 43, 44; Sergeant, 44
Cadawalader, General George, 8, 9, 17, 18, 19
Camp, 57, 63, 64, 74, 77, 81, 103, 106, 115, 161, 162, 163, 181; cooking in 144, at Gettysburg, 245; near Rappahannock, 113
Camp Distribution, 127, 128; fireworks at, 127
Camp hospital, 87
Camp Pennsylvania, 18
Canal boats, 48
Candelet, Sergeant John, 269
Cannons, 163
Capitol, 29
Carter, Sergeant, color bearer, 258
Carver Hospital, 146, 147
Castle Thunder, 252
Casualties, 148, 164; captured, 21; died, 21; killed, 21; wounded, 21
Cavalry, 49, 140
Cedar Mountain, Battle of, 32, 33, 37, 55, 71, 73, 85, 149, 197, 202, 222
Cedar Mountain, VA, 22
Cemetery Ridge, Gettysburg, 23
Central Virginia Railroad, 77
Centreville, VA, 83
Chadwick, Captain Francis, 142, 198, 204
Chambersberg St., Gettysburg, 51
Chancellorsville, Battle of, 21, 22, 33, 112, 113, 114, 115, 117, 224
Chantilly, Battle of, 21, 55, 197, 224, 240, 241
Chaplain, 90th P.V., 37, 39, 49, 50, 54, 75; taking money to Phila., 41
Charleston, S.C., 3; fighting at, 107
Chase, Secretary of the Treasury Salmon P., 31
Chestering, Colonel William H., 152
Chicago, ILL, 130
Chinn Ridge, 22, 44
Chorman, Colonel, 109
Christ Lutheran Church, 51
Christian Commission, 165
Christian, Colonel William, 104; forced to resign, 104
Cigars, 92, 157
Cincinnati, OH, 177
City Point, VA, 185
Civilian, fraternizing with, 264
Clarke, Captain, 188
Clemency rejected, Von Heinecke, 137
Cold Harbor, Battle of, 21
Cole, Private Edward, 34, 36, 49
Colonel McLean's regiment, 37
Colored troops, relieved by, 179
Commissary depot, Fredericksburg, VA, 30
Company A, 90th P.V., 48, 112, 147 160, 198, 212, 220, 243, 244, 245, 246, 247
Company B, 90th P.V., 83, 103, 141, 173, 175, 188, 189, 190, 198
Company C, 90th P.V., 9, 127, 158, 169, 186, 187, 192, 198
Company D, 90th P.V. 25, 71, 130, 139, 198, 199, 251
Company E, 90th P.V., 36, 198, 210, 215, 217, 269
Company F, 90TH P.V., 82, 83, 113, 130, 131, 139, 142. 149, 187, 188, 191, 198, 199
Company G, 90th P,V,, 38, 67, 68, 97, 177, 198
Company H, 90th P.V.,13, 17, 18, 27, 33, 44, 120, 121, 129, 152, 155, 157, 191, 194, 196, 198, 199, 200, 201, 202, 204, 205, 206, 207, 210, 212, 217, 248, 249, 252, 255
Company I, 90th P.V., 85, 92, 93, 198, 199
Company K, 90th P.V., 55, 112, 117, 182, 198, 199
Company drill, 105
Company papers, 159
Company payrolls, 167
Concealed powder, 18
Confederate Field Hospital, 261
Confederate Generals, 74
Confederate Prison Camps, 68
Confederate Surgeon, 261
Confederate wounded, 262

Confinement of soldiers, 87, 88
Congress, protest to, 14
Congressional Medal of Honor, 122
Connors, Captain, 149
Conscript replacements, 147
Conscription, 106
Consolidation of regiment, 192
Consul General of Hanover, 132
Contraband slaves, 31
Convalescent, camp, 93; soldiers, 88
Cooper, Corporal Abraham, 177, 178
Cooper, Mrs. Althea, 177
Copper smithing, 263
Corn Exchange Regiment, 126
Corps of Engineers, 64
Couch, Major General Darius, 188
Coulter, Colonel Richard, 104; request for assistance, 104; General, 248-249
Court of Inquiry, Major Sellers, 131
Crale, Private William, 86, 90, 91, 92, 93
Crawford's Division, 23, 168
Crawford, General Samuel, 23
Crosland, Private Lewis C., 41, 62, 73, 77, 83; wounded, 84, 85
Culpeper Court House, VA. 77, 146, 147, 153, 154, 157, 158, 209, 222, 253, 264
Curtin, Governor Andrew, 20, 24, 47, 87, 109, 110, 111, 169, 177, 194, 195, 197, 200, 201, 204, 208, 209, 216
Dallas, TX, 252
Davis, Captain, 140
Davis, Captain Jacob M., 103; Major Davis, 266
Davis, Captain John S., 120, 127, 128, 158, 192, 193
Davis, Captain William P., 119, 121, 204, 215, 217; Lieutenant, 198, 203, 205
Davis, Jeff, 13
Davis, Lieutenant Richard W., 129, 142, 149, 178, 179, 199, 203, 205, 212
Davis, Mrs Eleanor, 192
Deahl, Corporal David H., 191, 192
Deficient weapons, 17, 18, 163
Democrats, 24, 148
Department of Annapolis, 19
Department of Pennsylvania, 18
Department of the Susquehanna, 190
Descriptive Lists, 91, 93
Deserters, 39, 42, 47, 48, 73, 82, 106, 109, 172
Diarrhea, 37, 71, 97, 147, 149
Diary found, 42nd Mississippi, 124
Disability pension, 140
Disease, 66, 86
Division Hospital, 149
Division review, 106
Dix, General, 8, 15

Doctors, 90, 91, 146
Double Quick marching, 56
Draftees, 130, 131, 141, 147
Dress Parade, 105
Drill, 121
Drinkhouse, Corporal William, 38, 39
Drowning death, 46
Drunk, 69
Dry Tortugas, FLA, 134, 194
Duke, Lieutenant Charles Wilson, 1, 94, 96, 198
Duty, 60, 67
Dwyer, Private John, 146, 147
Dysentery, 150
Early, Major, Lee's staff, 241, 242
Ellis, Lieutenant William, 198, 204, 212
Emmittsburg, MD, 245
End of the war, 83, 84, 107, 150, 153, 161, 165, 167
England, 74
Enlisting underage, 108
Envelopes needed, 163
Equipment, canteens, 106; clothing payment, 108; firearms, 163; accidental discharge of, 32; firearm cleaning, 163; knapsacks, 36, 54, 57, 58, 105, 114; lacking, 81; overcoats, 92; shirts, 94, 167, 179; shoes, 62; stretchers, 112; tents, 36, 45, 46, 54, 58, 114, 161; underwear, 90, 93, 94
Ewell, General Richard, 124, 224
Excursion to camps, 70
Execution of deserters, 108, 130
Expected atrocities, 69
Expiration of 90 days service, 15
Express packages, 40, 57, 86, 130, 143
Fairfax Court House, VA, 224
Falmouth Station, 224
Falmouth, VA. 32, 34, 113, 115, 116; moving to, 110
Fayette, Private William, 1
Feather beds, 105
Ferry, Lieutenant Edward, 184, 198
Field, Hospital, 83; Confederate, 260
Final Papers, 11, 92, 147, 149
Fine tooth comb, 166
Fireworks, 70
Fitzhugh House, 21, 112
Flag of truce, 42
Floggings, negroes, 35
Florence, S.C., prison, 68
Foraging, 164
Forced marches, 58, 63,
Forrest Hall Prison, 185
Fort Delaware, 108
Fort Dushane, Petersburg, 186
Fort Lafayette, 250
Fort McHenry, 8, 13, 14
Fort Warren, Petersburg, 94
Fort Washington, 30

276

Fort Jefferson, Dry Tortugas, 194
Fort, building of, 171
Fortress Monroe, Va, 250
Forty Days, 23, 162
Frankford Arsenal, 126
Franklin Square, 6
Fraud, bounty, 151
Frederick Militia Co., telegram to, 10
Fredericksburg, Battle of, 1, 2, 21, 22, 30, 57, 96, 101, 168, 198, 200, 202, 205, 224; attack on, 94, 97, 99; heights recaptured, 119; moving to, 94
Fredericksburg, VA, 31, 33, 35, 36, 39, 43, 44, 46, 48, 49, 50, 53, 54, 55, 62, 96, 112, 119
Freight cars, 57
Fremont, General, 56
Fresh beef, 57
Fritz, Captain J. W., 17
Front Royal, battle near, 49, 59
Front Royal, VA, 49, 54, 55, 56, 57, 58, 60, 61, 62, 63, 73
Funeral Parade, President Harrison, 4
Furloughs, 61, 70, 90, 94, 132, 146
Gaines Mill, VA, 70, 74, 165; camp near, 165
Gallantry in action, 101
Gamble, George, 263
Gangrene, 162, 265
Gatchell, William H., 10
General Starvation, 111
Georgia, 3
Gerker, Captain Fred, 136
German Government intervention, 134
Germanna Ford, 254
Gettysburg, Battle of, 21, 22, 23, 33, 67, 90, 94, 159, 186, 224, 225, 243, 245; Battlefield Commission of, 246; charge at Cemetery by Louisiana Tigers, 244; civilians, 245, 246; field hospital,120; I Corps fighting, 124; Iversons charge,122; line of battle, 125 ;Marsh Creek, 247; O'Neal's charge, 122; Oak Ridge, 122; prisoners, 247, illegally paroled, 243; Sellers leads 90th, 124; soldiers hiding in, 244; supporting artillery, 125; wounded, 61; touring battlefield, 246
Gibney, Sergeant Thomas, alias Benner, 102
Giddons, Private James, alias Keating, 120
Gordonsville, VA, 77, 262
Gorgas, Captain John A., 26, 199
Gorgas, Lieutenant Edmund, 119
Gorting, Consul General of Hanover Adolph, 136
Gould, Private John Gould, 130, 144, 145. 162, 163, 165, 167, 168, 170, 172, captured Weldon R.R., 187-188, died in Florence, 188
Governor of MD, 7
Grant, Lieutenant General U.S., 150, 161, 165, 172, 178, 253, 255
Greenmount Cemetery, 18
Greencastle MD., 121
Griffith, General, 23, 67
Griffin, Lieutenant John, 110, 198, 204; insanity of wife, 109; obtaining commission, 109; wounded Fredericksburg, 109
Grindlock, Charles, 186
Groveton, Battle of, 197
Guard Duty, 87, 152
Guerrillas, 59, 141
Guilford Station, VA, 211
Guinea Station, Battle of, 21
Guyger, Private Nicholas, 183-185
Hagerstown, MD, 121
Halleck, Major General Henry, 178, 179
Hamilton, Private James, 9
Hand to hand fighting, 67
Hanging, for spying, 108
Happer, Captain, A. G., 263
Hard marching, 57, 69, 70, 74, 80, 106, 114, 126
Harris, Alva L., 170
Harris, Lieutenant John, 177, 182, 199
Harris, Private William H., 169
Harris, Sergeant Richard, 169, 170
Harrisburg, PA, 47, 121, 205, 207, 212, 217
Harrison, President William Henry, 4
Hartsuff, General, 104; brigade moves, 32; withdrawal at Antietam, 104
Hatch, General, 77
Hatcher's Run, Battle of, 21
Haviland, Lieutenant D.P., 101
Hay, John, 138
Hayes, Dr., 124
Hays, General Alexander, 254
Health, 29; heart disease, 46, 94
Hewlings, Lieutenant William, 198, 294
Hoecakes, 82, 246; exploding while cooking, 247
Hoffman, Dr. C., 25
Hoffman, Private Lucas, 151, 152, 155, 156, 157
Hollis, Private Frank, 53, 63, 65, 75, 92
Hooker, Major General Joseph, 22, 106, 108, 115, 240
Horn, Captain, 126
Horrors of war, 171-172
Hospitals, 91, 93, 97, 99, 112, 168, 169, 225, 263; good conditions in, 267; home state hospitals, 89;

277

hospital tent, 112; poor care, 87, 89
House of Representatives, Resolution, 14
Howell, Chaplain Horatio, 41, 51, 53, 56, 69
Hughes, Private John, 130
Ill, sharing tents while, 78
Immigrants, Irish Catholics, 5
Inauguration of Lincoln, 10
Insanity, 152
Inspections, 37, 65
Instructing recruits, 20
Insult to the flag, 74
Intoxication, death from, 131
Invalid Corps, 130, 139
Invasion of Maryland, 224
Irish Brigade, 163
Jackaway, Private Samuel, 112
Jackson, General Thomas, Stonewall, 22, 32, 49, 50, 53, 54, 55, 59, 60, 63, 74, 83, 84, 92, 117, 223, 240
Jacobus, Captain Peter H., 82, 184
James River, 250
Jenkins, Private Edward, court martial, escape from guard house, 188-190, postwar arrests, 190
Jenkins, Mrs. Christine, 188
Jennings, Private Frank, 220, 221; corporal, 224; death wish of, 222; discharged, 230; enlists, 221; furlough, 229; marital problems, 221-222; sergeant; 220, 225; reenlisted, 220; Salisbury prison camp, 220
Jersey City, N.J., 232
Jerusalem Plank, Road, Petersburg, 21
Jewell, Lieutenant George, 199
Johnny Reb, 114
Jones, Maria, 125, 126
Jones Private William, 46, 121, 122, 125, 140, 153, 157, 158; died, 158; drafted, 125-126
Judge Advocate, Army of Potomac, 137
Judiciary Square General Hospital, 47
Kane, Marshal George, arrest of, 9, 10, 12, 13, 14, 15, 19
Kane, Private Daniel, aka George, 126
Kearny, Major General, 242; killed at Chantilly, 241; remains received, 241; return of body, 240
Keating, Mrs. James, 119, 120
Keating, Private James, 120; killed at Gettysburg, 119
Kellar, Private G. B., 47
Kelly's Ford, VA, 144, 149
Kenly, Colonel John, 20, 250
Kenner, Captain Henry C., 263
King George County, VA, 206
Kitts, Sergeant George, 113
Kossuth hat, 166
Lack of shoes, 81

Lancaster, PA, 61
Lang, Mrs. Frederick, 149
Lang Private Frederick, 149-150
Laurel Hill, Battle of, 21, 23, 177
Leave of absence, 142, 158
Lee's army, 145
Lee, General Robert E., 74, 165, 240, 241, 243, 253, 255
Leech Lieutenant Colonel William, 83, 201, 208
Lehr, Samuel, 109, 110
Lelar, Corporal William, 80; private, 27
Letherbury, Private Henry, 80, 82
Libby Prison, 226, 227, 243, 249, 250, 251, 267
Lice infestation, 144, 145, 164
Lincoln, President Abraham, 3, 10, 14, 32, 106, 134, 137, 138, 184, 185, 229
Line of battle, 112, 113, 117, 124, 140, 171
Log cabins, 106
Log houses, 161
Long Bridge, Washington, 30
Longstreet, General James, 82, 223
Louisiana, 3
Louisiana Tigers, 244
Lowell's Commercial College, New York, 230
Lyle, Captain Peter, 5
Lyle, Colonel Peter, 6, 12, 18, 19, 20, 24, 31, 36, 67, 82, 101, 103, 104, 119, 124, 147, 148, 158, 159, 182, 196, 200, 210, 206, 211, 216, 218, 219; assumed brigade command Bull Run, 83; cheers for, 115; complaint of conduct, 217; died, 148; dysentery, 148; objects to Watson promotion, 110; Sheriff of Philadelphia, 148; support of his officers, 204; reported killed, 164
Lynchburg Locomotive Works, 263
Lynchburg, VA, 263, 264
Magee, Captain John, 24
Mahone's Division, 220
Mahone, General William, 220
Mail, 47, 48, 82
Manassas, VA, 48, 49, 53, 63, 64, 66, 71, 73
Manley, Private James, 13
Marching, 36, 50, 53, 54, 55, 58, 113; marching orders, 179
Maryland, 15
Maryland Brigade, Union, 159
Maryland Invasion, 1864, 174
Maryland Invasion, 83
Maryland Legislature, 10
Mason, Private Matthew, 27, 28, 30, 45, 46, 48, 56, 58, 69, 70, 78, 80
Mathes, Private Henry, 143, 150, 151, 154, 155, 160, 161, 162
McClellan, Major General George, 20,

30, 74, 222, 223; army of 32 reported in Richmond, 71; falls back from Richmond, 222
McDowell's Corps, 30, 59
McDowell Division, 42, 45
McDowell, Major General Irvin, 30, 31, 64, 74, relieved from command, 83
McGowan, Private Jack, 251-252
McKelvy, Lieutenant Colonel Samuel, 128
McMasters, Lieutenant, 250
Meade, Major General George, 129, 137, 138, 145, 207, 209
Meade, Lieutenant James, 198; not promoted, 215
Megee, Colonel George, 17
Mellor, Private James, 168
Merrimac, 37
Mervin, A. M., 87
Mexican War, 5, 64, 240, 241
Miller, Private Samuel, killed 112
Milton, PA, 146
Mine Run, Battle, 21; campaign,144-145
Missing in action, 37
Mississippi, 3
Mitchell's Station, VA, 158, 160
Moffett, Dr. George B., 262
Monroe County, PA, 56, 96
Monteith, Captain George, 172
Moore, Lieutenant James, 199
Moore, Lieutenant Samuel, 198, 204
Moran, Captain, 184
Morehead, Colonel, 169
Morin, Lieutenant Anthony, 37, 71, 73
Mortars, 175
Mount Vernon, 30
Mud March, 187
Musket volleys, 171
Muster out, 15, 24, 148
Muster for pay, 105
Myers, Captain Wilbur T., 183
National Guards, 4, 6, 8, 12, 13, 15, 20, 24, 31, 33, 36, 77, 83, 126, 183, 200, 211, 221, 250; armory, 43, 44, 53, 54, 71, 75, 182, cost of construction, 75; battalion, 77
Negro Troops, 161
Negroes, condition of, 34
Neill, Captain Thomas H., 19
New Berne, N.C., Battle of, 38
New year's Celebration, 146
New York,136, 255
New York Ledger, 150
Newkurnt, Colonel, 126
Newspapers, 79, 126, 157, 163, 164
Newton, Major General John, 137
Nicetown Hospital, Philadelphia, 137
Nicetown, camp in, 119
Norfolk, VA. 37
Norristown, PA., 25
North Anna Campaign, 21
North Carolina, 3, 165, 168

Northrup, Private Rufus, 243-247; captured at Gettysburg, 243-244
O'Keefe, Private William, 48
Oak Ridge, Gettysburg, 22, 33
Oakley, Private, 8
Officer's wives, 154
Orange & Alexandria Railroad, 77
Orange Courthouse Railroad Station, 262
Ord, General, 54
Ordinance of secession, 3
Paper needed, 163
Parole of prisoners 228, 229, 265
Patapsco River, 9
Patterson Park, Baltimore, 27
Patterson, General, 9, 18
Paul's Brigade, Lyle commands, 124
Paxson, Private Isaac, 181, died in Salisbury prison
Paydays, 33, 62, 66, 140, 141, 143, 151, 153
Paymasters, 36, 50
Pegram's Battery, 71,
Pennsylvania, 15, 83, 87, 89
Pennsylvania Avenue, Washington, 29
Pennsylvania, Lee's invasion, 84, 85, 122
Pennsylvania Militia, 4, 147, 148, 200, 202, 250, 251
Pennsylvania Railroad, 232, 237
Pension Application, 34
Pension controversy, 166-167
Perryville, MD, 6
Petersburg, Battle of, 21, 23, 162-163; artillery at, 174; attack on, 166; fortifications at, 174, siege of, 162
Petersburg, VA, 167, 169, 171, 172, 173, 179, 226
Philadelphia, PA, 4, 5, 15, 17, 18, 20, 21, 24, 29, 36, 41, 55, 56, 58, 63, 69, 70, 84, 87, 88, 94, 96, 103, 109, 113, 119, 129, 132, 139, 142, 147, 148, 158, 163, 168, 170, 183, 184, 185, 189, 191, 193, 200, 201, 202, 205, 211, 216, 232, 238, 248, 253, 263, 267; pension agents in, 121; death records, 143; draft in, 125; return of body of Sgt. Miller to, 113; Uhlmann's Hotel in, 132
Philadelphia Evening Bulletin, 65
Philadelphia Inquirer, 116
Phillips, Sergeant William, 36, 70, 71, 73; death of, 73; ordered to fall out, 71
Photographs, 69, 79, 108, 126, 144, 167
Picket, 41, 56, 58, 78, 105, 110, 111, 115, 117, 141, 143, 157, 161; trading by, 167, 174
Picketts Charge, repulsed, 120
Piedmont Station, VA, 54
Piedport, Va, 57

279

Piles, 81,
Pittsburgh, PA, 249, 256
Plank Road, Wilderness, 254
Police Board, arrest of, Baltimore, 14
Police Department, Baltimore, 12, 14, 15
Politics, 25, 26, 89,
Pollocks Hospital, Fredericksburg, 96, 99
Pontoon bridges, 113
Pope, Major General John, 64, 74, 75, 80, 222, 224, 242; orders of, 77
Poplar Springs, Battle of, 21
Port Republic, VA, 63
Porter, Major General Fitz John, 18, 223
Post Office, Baltimore, 9, 14
Postage stamps needed, 28, 35, 37, 58, 71, 82, 140, 153; sale of stamps, 59
Potomac River, 30, 94, 124, 171, 224
Pottsville Miner's Journal, 42
Pottsville, PA. 42, 85
Pratt's Point, VA, 101
Prayers, 81
Preparations for battle, 49
Prisoners of war, 142; casualties, 175; confiscating money of, 126; escape from Libby Prison, 249-252; hiding money, 227, 264; moved to Richmond, 265; paroled, 243; poor rations & water, 226, 227; transport by rail, 265, 266
Promotions, 139, 169, 196, 197, 200, 212; denial of politics in, 204; officers recommendations in, 111; politics in, 111, 212; requested, 199; recommendations for, 215
Proof of widow's claim, 103
Providence, R.I., 222
Provost guard, 163
Provost Marshal, 133, 139 Baltimore, 10, 20
Quakers, 61
Quayle, Corporal William, 243, 249-252
Railroad depot burned, Aquia Creek, 30
Railroad tracks destroyed, 30
Railroad, travel by, 54
Railroad iron, unloading, 48
Railroad, rebels destroy, 141
Rain and mud, 77, 124
Raleigh, North Carolina, 229
Rapidan River, 130, 132, 173, 222, 254, 264; crossing, 141
Rappahannock River, 39, 41, 42, 43, 46, 112, 113, 114, 115, 222; crossing, 113
Rappahannock Station, 21, 55, 80, 197, 251
Rappahannock Station, VA, 126, 208
Rations, 81, 115, 116; fresh beef, 106; lack of, 80, 164; plenty of, 94
Rau, Corporal John, 186-187
Rauh's Hotel, New York. 132
Raymond, Captain Nathan, 138, 139, 199; Lieutenant, 83
Reading, PA, 25
Reading Railroad, 42
Ream's Station, Battle of, 21
Rebels, 46, 59, 110, 111, 113, 114, 115, 117, 130, 161, 220, 244, 251; crossing the river, 106; desert to Union pickets,111; driven to Rapidan, 142; prisoners of war, 83, 116, 162-164; starving, 111
Recruiting, 24, 47, 51, 201, 202, 205, 214
Reed, Private John, 194-195
Reenlistment of soldiers,119, 150
Regiment, breaking up, 108
Regiment reorganized, 211
Regimental Colors, in mourning, 80
Regimental mail, 80
Regimental politics, 24
Regiment, good health, 77
Regulars, 83
Reilly, Lieutenant John F., 198
Relief money, 126
Republicans, 24, 25
Request for Court Martial, 128
Resignation, medical, 139
Review of troops, President Lincoln, 106
Reynolds, Major General John, 114, 124, 224, 246
Richards, J. S., ESQ., 25
Richmond, VA., 30, 40, 45, 115, 181, 184, 184, 222, 226; marching to, 56; moving to, 45, 57, 59, 66; prisoner at, 101
Rickett's, Major General James, 241
Rickett's Brigade, 37, 45, 56
Rickett's Division, 92
Ricketts, Charles, 235, 236, 237, 238; alcoholism of, 233; attempts to reconcile, 236, 237; claimed to stop drinking, 237; death of father-in-law, 237; disappearance of, 238-239; jobs, 234, 237; Lieutenant, 198, 204, 232, 234; marriage, 232; separation, 232; suicide attempt, 233-234; travel to the orient, 238
Ricketts, George, 232, 235
Ricketts, Helen, 234, 235, 237
Rifle pits, 65, 117, 163, 164
Riley, Lieutenant John, 149, 204
Riots, Philadelphia, 1844, 5
Robbery of prisoner, 189
Robbery of wounded, 258-259
Robbins, Private William, 106
Robinson's Division, 103, 177
Robinson, General John, 114, 254
Robinson, Private Theodore, 88, 89

280

Rockets, 31
Roger's Farm, Gettysburg, 246
Roll call, 105
Roney, Quartermaster Samuel B., 198
Rose, Private John 45, 48; drowned, 48
Runaway teams, 73
Rush, Captain, 27, 44, 198, 202
Salisbury Prison Camp 97, 168, 174, 175, 227; burials, 228; conditions at, 227-228; deaths, 227-228; escape attempt, 228; hospital, 228
Sanitary Commission, 261
Scales' Brigade, attack of, 122
Scarlet fever, 192
Schenck, General, 139
Schofield, Major General John, 219
Schooners, 48
Schuykill County, PA, 42, 84
Scott, Lieutenant General Winfield, 8, 10, 19
Secessionists, 70, 77; sympathizers, 84
Secretary of War, 10, 169, 211, 219; requested to intervene, 136; Stanton, 31, 32, 136, 250
Sedgwick's Corps, 119
Siege tactics, 165
Sellers, Major Alfred, 97, 99, 124, 125, 128, 196, 201, 203, 241; board of inquiry, 130; charges, 129; relieved of duty, 129; resigned, 209
Seminary Ridge, Gettysburg, 90, 243, 247
Sending money home, 35, 37, 39, 40, 43, 44, 49, 51, 53, 54, 55, 56, 59, 62, 69, 74, 75, 103, 107, 108, 110, 126, 130, 140, 141, 143, 153, 154, 161, 179, 188
Shaved heads, 37
Shay, Corporal, 93
Shenandoah River, 53, 57, 58; collapse of bridges, 55, 58, 63
Shenandoah Valley, 32, 60, 222
Sherman's Battery, 64
Sherman, Major General William T., 174
Shields, General, 49, 56, 59
Shippensville, PA, 24
Shoemaker, Dr. T.N.E., 25
Sickness in camp, 78
Sigafoos, Private Jehill, 188
Signal Corps, 31
Skirmish line, 120, 163, 259
Smedley, Corporal Charles, 61, 67, 68; Private, 60, 66, 67
Smedley, Joel, 68
Smithfield Township, 96
Snether, Mr., 10
Snyder, Daniel, ESQ., 25, 108; arrest as a spy, 108
Snyder, Mr., 182
Snyder, Private Henry, 56, 58, 59, 60, 61, 68, 94, 95, 107, 109, 110, Sergeant, 56, 111, 179, 181, 182
Soldier, struck by shell, 165
Soldier's bones, 64
Soldier's life, 89
Soldier's pay, 89
Soldier's Rest, 29
Soldier's Retreat, 29
South Anna, Skirmish, 21
South Carolina, 3, 188
South Mountain, Battle of 21, 197, 224
Special Order#19, 19
Special Order#34, 18
Spotsylvania, Battle of, 21, 23, 177, 248
Spotz, Dr. J., 25
Spring Garden, Philadelphia
St. Elizabeth's Hospital for the Insane, 152, 156
Staples, Private John W., 108
Star Spangled Banner, 37
Stars and stripes, 84
State Legislature, PA, 200, 202
Steamboats, 31, 48
Steinmetz, Private Edward, 172-173
Stewart's Battery B, 122
Stones River, Battle of, 169
Straggling, 48, 81
Street, Mrs. Catherine, 187, 188, 191
Street, William J., 191
Stuart House, 240
Stulen, Private John, 248, 249, 252, 255; assigned as orderly, 253; delivers orders, 255; detail ends, 255; lost in the Wilderness, 254; wounded at Fredericksburg, 248
Stutzman, Corporal John, 107, 113, 116, 146, 174-175; death in Salisbury, 175; wounded in the Wilderness, 175; Private, 105, 112
Substitutes, 126, 131, 147, 150, 151, 155
Sulphur Springs, Skirmish, 21
Sunday Dispatch, 126
Sunstroke, 70, 94, 152
Super, Lieutenant Jesse, 198, 204
Supplies, Confederate, 77
Surgeon, 87, 152; Certificate of Disability, 32, 89, 93, 94, 140
Survivor's Association, 90th P.V., 256, 257, 268
Survivor's Pension, 73
Suthen, Dr., 25
Sutler, 94, 153
Sutton, Private, 247
Sweigert, Private, 2
Switz, Private William, AKA Smitz, Schmidt, 132, 134; execution of, 133-135
Swollen feet, 81
Target practice, 31
Tarr, Captain, 159
Taylor, Colonel J.H., 127

281

Tennessee, fighting in, 107
Term of service, expires, 97
Theft from mail, 40
Thomas, Aide de Camp, Samuel B., 207, 209, 215
Thomas, Brigadier General Lorenzo, 139
Thoroughfare Gap, Battle of, 21, 82, 197
Thoroughfare Gap, VA, 223
Three year's service, 20, 21, 147
Three month's service, 3, 47, 122 169, 211, 218
Tobacco, 165, 166
Todd's Tavern, Battle of, 21
Tower's Brigade, 44, 81
Tower, Brigadier General Zealous B., 81, 83
Townsend, Assistant Adjutant General, 128
Traitors, 84
Transportation of gun, 19
Transports, 171
Treatment of draftees, 130
Trench warfare, 23, 114; near Richmond, 164
Troops arriving, 161
Troops to PA, 171
Tuberculosis, 93
Turner, Major, commanding Libby Prison, 250
Typhoid Fever, 66, 78, 85, 94, 109, 169; death from, 78; recovery from, 90, 91
U.S. Army, 89, 139, 243
U.S. Army General Hospital, 151, 155
U.S. Government, 121
U.S. Mail, 40
U.S. Military Telegraph, 138
Unemployment, 103
Uniforms, shirts needed, 144
Union soldier, spirit of, 84
United States, 3
Unloading railroad iron, 31
Valium, Surgeon Edward P., 47
Van Buren, death of President, 80
Veteran regiments, 147, 148
Vincent, Major Thomas, A.A.G., 211
Virginia, 65, 265
Visits to sick, 87
Von Heinecke, Private Edward, AKA Barber, 132, 136, 137, 138; arrival in New York, 132; arrival of wife, 132; deserter, 132; execution scheduled, 136-137; language barrier, 138; released from sentence, 134; request for respite, 138; travels to Philadelphia, 132
Wadsworth, General, 255
Wagon train, 164
Wagons, 36, 141
War Department, 129, 138, 147, 177, 190; policy of, 147

War news, 28
Warm weather, 77, 161
Warning deserters, 109
Warren, Major General Governor K., 145, 174, 232
Warrenton, VA, 68, 69, 70, 73, 74, 75, 77, 78, 80, 92, 222
Washington, D.C., 29, 33, 36, 47, 54, 63, 66, 67, 70, 97, 103, 127, 128, 136, 138, 139, 146, 147, 152, 154, 160, 169, 177, 185, 190, 224, 250, 267; defenses of, 241
Watson, Captain George, 208, 218, 256, 257; arrested, 217; assisted at Libby, 266; assisted by slaves, 263; assisted by strangers, 263, 266, 267, 268; captured & wounded, 217; charges withdrawn, 209; command of Color Company, 217; commended, 201, 202; commission arrives, 196; commission issued, 205; commission withheld, 205, 206, 212, 214; complaint to Governor Curtin, 206; diarrhea, 263; discredited, 205; discharged from hospital, 267; first aid training, 258; Governor request leave for, 207; injustice to, 202, 205; leave, 208; leg amputated, 196, 215-216, 260, 261, 267, 268; loaned money, 263; Lieutenant, 129, 196, 200, 206, 207, 208, 209, 218; medical care of, 268; obtained food, 263, 266; offered Captaincy, Co. E, 215, 218; Paying for assistance, 266; Problems with crutches, 265; promotion controversy, 110, 129; promoted, 219; purchased crutches, 263; recovers from wounds, 216; refused promotion, 210; requested Governor's help, 203, 206, 216, 218; sent to Negro Hospital, 265; support of administration, 201, 203; wounded, 196, 215-216; under arrest, 208, 209
Weldon Railroad, Battle of, 23, 97, 157, 158, 168, 174, 175, 181, 182, 187, 191, 220, 225, 226; artillery fire at, 225; digging trenches 226; regiment overrun, 226
Westerman, Private Peter, 186-187
Western Army, 161
Westminister, MD, 244, 247
White Oak Church, 214
White Oak Swamp, Battle of, 21
Wilderness, Battle of, 21, 23, 67, 97, 107, 125, 141, 157, 162, 188, 224, 225, 252, 253, 254, 255, 257, 258, 259. 260
Wildy, Mr. Richard, 200
Wilmington, N.C., 229
Winter quarters, 145
Wise, Corporal Frank, 33, 34, 39, 44

50, 51
Wives of dead soldiers, fraudulent claims, 103
Wollenweber, Private Lewis, 54, 55, 97; died of wounds, 99
Woodcutting, 31
Wounded prisoners, 261, 262; escape of 261; exposed to weather, 261; infested with lice, 262; moved by ambulance, 262; obtain weapons, 261, 262, 263; robbery of, 259; transported to Lynchburg, 262
Wright, Mr. James, 96
Wright, Private William, 96, 97
Writing materials needed, 165
Yorktown, VA. 30
Zell, Lieutenant Peter H. Zell, 199
Zilsay, Hospital Clerk James, 86

NUMBERED UNITS

1st Dragoons, 241
1st Maryland, 20, 250
1st Massachusetts, 246
1st Regiment, 1st Brigade, 1st Division, PA State Militia, 4,
2nd Regiment, 1st Brigade, 1st Division, Pa State Militia, 5, 17
3rd Delaware, 194
4th Delaware, 105
4th Maryland, 39
4th U.S. Cavalry, 264
5th Texas, 105
6th Massachusetts, 6
7th New York, 5
11th P.V., 44, 150, 192, 221, 229, 263
12th Massachusetts, 101, 147
15th PA Cavalry, 169
19th P.V., 4, 6, 8, 14, 18, 20, 232, 251
31st PA Militia, 126
44th PA Militia, 121, 122, 125
49th Virginia, 262
57th P.V., 241
71st P.V., 169
88th P.V., 124, 147, 150
90th P.V., 21, 22, 23, 31, 32, 33, 41, 42, 44, 46, 47, 49, 51, 61, 65, 67, 74, 79, 80, 83, 84, 85, 88, 90, 92, 97, 99, 101, 102, 103, 104, 109, 111, 112, 119, 121, 124, 126, 127, 129, 137, 139, 141, 142, 147, 149, 152, 154, 156, 157, 158, 160, 162, 168, 169, 170, 173, 175, 177, 178, 182, 183, 184, 186, 188, 190, 191, 192, 194, 197, 200, 201, 204, 206, 207, 208, 209, 211, 214, 216, 218, 219, 220, 232, 241, 242, 243, 244, 245, 246, 247, 248, 249, 251, 252, 253, 255, 256, 257, 259, 268, 269; addressed by General Pope, 222; assisted Colonel Coulter, 104; dislike of, 155; leave Philadelphia, 222; poor condition of troops, 223; promotions 154, 160; request transfer of draftees 210, retired to Cemetery Ridge, 122
91st P.V., 154
94th North Carolina, 167
97th New York, 150
136th P.V., 115, 117, 119; officer killed, 117; mustered out, 115

I Army Corps, 22, 23, 106, 112, 124, 137, 148, 210, 224, 253; artillery, 122; consolidated with V Corps, 253; generals intervene in Barber case, 134; moves into Gettysburg, 245; retreat through Gettysburg, 247; review, 106; 2nd Brigade, 2nd Division of, 101, 131, 200, 211
II Army Corps, 163
III Army Corps, 117, 225
V Army Corps, 23, 148, 153, 232; Crawford's Division of, 220; review, 154
VI Army Corps, 119
VIII Army Corps, 152
XI Army Corps, collapse of, 113, 114, 224